Schiff— Binghamton

# TOWARDS A NEW AMERICAN POETICS: *ESSAYS & INTERVIEWS*

charles olson

robert duncan

gary snyder

robert creeley

robert bly

allen Ginsberg

*by* ekbert Faas

Black Sparrow Press : santa Barbara : 1979

LIBRARY OF CONGRESS CATALOGING IN PUBLICATION DATA

Faas, Ekbert.
   Towards a new American poetics.

   Bibliography: p.
   1. American poetry—20th century—History and criticism. 2. Poets, American—20th century—Interviews. 3. Poetics. I. Title.
PS325.F3      811'.5'409           78-1559
ISBN 0-87685-389-0
ISBN 0-87685-388-2 pbk.


Second Printing

*For my wife Barbara*

## Prefatory Note

As a general rule, the following essays were completed before the interviews and, to allow for a double perspective, left unchanged even where my findings seemed to be at variance with the poets' responses. At the same time I am deeply aware of the debt I owe Robert Duncan, Gary Snyder, Robert Creeley, Robert Bly and Allen Ginsberg for the many new insights which have given final shape to this study. The Preamble, in particular, tentative as it may be in trying to map the groundwork for the following sections, could hardly have been written without the liberal education I have continued to enjoy since my first talks with Duncan and Snyder in the summer of 1973.

I should also like to express my gratitude to the *American Council of Learned Societies* for supporting my 1972-4 research period in New York City, to the *Canada Council* for generous financial support, to Diana Gay of the Poetry Collection at SUNY, Buffalo, for helping me with the bibliographical work, to Seamus Cooney for his fine editorial advice and, finally, to Barbara Lecker for her help and encouragement all along the way.

E.F

# Contents

Preamble  9

Charles Olson
 Essay  39

Robert Duncan
 Interview  55

Gary Snyder
 Essay  91
 Interview  105

Robert Creeley
 Essay  147
 Interview  165

Robert Bly
 Essay  203
 Interview  223

Allen Ginsberg
 Essay  249
 Interview  269

Bibliography & Abbreviated References  289

# PREAMBLE

Poetic inspiration, as Lu Chi recognized ca. 300 A.D., must take its own course:

> When it comes, it cannot be checked;
> When it goes, it cannot be stopped.
>
> (Li,T,73)*

Far from being an imitation of nature, art embodies the "resonance or vibration of the vitalizing spirit and movement of life" (*ch'i-yün shêng-tung,* Si,A,21-2), and by its spontaneous self-realization comes as a surprise even to those who are creating it. According to one Chinese painter-critic, "there is no knowing how it will take shape . . . it always goes when it should go and stops when it has to stop" (Bu,L,35). "When I begin to paint," comments another, ". . . I entirely forget that it is myself who holds the brush" (Ch,C,204). "How is the impersonality of the [cosmic] Creator any different from this?" asks a third (Bu,L,39).

Of course, the artist uses craft. But only in order to turn himself into a perfect medium for the self-expression of the life-force (*ch'i*) which breathes in him as in nature. Thus it may take a painter years to learn how to trust his hand (*hsin-shou*) before his brush-strokes turn into "obedient servants to the spirit of his object" so that the latter "makes its own picture" (Su,M,32). Yet the aim of this disciplined spontaneity is the very transcendence of craft. "[H]e who, when writing a poem, insists on its form, is surely far from being a poet," wrote Su Tung-p'o (Ch,C,210). And whatever forms the poem will assume organically as an extension of its contents, must, as Tung Yu wrote, emerge "like the unfolding and blooming of leaves and flowers" (Bu,L,56).

The final aim of such art is an approximation of *śūnyatā,* the ultimate "void of inexhaustible contents" (Su,M,28), and a reenactment of its cyclic emanations. A literary composition, writes Lu Chi,

---

* For an alphabetical list of the bibliographical abbreviations used in the Preamble and in the following essays, see BIBLIOGRAPHY & ABBREVIATED REFERENCES at the end of this study.

is "created by tasking the Great Void, / . . . 'tis sound rung out of Profound Silence," while at the same time being "the embodiment of endless change" (Bi,A,207,209). Yet there are few artists like Ni Tsan (1301-1374) or Wang Wei (699-761?) who have left unquestionable evidence of such enlightenment. For most, the pursuit of literature and art is simply "a vehicle of the Way" *(wen yi tsai Tao)* which, besides the notion that poetry expresses "the intent of the heart [or mind]" *(shih yen chih)*, is the most widely quoted principle of Chinese poetics (Li,T,69,114). And the Way is as long as the mind is deep, comprising, as Buddhist philosophers knew long before Carl Jung, not only the personal "mind-system," but the huge memory storehouse of the "Universal Mind" in which "discriminations, desires, attachments and deeds" have been collecting "since beginningless time" and which "like a magician . . . causes phantom things and people to appear and move about" *(Laṅkāvatāra-sūtra,* Go,B,300). Lieh Tzu has given striking testimony to what may happen to the quester-artist somewhere along the middle of the Way. After nine years of study, he writes, his self

> both within and without, has been transformed . . . My eye becomes my ear, my ear becomes my nose, my nose my mouth. (Ch,C,87)

No wonder that Chinese poetry, long before our own, managed to cover the full spectrum of human consciousness from the rational mind through the subconscious towards mystical illumination. The following lines by Li Ho (791-817) give an example of the middle realm with its wondrous phantasmagoria:

> When the wind brushes the cassia leaves and a cassia seed
>     drops
> The blue racoon weeps blood and the cold fox dies.
> Dragons painted on the ancient wall with tails of inlaid gold
> The God of Rain rides into the autumn pool;
> And the owl a hundred years old, which changed to a goblin of
>     the trees,
> Hears the sound of laughter as green flames start up inside its
>     nest.[1]*

All this may strike a familiar chord to the unprejudiced observer of twentieth century art and help rectify the distorting perspective of those who continue to define art as *"form created by a human, intellectual act"* (E. Kahler) or criticism as a concern "with the problem of

*Notes for this section on p. 33.

unity—the kind of whole which the literary work forms or fails to form" (Cleanth Brooks).[2] Yet even though we may ignore a non-Western body of æsthetics like the Chinese, there is no reason why modern poetry, for instance, should continue to suffer Procrustean mutilations at the hand of critics who, in slavish adherence to such obsolete Aristotelian concepts, simply reduce their study objects, say, to the first 84 of Pound's *Cantos* or to the first four books of Williams' *Paterson*.[3] Pound's life-long quarrel with critics clamoring for symmetry, plot and form, or Williams' comment "that there can be no end to such a story as I have envisioned" in *Paterson* (W,P,7) ought to be sufficient caveats against such critical malfeasance. Pound and Williams may have failed to provide traditional Western æsthetics with a full-fledged alternative for the interpretation of their own works. But something close to it seems to emerge when their workshop poetics are placed within the wider context of similar theories by other poets, artists and composers or when they are viewed through the perspective of Olson, who as Pound's and Williams' disciple brought this evolving new æsthetics in progress to its most comprehensive synthesis to date.

These developments which, in Olson's phrase, point towards an open form art no longer of "mimesis but [of] kinesis" (O,W,148) are the subject of a previous study[4] to which the present volume is a sequel. As open-ended as its predecessor, it attempts to graph several further evolutions of the new art by focusing on some of its major practitioners amongst American poets. The opening essay on Olson, an adapted version of the previous volume's concluding chapter, should map some of the groundwork supporting the subsequent interviews and monographs. This additional preamble may help clarify several further premises, trace connections to recent American poetry in general, survey the individual sections on Duncan, Creeley, Snyder, Bly and Ginsberg, and hint at some possible future developments.

In terms of obvious simplification, the new art and æsthetics may be said to reflect a non-anthropocentric, a-teleological and frequently monistic understanding of life. As such it in many ways seems closer to notions like the classical Chinese ones referred to above than to the orthodox thought patterns of our post-Aristotelian and Judæo-Christian heritage. This is not to invoke the mouldy cliché of a marriage between East and West but rather the concept, held by Robert Duncan, of multiphasic modern man as he emerges into a global culture for the first time in history. Present-day æsthetics is an eclectic hybrid of the primitive and civilized, the old and new—a constantly widening conglomerate made up of scrappy bits of information ranging from quantum mechanics to Shamanism or biology. And the forces behind its ever changing patterns, which have caused the most drastic reorientation of Western art since its beginnings, are all the more elusive as they are unprecedented. Any attempt to locate them—like the effort to describe the house in which we live—will therefore have to proceed not only from within but from without. Primitive culture can throw light on obvious neo-Primitive symptoms in our own, as it tries to reclaim some of the vital primordial powers suppressed by our hyper-rationalist tradition. Yet now that the new art, after its iconoclastic *Sturm und Drang* phase, is apparently coming to rest in a period of self-consolidation, its central notions seem to find more and more analogues amongst the high cultures of the East. The few examples chosen here will also try to indicate the scope of the new æsthetics and some of its immediate origins in our own tradition.

§    §    §

The latter, of course, lie in the Romantic period when the arts, to use Shelley's phrase, arose "as it were from a new birth" (Ab,S,11). Shelley himself unwittingly echoes Lu Chi where, in opposition to a rationalist understanding of the poetic imagination, he likens "the mind in creation" to "a fading coal, which some invisible influence, like an inconstant wind, awakens to transitory brightness." As far as inspiration is concerned, in other words,

> the conscious portions of our natures are unprophetic either
> of its approach or its departure. (Ab,M,192)

This anti-mimetic, neo-Heraclitean understanding of art as an enactment of *panta rhei*, in which modern æsthetics again resembles the Chinese, has found a succinct formula in D. H. Lawrence's description of poetry as "life surging itself into utterance at its very well-head" (La,C,87). Even this concept, according to which nature finally comes to realize itself to the creator's bewildered surprise (e.g. Jackson Pollock's "When I am *in* my painting, I'm not aware of what I'm doing. It is only after a sort of 'get acquainted' period that I see what I have been about," O'C,P,40), can be traced back to the Romantics. Theoretically speaking, it is implicit in Coleridge's definition of the imagination as "a repetition in the finite mind of the eternal act of creation in the infinite I AM" (Ce,B,167), and at least two English poets, less obsessed with their egos than Coleridge, also bear witness to the total self-abandonment which according to various Chinese literati should accompany this reenactment of cosmic

creativity. Blake wrote his poem *Milton* "from immediate Dictation
. . . without Premeditation and even against [his] Will" while Keats'
own creations often "struck him with astonishment and seemed
rather the production of another person than his own"
(Ab,M,214,215). Keats, whom Olson considered as his most important Romantic predecessor, describes this egolessness of the "came-
leon Poet" as the *"Negative Capability"* by which "he is continually . . .
filling some other Body" (K,L,71,226-7). And anticipating Olson's
"form is never more than an extension of content" (O,W,16), he
finds an image directly reminiscent of Tung Yu's. If poetry, he wrote,
"comes not as naturally as the Leaves to a tree it had better not come
at all" (K,L,107).

Before we reach contemporaries like Snyder or Creeley, painter
Mark Tobey or composer John Cage, we find little genuine mysticism in post-Romantic Western art that could compare with Wang
Wei's or Ni Tsan's translucid approximations of *śūnyatā*. Like
Gottfried Benn, Piet Mondrian or today's minimal artists, Mallarmé,
following his sudden discovery of "Nothingness, which [he] found
without any prior knowledge of Buddhism" (M,E,88), went astray in
a mysticism *à rebours*. For in his coercive attempt to make the ultimate
void of inexhaustible contents reveal itself in his "Sumptuous Allegories of Nothingness" (M,E,92) or "silent poem[s], all white"
(M,Œ,367), Mallarmé only displayed his one-sided and hence erroneous apprehension of the ultimate paradox. Yet long before the
Surrealists, in their *Second Manifesto* of 1930, came to surmise that
beyond their subconscious phantasmagoria there may be a point
from which "the real and the imaginary, the past and the future . . .
cease to be perceived as contradictions" (Br,M,76-7), there was a
"terrible worker" who tried to hew his Way through these subliminal
jungles towards the light beyond. Like today's psychedelic artists,
Rimbaud proceeded by "a long, gigantic and deliberate *derangement
of all the senses,*" which resulted in a total transformation of his ego
reminiscent of the surreal experiences recorded by Lieh Tzu:

> It is wrong to say: I think. One ought to say: people think me.
> . . . For *I* is someone else ("Car *JE* est un autre."). If brass wakes
> up a trumpet, it is not its fault.

Rimbaud's new understanding of form as retrieved from the depths
of the "universal soul" ("l'âme universelle") in which he immersed
himself, again anticipates 20th century art theories even as it harks
back to comparable notions which the East has held for centuries: "if
what he brings back from *down there* has form, he gives form; if it is
formless, he gives formlessness" (R,W,303-9). Rimbaud, like his
Chinese peer Li Ho, excelled in both—in the conscious and formally

artistic portrayal of everyday reality as much as in the turbulent poetic enactments of his subconscious fantasies.

§    §    §

Rimbaud along with Keats and many other artists, scientists and thinkers provided some of the mainstays for Olson's theory of projective verse. This major effort of polyhistoric syncretism, as we shall see, draws upon a phenomenal range of information from nuclear physics to anthropology or recently unearthed non-Western sources and combines the practical know-how poetics of Pound and Williams with the visionary insights of D. H. Lawrence. The appearance of Olson's famous essay in 1950 paved the way for the eventual ascendance of the new art and æsthetics over the Eliot-dominated New Critical literary hierarchy which still controls most universities. When Donald Allen, in 1960, assembled the then active practitioners of open form poetry in his influential anthology *The New American Poetry,* Kenneth Rexroth was about the only well-known critic to come to its support, while James Dickey denounced it as presaging "the death of all authentic expression in this generation" (Di,B,6). It was quite another matter, when, nine years later, S. Berg and R. Mezey brought out their *Naked Poetry: Recent American Poetry in Open Forms,* which quietly took its place beside the major anthologies of our time. Excluding Olson and Duncan, the editors were right in feeling "like intruders," and it is easy to guess why they quickly abandoned their "original plan to discuss the theory and practise" of open form. Yet despite such shortcomings, now partly amended by the inclusion of Duncan in the second edition (1975), they were far from wrong in gathering Rexroth, Ginsberg and Creeley under one cover with such poets as Lowell, Wright or Kinnell. In fact, it comes as a surprise that the unofficial poet laureate of the Carter administration is missing from the volume.

For although Dickey has continued to denounce Olson, Duncan and other open form poets and theoreticians, he by 1964 "discovered" the "open," "conclusionless," "ungeneralizing" poem for himself—

> a poem which would have none of the neatness of most of those poems we call "works of art" but would have the capacity to involve the reader in it, in all its imperfections and impurities, rather than offering him a (supposedly) perfected and perfect work for contemplation, judgment, and evaluation. (Di,B,290)

And when all is said, one has to grant that some of Dickey's poems since *Buckdancer's Choice* (1965) belong to the major achievements of open form poetry in America. Paralleling his recent development Dickey also turned into an ever more active and articulate apologist of the new æsthetics, now denouncing "all marmoreal, closed to-be-contemplated kinds of poems" and instead speaking of poetry as

> a minute part of the Heraclitean flux, and of the object of the poem as not to slow or fix or limit the flux at all but to try as it can to preserve and implement the "fluxness," the flow, and show this moving through the poem, coming in at the beginning and going back out, after the end, into the larger, non-verbal universe whence it came. (Di,S,173-4)

A no less dramatic change marks the career of Robert Lowell, who to many, and in particular to academic critics, has inherited the mantle of T. S. Eliot. What seems like a *volte face* in Dickey's case, however, corresponds to a much earlier and more deep-rooted change of artistic sensibility in Lowell's. Curiously enough, Lowell was one of the first to acknowledge the importance of *Paterson* and in fact, as he tells us, wrote his earliest, unpublished poetry in Williams' manner (Sc,P,258). Influenced by the New Critics, however, he subsequently joined the "university poets" in their long feud with the followers of the older master:

> My own group, that of Tate and Ransom, was all for the high discipline, for putting on the full armor of the past (L,W,535) . . . both Tate and I felt that we wanted our formal patterns to seem a hardship. (Sc,P,244)

His religious conversion at age twenty-three reinforced these formalistic tendencies. "Catholicism," as he said in 1961, "gave me some kind of form, and I could begin a poem and build it to a climax" (Sc,P,260). Thus, "The Quaker Graveyard in Nantucket," the most celebrated of his early poems collected in *Land of Unlikeness* (1944) and *Lord Weary's Castle* (1946), follows a traditional genre, the funeral elegy, with its sequence from exclamations of grief to the *consolatio*, and is formally modelled on Milton's "Lycidas."[5] Yet the final lines with their dogged affirmation of suffering, death and destruction sound like a cry of despair rather than of consolation:

> When the Lord God formed man from the sea's slime
> And breathed into his face the breath of life,

And blue-lung'd combers lumbered to the kill.
The Lord survives the rainbow of His will.

Here as elsewhere, Lowell's early poetry seems to portray the world of a Christian living in fear of eternal damnation, yet bereft of all hopes of salvation. The later poetry reads like a secularized psychograph of this Kafkaesque nightmare or, in Ted Hughes's words, evokes "a torture cell walled with family portraits, with the daily newspaper coming under the door."[6] The first hints of such change are to be found in the "strange autobiographical phantas-magoria" (David Daiches)[7] of *The Mills of the Kavanaughs* (1951). As the largely confessional content hides under fictitious characters and localities, so a new creative impulse seems to writhe in the fetters of the tortuous narratives and monologues. Yet Lowell still clings to traditional concepts. While acknowledging the existence of these "amazing new poems" which can absorb everything—"quotations from John of the Cross, usury, statistics, conversations and news-paper clippings"—he criticizes *The Waste Land* and the *Cantos* for their lack of "plot and character, just those things long poems have usually relied upon" (L,B,620).

The mid-fifties, a time crucial for the final emergence of open form poetry in the wake of Olson's projective verse poetry and theorizing, was a period of religious and creative crisis for Lowell—"six or seven years ineptitude—a slack of eternity" (L,IR,12). The religious outcome is announced on the very first page of *Life Studies* (1959) which like a sudden windfall put an end to that sterility:

Much against my will,
I left the City of God where it belongs.

The outburst of creativity unleashed by these changes came as a total surprise to the poet himself. Soon, however, Lowell began to recognize that his own development was part of a much larger one, and that young poets had grown "more conscious of the burden and the hardening of this old formalism . . . And once more, Dr. Williams [became] a model and a liberator" (L,W,535-6). This modest bow before the older poet, however, should not blind us to the independence of Lowell's own achievement. What the poet tells us about the actual genesis of *Life Studies* testifies to a period of solitary experiment, trial and error rather than of apprenticeship. Some of the poems published in the collection were first written in the rhymes and prosodies of the early style, until Lowell realized that this "regularity just seemed to ruin the honesty of sentiment" (Sc,P,246-7). And it was not until he temporarily abandoned the writing of verse in favor of prose that he finally found his new poetic voice. Working on his autobiography (partly published in *Life Studies*, New York, 1960) and having to write within the crippling limitations of discursive continuity, he was driven back to poetry.

> I found it got awfully tedious working out transitions and putting in things that didn't seem very important but were necessary to the prose continuity. Also I found it hard to revise. Cutting it down into small bits, I could work on it much more carefully and make fast transitions. (Sc,P,247)

The impulse of ruthless self-scrutiny which thus broke the fetters of both traditional prosody and prose also accounts for the influx of a new subject matter into modern poetry.

It is misunderstanding "confessional" poetry to claim that the better poems written in that genre achieve a "fusion of the private and the culturally symbolic" (M. L. Rosenthal).[8] Although such may be the case at times, it is more appropriate to say that confessional poetry is a new phenomenon in Western literary history for the very reason that it allows the privately autobiographical to become the central subject matter of poetry. In contrast to recent confessionalism, Romantic subjectivity was only a springboard towards the absolute, and the demand for sincerity had a claim on those emotions alone which would lead the way to that goal. When private confessionalism began to invade poetry with the breakdown of the Romantic ideal, the poets themselves were the first to denounce it as a degeneration of the earlier mode. This was the case with Browning, who after *Pauline: A Fragment of a Confession* (1833) escaped into more objective genres and, most notably, into the dramatic monologue, which the author could claim contained "so many utterances of so many imaginary persons, not mine."[9] Due to the influence of T. S. Eliot, to whom poetry was "an escape from personality" rather than an expression of it (E,W,58), such prudishness continued to dominate Anglo-American poetry in our century, and it is only since *Life Studies* that the portrayal of one's private agonies and neuroses has ceased to be considered a breach of poetic decorum. Lowell's "Skunk Hour," the celebrated masterpiece of the volume, for instance, gives us the poet's self-portrait as a mentally unbalanced voyeur. Yet out of the "Existentialist night" of his despair the speaker seems to be reaching out for a new religious awareness rooted in life itself. "Somewhere in my mind," the poet recalled later,

> was a passage from Sartre or Camus about reaching some point of final darkness where the one free act is suicide. Out of this comes the march and affirmation, an ambiguous one, of my skunks in the last two stanzas.[10]

Lowell himself has commented on the influence his action painter friends exerted on the writing of *Life Studies*.[11] Yet the full efflorescence of the new impulse they encouraged was yet to come. In *Life Studies* Lowell still hoped "that each poem might seem as . . . single-surfaced as a photograph," and the following collections, *For the Union Dead* (1964) and *Near the Ocean* (1967), only modified and expanded upon the earlier style. The *Notebook* poems, however, mark a new breakthrough:

> Words came rapidly, almost four hundred sonnets in four years—a calendar of workdays. I did nothing but write; I was thinking lines even when teaching or playing tennis . . . Ideas sprang from the bushes, my head . . . As I have said, I wished to describe the immediate instant. (L,IR,14)

It is no wonder then that the publishing history of the book came to resemble that of *Paterson,* which, as Williams recognized after the completion of the four books he had planned, was a "story" he would never finish. In the 1969 edition Lowell still seems to cling to an overall closed conception of the sequence. Yet the inadvertent self-contradictions contained in the "Afterthought" already seem to indicate what was to follow:

> as my title intends, the poems in this book are written as one poem, jagged in pattern, but not a conglomeration or se-quence of related material . . . The separate poems and sections are opportunist and inspired by impulse. Accident threw up subjects, and the plot swallowed them—famished for human chances.

What happened during 1969 must have come as a surprise to Lowell just as the writing of *Paterson,* Book V did to Williams. In a "Note to the New Edition," dated January, 1970, the poet admits that his "one poem" had undergone severe changes and expansions. "About a hundred of the old poems have been changed . . . More than ninety new poems have been added . . . I couldn't stop writing, and have handled my published book as if it were manuscript."

Lowell's development, although more dramatic than that of most of his peers, is no less than typical for the majority of contem-porary American poets. It would be easy to document similar changes in the work of James Wright, W. S. Merwin, or Sylvia Plath, to name only some of the more important ones. The most obvious indication of the general revolution they bear witness to is the fact that the writing of verse in regular rhyme, meter and stanza has by now almost become an anachronism. Yet however interesting such individual changes may be in signaling the final ascendance of open form poetry, they are less significant than the contributions of poets like those discussed in this volume who in one way or another have devoted their lifework to the pursuit of the new art.

§    §    §

Ironically, the artistic conversions of poets like Dickey and Lowell find a diagonal counterpart in an evolving new attitude amongst their previous opponents, many of whom seem increasingly inclined towards a reassimilation of more traditional modes of expression. As Duncan said in a 1969 interview, "I'm not going to take the closed form versus the open form because I want both, and I'll make open forms that have closed forms in them and closed forms that are open" (D,I). Of course, Duncan has always held on to tradition far more than his friend Olson, for instance, or most other Black Mountain poets. But this conservational attitude ("I'm always immensely conservative of everything," as he says, D,I) seems to find numerous analogues in recent statements made by his contemporaries. Denise Levertov's "Some Notes on Organic Form" (1965), for instance, refers back to Hopkins' "inscape," which itself derives from Duns Scotus' *hæcceïtas* principle of individuation as well as from Plato's idealistic philosophy. Both these elements are clearly evident in Levertov's own use of the æsthetic vocabulary provided by her Victorian predecessor:

> Gerard Manley Hopkins invented the word "inscape" to de-
> note intrinsic form, the pattern of essential characteristics
> both in single objects and (what is more interesting) in objects
> in a state of relation to each other, and the word "instress" to
> denote . . . the apperception of inscape. (Lv,P,7)

Equally mimetic rather than projective in its basic metaphysical assumptions is Levertov's concept of "organic form" proper which, as she claims, arises "out of fidelity to instress"—

> a design that is the form of the poem—both its total form, its
> length and pace and tone, and the form of its parts (e.g., the
> rhythmic relationships of syllables within the line, and of line
> to line; the sonic relationships of vowels and consonants; the
> recurrence of images, the play of associations, etc.). (Lv,P,10)

Less traditional in their philosophical assumptions but equally tradition-*oriented* are recent experiments, or at least speculations about a possible reintegration of rhyme, meter and stanza into open form poetry. Led by Pound's "paradigm tracing the degeneration of Poesy from Greek dance-foot chorus thru minstrel song thru 1900 abstract voiceless page," Allen Ginsberg, as early as 1966, proclaimed a new era of poetry "returned to song and song forms" (B-M,P,221) and recently contributed a whole volume of his own songs entitled *First Blues, Rags, Ballads & Harmonium Songs 1971-74* (1975) to the new development. Similarly, Bly raised the question of how the "sound sensuality" lost by discarding rhyme and meter can be brought back into the open form poem,[12] while Snyder suggested that "using ballad meter and using any of a number of easily available forms surely has its value, just as it's very difficult to sing songs that don't have these forms." Generally speaking, Snyder, like Duncan, has

> no antipathy as such to closed form. Like, anything that works, I'll use. I'm impressed by the fact that almost all the poems that I can remember by heart are poems with regular meters that rhyme.[13]

In their search for the appropriate formal models, poets today, of course, no longer confine themselves to Eliot's claustrophobic concept of a tradition which will only survive by a "continued veneration of our ancestors . . . in the literatures of Greece, Rome and Israel" (E,P,211). No matter where they place their individual emphases, they instead draw on the heritage of world culture comprising Western, Eastern and Primitive. As Duncan puts it, "we are coming from what were once national traditions . . . into . . . a community of meanings . . . A psyche will be formed having roots in all the old cultures" (D,C,17).

It is true that the diverse cultural orientations of poets frequently result in what may appear to be radical disagreement rather than common pursuit. Duncan, for instance, has criticized Snyder for his single-minded exclusion of most of Western culture, or Pound and Olson for ignoring Christianity;[14] Snyder in his turn has called Charles Olson "an apologist for Western culture" (S,IA,111), while Robert Bly, advocating a poetry inspired by Spanish and South American Surrealism, criticized American poets generally for their "elegant isolationism" (B,S,6,22) and the "Black Mountaineers" for continuing to foster the American "formalist obsession":

> The Olsonite poets are always approaching poetry through technique; Creeley is a perfect example. All their talk about technique is academic, and a repetition, in a different decade and different terms, of the Tate-Ransom nostalgia for jails. (B-M,P,163)

Yet more important than such disagreement is the intellectual fervor which inspires it, and which, if viewed without the understandable party prejudice, seems to contribute to a common goal.

For by relating the new art and æsthetics to ever new strands of world culture, each individual poet helps transform the once icono-clastic movement into an unprecedented world poetry deriving its roots from all the various layers of man's consciousness. A major landmark in this direction was *Technicians of the Sacred* (1968) in which Jerome Rothenberg relates, as his subtitle puts it, *A Range of Poetries from Africa, America, Asia & Oceania* to modern poetry, trying to show "some of the ways in which primitive poetry & thought are close to an impulse toward unity in our time." Such ways are the " 'pre'-literate" as compared to the "post-literate" (McLuhan) situation of poetry; "a highly developed process of image-thinking"; an " 'intermedia' situation" whereby poetry operates "through song, non-verbal sound, visual signs, & the varied activities of the ritual event"; the "recognition of a 'physical' basis for the poem within a man's body"; or, most importantly, the notion of the poet as shaman (Rg,T,xxiii-xxiv). Considering the early discovery of Primitive sculpture, this integration of Primitive poetry into the mainstream of Modernism had long been overdue, and as a consequence its impact on American and British poets came to be felt all the more strongly. Many poems from Gary Snyder's more recent work, for instance, would hardly exist without this model, which Rothenberg was quick to reinforce by subsequent publications such as *Shaking the Pumpkin* (1972), containing traditional poetry of the North American Indians, and the anthology *America a Prophecy* (1974), edited in collaboration with George Quasha and subtitled *A New Reading of American Poetry from Pre-Columbian Times to the Present.* Although the first of its kind, this anthology, as the editors themselves seem to realize, is itself only one more step towards the goal which it sets itself in the introduction:

> When we understand . . . tradition as an active force, we are able to make genuine use of the discoveries of archæologists, linguists, anthropologists, historians, and translators . . . The spread of information about the past and the culturally re-mote has made the present generation, in Gary Snyder's words, "the first human beings in history to have all of man's culture available to our study" and to be "free enough of the weight of traditional cultures to seek out a larger identity." (Rg,A,xxx)

A major contribution to this larger identity was, of course, made by Gary Snyder himself, who in his essays and poems expanded the range of modern poetry to receive the impulse not only of "the most archaic values on earth" but more specifically of Far Eastern art and philosophy. If Eliot called Pound "the inventor of Chinese poetry" for his time (P,P,14), there is reason to pay similar tribute to Snyder in our own. Probably no Western poet before him spent equal time in study and meditation in order to penetrate the secrets of Buddhist mysticism, and certainly no one emerged with similar results. The most obvious sign of this lies in the very fact that Snyder's poems have little in common with most of what is known to us of Far Eastern poetry in translation or imitation. The elliptic terseness of his lines never yields to facile mellifluousness or grace, and especially where Snyder equals the transparent luminosity of a Han-shan or Wang Wei—"going out into emptiness and into the formless" while resting on "an absolute foundation of human experience and insight" (S,IR, 64, 68)—the achievement is the obvious result of an arduous struggle with the insufficiencies of our language:

> The corrugated roof
> Booms and fades night-long to
>
>      million-darted rain
>   squalls    and
>
>     outside
>
>     lightning
>
> Photographs in the brain
> Wind-bent bamboo.
>              through
>
>     the plank shutter
>       set
>
> Half-open    on eternity.
>                   (S,W,28)

Robert Creeley, albeit as the result of a totally different development, has achieved a similar fusion of almost pre-conceptual concreteness and mystical luminosity in more recent poems such as "The Moon"—

>     a lovely
>
> bright clarity and perfect

roundness, isolate,
riding as they say the
black sky.
            (C,F,59)

While Snyder's career has been one of single-minded study and
growth within non-Western culture, Creeley's parallels and, in a
sudden transformation during the early sixties, transcends the work
of others such as Mallarmé, Robbe-Grillet, or the minimal artists. A
prose work like "3 Fate Tales" seems to take place in an "eternal *now*"
(Robbe-Grillet, R-G,R,134) or repeatable arbitrariness; the early
poetry—the "poem supreme, addressed to / emptiness" (C,P,29)—
seems to follow a poetics of *"abolition"* and *"élimination"* like that of
Mallarmé who after his sudden 1866 revelation of Nothingness tried
to write the "silent poem, all white." Similarly, Creeley for several
years seemed to work "toward a final obliteration of himself"
(C,G,39), mainly by such means as abstract vocabulary, simple word
repetition, repetitive relocation of phrasing and the faltering staccato movement of his speaking voice, which "despairs of its own /
statement, wants to / turn away, endlessly / to turn away" (C,P,159).

What for Mallarmé remained an aim in itself, however, only
served as a starting point for Creeley. Although

All [he] knew or know[s]
began with this—
emptiness
            (C,F,95)

he gradually came to realize that the latter is ultimately a void of
inexhaustible contents, or, speaking in his own words, that "There
is / a silence / to fill" and that "It is possible, in words, to speak / of
what has happened—a sense / of there and here, now / and then"
(C,W,106,122). "Before a man studies Zen," wrote Seigen Ishin,

> to him mountains are mountains and waters are waters; after
> he gets an insight into the truth of Zen . . . mountains to him
> are not mountains and waters are not waters; but after this
> when he really attains to the abode of rest, mountains are once
> more mountains and waters are waters. (Su,Z,24)

During the sixties Creeley seemed like a man about to enter the third
stage, trying to recapture the 'Small facts / of eyes, hair / blonde,
face" or tentatively positing his own identity: "Here I / am. There /
you are" (C,F,43,53). And before long, figures and objects of an
often unearthly concreteness which now are recorded as a continuous "day book or journal . . . to deal with reality over a man's
life" (C,C,17) began to emerge from the maze of disembodied

abstractions so typical of the poet's earlier mode.

While Creeley gradually came to locate himself, although half unawares, within a specific strand of Western spiritual history, Robert Bly, from his very beginnings, made himself the forceful apologist of another. Surrealism, despite the isolated efforts of a David Gascoyne or a Philip Lamantia, had never been able to hold its own against the overwhelmingly Objectivist orientation of poetry in England and America. This is why Bly, in the late fifties, came to announce that American poetry was cut off from "the greatest tradition of all modern poetry, and the *avant-garde* for a century" which is characterized by "the heavy use of images" (B,F,2,14). Because the "other poetries have passed through surrealism; we have not" (B,F,3,7).

Yet Bly is no follower of Breton and *écriture automatique* and in his own poetry tries to transcend the psychographic one-sidedness of his French predecessors by following the model of such Spanish and South American Surrealists as Lorca and Neruda. Analogously, Bly evolved his Surrealistic mode by writing, not so much about himself, but about the life of his country, which according to his programmatic essay "On Political Poetry" (*The Nation,* April 24, 1967) "can be imagined as a psyche larger than the psyche of anyone living." As in the powerful "Counting Small-Boned Bodies" whose Surrealistic imagery is contained within an obvious rhetorical framework, Bly usually refuses to yield his imaginative control to the autonomous flow of subconscious imagery:

> Let's count the bodies over again.

> If we could only make the bodies smaller,
> The size of skulls,
> We could make a whole plain white with skulls in the moon-
>     light!

> If we could only make the bodies smaller,
> Maybe we could get
> A whole year's kill in front of us on a desk!

> If we could only make the bodies smaller,
> We could fit
> A body into a finger-ring, for a keepsake forever.

> (B,L,32)

Bly's single-minded belligerence in defense of Surrealism and against the "formalist obsession" of American poetry has performed a salutary function, and as his influence increased he started to mellow in his attitude towards others and to adopt elements from poetries he had initially opposed. A recent poem such as "The Teeth Mother Naked at Last" (1973) combines the earlier Surrealism with Pound's fragmentation techniques and Ginsberg's Whitmanesque rhetoric. In 1974 Bly suddenly spoke of Olson as the man who "wonderfully understood . . . that the roots of form go back to the body and its breath" (B,R,33) and in 1972 he hailed Ginsberg whom he had earlier criticized for his "unkindness" or "fear of the uncon-scious" (B,S,5,70) as "the rebirth of a very powerful spiritual man" and as a fellow traveller in a common pursuit who, unlike Gary Snyder or himself, had gained his access to a new consciousness "not through the Tibetans and Japanese—but through the Hindus" (B,IL,54). Buddhism, from which, as Bly himself said in 1972, he had "learned most" during the previous decade (B,IL,50), played an important role in this development.

In the light of its philosophy, Bly would probably agree that Surrealism and Objectism are complementary rather than opposed to each other, and hence share the attitude which arose from Creeley's earlier "battle against objectivism." As Creeley had explained in a marginal comment to his "Note on the Objective" (1951), sent to Olson shortly before its publication, "to be *objective* . . . MEANS to be so *subjective* that the possession of content . . . is complete enough for the poet to hand over." But he soon realized that his notion of the "*subjective* in a more basic character" was merely, as it were, the photographic negative of Olson's Objectism; or in other words that "subjective" and "objective" are both mislead-ing and obsolete concepts in a description of the new consciousness. As Creeley concluded in the final paragraph of his "Note," it there-fore is "perhaps best to junk both terms" and to replace them with a more neutral and monistic vocabulary as in "a man and his objects must both be presences in this field of force we call a poem" (C,G,18-19).

It may well be that Ginsberg and Duncan are the two poets to most reorient open form poetry since Olson. Their joint contribu-tion lies in a new emphasis on those underground Western traditions which are only now, with the help of scholars such as Frances Yates, beginning to assume their rightful place in our spiritual and artistic consciousness. Following their lead it may become possible to relo-cate within our own heritage what in the iconoclastic theorizing of a Pound, Lawrence or Olson was largely derived from non-Western sources. For "underneath the academic and public traditions of the West," as Ginsberg points out,

> there's always been the esoteric private hermetic stream. Go
> back through the great Western poets—Whitman, Emerson,

Shelley, Coleridge, Blake—back through Boehme, all the way
back to Pythagoras who said, "Everything we see when awake
is death; and when asleep, dream." This Gnostic transmission
. . . proceeds originally out of the same middle Eastern consciousness that also travelled into the Orient . . . So the whole
argument about the Orient being alien to us is in essence
silly—and not interesting—because it assumes that Western
thought is all hard Jehovah Christ the Church liberal
humanism but forgets the more interesting thought. Shakespeare's "our little life is rounded by a sleep" and "we are such
things as dreams are made of" is, precisely, the same statement
about the nature of suchness, the nature of existence, as the
Prajna-paramita Sutra, the "highest perfect wisdom" Buddhist sutra. (G,IO,16-7)

Ginsberg himself admits to having borrowed most of these ideas
from a friend who may well be the most erudite among the major
poets in present-day North America, Robert Duncan. Duncan is
frequently misnamed a follower of Olson despite the fact that even
during the latter's most influential period he frequently dissociated
himself from the older poet, who himself had expressed suspicion of
Duncan's particular areas of interest. In "Against Wisdom as Such,"
for instance, a reply to Duncan's 1953 self-description as "a poet,
self-declared, manqué," Olson referred to Duncan's San Francisco
as "an école des Sages ou Mages as ominous as Ojai, L.A." (O,U,67).
In his turn, Duncan published a programmatic statement concerning his "radical disagreement" with Olson in *The Black Mountain
Review* of summer 1955 (pp. 209-12), acknowledging Olson's criticism ("He suspects, and rightly, that I indulge myself in pretentious
fictions") and declaring his own allegiance to the Romantics, particularly concerning the belief "that form is Form, a spirit in itself."

Duncan's concept of his "Romanticism" was well established by
the time he first met Olson in 1947. The foster-child in a household
of middle-class occultists, he could often, after having been put to
bed, hear his parents and their associates from the *Hermetic Brotherhood* in an adjacent room—"speaking in hushed or deepened voices,
or speaking in voices that were not their own" (D,T,14). Contem-
poraneous with Yeats' *Order of the Golden Dawn*, the *Brotherhood* drew
its inspiration from a multiplicity of sources: "The theosophy of
Plutarch, Plotinus and Pseudo-Dionysius the Areopagite, the hermeticism of Pico della Mirandola, or *The Light of Asia* and the
*Bhagavad-Gita*, joined in the confusion of texts and testimonies of
libraries that could include accounts written by trance-mediums of
travel past time or far planets, manuals of practical astrology and

numerology." Thus Duncan "heard of guardian angels and of genii, of vision in dreams and truth in fairy tales, long before Jung expounded the gnosis or Henri Corbin revived and translated the Recitals of Avicenna" (D,S,6). From such childhood impressions Duncan evolved his idiosyncratic sense of a new poetic tradition—an oddly erudite conglomerate of all that was half or totally heretical in the course of Western cultural history.

> From Alexandria of the Roman era, where the master of Yoga and the Zoroastrian mage met with the professor of a god-magicking neo-Platonism; from Spain and the Provence, where, in the eleventh and twelfth centuries, Arab, Jew, and Cathar, mixed a rich culture, producing in the dialectic of its psychology . . . the inspiration of mystics, gothic masons, and two schools of a poetic mystery—the *trobar clus* and the Grail romance; from the Academy of Cosimo de' Medici in the fifteenth century where, following the teaching of Gemistos Pletho, Ficino and Pico della Mirandola mixed the Emperor Julian's orations and the conversations of Moses of Leon's *Zohar* to set into motion the ideas of a Christian Kabbalism and the practises of a demonic and spiritual magic; from the speculative symbolism and legendary history of fifteenth century alchemy and astrology; from the brotherhoods of the seventeenth century—the Freemasons, the Rosicrucians, or such religious sects as the Brothers and Sisters of the Free Spirit, that Adamite mystery in which as Fränger argues, Bosch was initiate, or the "Hidden Seed" of the Moravian Brethren after the Thirty Years War; from such sources the Romantic Movement in the eighteenth and nineteenth centuries inherited and made up its "tradition."   (D,A,50-1)

Such thinking opened the way to a new understanding of Whitman and Blake, whose integration into the mainstream of modernist poetry may well turn out to be the major development in American literary history since mid-century.

In 1954, the year preceding his declaration of independence from Olson, Robert Duncan, who was "already a convert to the Romantic spirit," suddenly, during a reading given by poetess Helen Adam, discovered the possibility of a new poetry in the "sublime and visionary manner [of Blake]." This experience finally broke, as he puts it, "the husk of [his] modernist pride" or previous "conviction that what mattered was the literary or artistic achievement" instead of the "wonder of the world of the poem itself" (D,T, 41-2). But before his final evolution into a major poet as apparent in *The Opening of the Field* (1960), Duncan absorbed the even more crucial influence of Whitman, who quickly gained a dimension capable of subsuming the previous impact of more recent poets under his all encompassing poetics of "the grand ensemble." As Duncan relates himself, "*Leaves of Grass* was kept as a bedside book" in the course of writing *The Opening of the Field* while "Williams' language of objects and Pound's ideogrammatic method were transformed in the light of Whitman's hieroglyphic of the ensemble." To a mind familiar with the Hindu *ātman* concept, even the Coleridgean notion of the self as the "only entrance to all facts" (Whitman, Wn,L,487) now appears in a positive light. "In Whitman," Duncan writes, "there is no ambiguity about the source of *meaning*. It flows from a 'Me myself' that exists in the authenticity of the universe." The very notion which, in the wake of Romantic philosophy, had proved so fatal a legacy to writers from Coleridge to Pater, now turns Whitman into a guide to the poets of the future:

> Back of our own contemporary arts of the collagist, the assembler of forms, is the ancestral, protean concept, wider and deeper, of the poet as devotee of the ensemble. Back of the field as it appears in Olson's proposition of composition by field is the concept of the cosmos as a field of fields. Our field in which we see the form of the poem happening belongs ultimately to ... the grand ensemble Whitman evokes. (D,W,78,100)

A fusion of influences similar to that which informed *The Opening of the Field* marks the genesis of a poem whose general influence seems to emulate the previous impact of *The Waste Land*. Ginsberg's *Howl*, whose reading at the San Francisco *Six Gallery* in 1956 virtually launched the Beat movement, was written in a rapid outburst of creativity—but after a long period of gestation. The earliest impulse derived from his 1948 Blake vision which had left Ginsberg with the conviction that he "was born to realize . . . the spirit of the universe" (Pl,W,304). Reading one of Blake's poems,

> he heard a deep ancient voice, which he identified as Blake's, as the Creator's, pronouncing the poem, bringing him into a deepening understanding of the poem and the universe. (G,A,15)

Almost a decade of experimenting had to elapse before Ginsberg found the poetic means to turn such visions into poetry. Unaware of Olson's "Projective Verse" essay at the time, he relied on

Kerouac's similar "theory of breath as measure" (Ke, IR, 83) and on the "eccentric modulations of long-line composition displayed" by Blake, Whitman and others (B-M,P,221). *Howl* was to convert this theory into practise. "Ideally each line" in that poem, as the poet pointed out, is "a single breath unit." But there were other more general influences. As Ginsberg remembered in 1959,

> I realized at the time that Whitman's form had rarely been further explored (improved on even) in the U.S. Whitman always a mountain too vast to be seen. Everybody assumes (with Pound?) (except Jeffers) that his line is a big freakish uncontrollable necessary prosaic goof. No attempt's been made to use it in the light of early XX Century organization of new speech-rhythm prosody to *build up* large organic structures. (A,P,416)

Since then, Ginsberg's major formal concern has been exploring the relations "between poetry and mantra chanting by means of the yoga of breath" (G,IS,12), and trying to evolve a language whose psycho-physiological impact would even affect today's political arena or, in Ginsberg's own words, would "make every hard hat vibrate with delight." Blake, who more than two decades earlier had sent Ginsberg on his poetic quest, again became the major influence at this stage. It was "The Sick Rose"—"with the voice of Blake reading it" to him in his Harlem flat—which had brought about Ginsberg's first cosmic vision. Because Blake's poem, as Ginsberg now came to realize, was an example of "pure Mantra" within English poetry— "as penetrant & capable of causing Transcendental Knowledge as any Hindu Hare Krishna or Hari Om Namo Shivaye." So, Ginsberg finally set about to reinvent Blake's unrecorded melodies to the *Songs of Innocence & Experience*, in the belief that "only the prophetic priestly consciousness of the Bard—Blake, Whitman or our own new selves—can Steady our gaze into the Fiery eyes of the Tygers of the Wrath to Come" (G,B).

As Ginsberg would be the first to admit, the genealogy table of Western poets with "the prophetic priestly consciousness of the Bard," of course, goes back much further than to Blake. Within the Hermetic tradition, for instance, Orphic incantations formed a common practise of the Magus, and where Ginsberg uses his Indian harmonium, Ficino, who around 1463 translated the Greek *Corpus Hermeticum* into Latin, is said to have accompanied his singing of the *Orphica* on a *lira da braccio* decorated with the figure of Orpheus taming the animals (Y,B,78,80). For as Pico della Mirandola pointed out in his *Conclusiones Orphicæ*,

> nothing is more efficacious than the Hymns of Orpheus, if
> there be applied to them suitable music, and disposition of
> soul, and the other circumstances known to the wise. (Y,B,79)

By the time Pico declared Cabalistic magic as an indispensable part
of such chanting, its ultimate orientation became even clearer. It was
geared towards the Absolute which Ficino had described as "God
[who] is nothing, and yet . . . is all" or which in Pico's Cabalistic
conviction was the Ensoph with its ten Sephiroth emanations but
which in itself "is the Nothing, the unnameable, unknown *Deus
Absconditus*." As Pico added elsewhere: "Idem est nox apud Or-
pheum, & Ensoph in Cabala" ("The night in Orphism is the same as
the Ensoph in Cabala," Y,B,125,126). Through Giordano Bruno or
Philippe Du Plessis Mornay, friend and favorite theologian to Sir
Philip Sidney, who translated the French philosopher's *De la vérité de
la religion chrétienne* (1581) into English, such knowledge must also
have reached William Shakespeare (Y,B,177-8).

It is easy to see how much these notions resemble the Eastern
concept of the ultimate void of inexhaustible contents and its
analogues in contemporary open art theories. And as *śūnyatā* finds
its psycho-physiological counterpart in "extinction" (*nirvāṇa*), so did
the "Orphic night" correspond to what Pico, in his *Conclusiones
Cabalistæ*, and, even more significantly, in his commentary on Beni-
vieni's *Canzona de Amore,* calls "mors osculi": "In a supreme trance,"
as Frances Yates paraphrases,

> in which the soul is separated from the body, the Cabalist can
> communicate with God . . . in an ecstacy so intense that it
> sometimes results, accidentally, in the death of the body, a way
> of dying called the Death of the Kiss. (Y,B,99)

Equally striking are the resemblances which emerge when we compare Eastern and Modernist notions of both cosmic and artistic
creativity with those of the neo-Platonists and Hermeticists. According to Proclus, an influential systematizer of Plotinus' philosophy,
"all things proceed in a ciriuit . . . originating from the unmoved and
to the unmoved again returning" (Ab, S, 149). Or as the *Corpus
Hermeticum* proclaims in talking about "the nurse of all beings . . .
who gives birth to all things":

> Whether you speak of matter or bodies or substance, know
> that these things are energies of God, of God who is the All.
> (Y,B,34)

Man, the *magnum miraculum* "brother" to the creative World-

Demiurge, is capable of recreating these cosmic processes in his imagination. As Pico states in his *Oration on the Dignity of Man*,

> he passes into the nature of a god as though he were himself a god; he has familiarity with the race of demons, knowing that he is issued from the same origin. (Y,B,28)

To Bruno this imagination, as the most powerful inner sense, becomes "the sole gate to all internal affections and the link of links." As he came to believe, following the neo-Platonist poet Synesius' study *De somniis*, much of its power is derived from dreams through which the divinities communicate with man (Y,B,266,335).

By the time Bruno enunciated these ideas in England and on the Continent, the Inquisition, which was to send him to the stake in 1600, had already started to win its battle against the new philosophers. Their final efforts to join forces on a European level, in which Shakespeare and his friends seem to have taken an active part, were crushed by the defeat of the Winter King and Queen of Bohemia at the Battle of the White Mountain (1620) and ultimately drowned in the spiritual devastations of the Thirty Years' War. This, Frances Yates suggests (Y,S,21), may have been the tempest dreaded by Shakespeare, who would have been equally aghast at the subsequent era of "Enlightenment." As Robert Duncan writes,

> The neo-Platonism and Hermeticism or Rosicrucianism of the early 16th century that carried men's religious thought across barriers of church and Bible into realms of imaginative synthesis were put into the quarantine of irrational contagions. Only the ideal of rationalism, projecting its shame-taboo against what reasonable men did not conclude upon, held off the knowledge that the revelation of the soul was written in many religions and the traces of many experiences. Churchgoer or atheist, the rational man was immune to psychic information. A ghost or two, perhaps, but not the gods. (D,F,68-9)

So persistent was rationalist supremacy that even during the Romantic period when William Blake, inspired by Thomas Taylor's various translations of Orphic and Hermetic writings, revived the ancient wisdom in his poetry and art, such efforts were either ignored or attacked as "a farrago of nonsense" or "the wild effusions of a distempered brain." Similar conflict surrounds Coleridge's definition of the imagination "or esemplastic power" from the famous fragmentary 13th chapter of the *Biographia Literaria*. Auspiciously introduced by a motto culled from Synesius' Hymns and indirectly characterized as "An orphic tale indeed, / . . . / To a *strange* music chaunted!," this crucial landmark in the evolution of the new arts reads like Hermetic theorizing on the imagination put in a nutshell:

> The primary imagination I hold to be the living power and prime agent of all human perception, and as a repetition in the finite mind of the eternal act of creation in the infinite I AM. The secondary I consider as an echo of the former . . . It dissolves, diffuses, dissipates, in order to re-create. (Ce,B,162,165,167)

Yet even Coleridge remained a slave to the Zeitgeist of his era, joined his rationalist contemporaries in their attacks on Taylor's neo-Platonism,[15] and finally, as he grew older and more orthodox, crossed out the crucial "a repetition in the finite mind of the eternal act of creation in the infinite I AM" in a copy of the *Biographia Literaria* annotated in his own hand.[16]

Such rationalism also dominated Victorian Europe. And even Yeats who, unlike Coleridge, intensified his youthful studies of Hermetic philosophy as he grew older, did not develop a following to hold its own against the renewed onslaught of critical orthodoxy led by T. S. Eliot and his New Critical followers in our century. But by now their often fatal influence on poets and artists has been broken by a new understanding of art as a reenactment of nature in process, achieved by projective empathy and psycho-physiological spontaneity, rather than as an imitation of reality in stasis, perpetrated by imposing upon its subject a unity or *"form created by a human, intellectual act"* (E. Kahler).

In understandable reaction against the orthodox critical establishment, these insights often tended to evolve by a radical rejection of our cultural heritage and a wholesale adoption of related notions from non-Western cultures. Yet in the light of the recently unearthed treasures of unorthodox Western thought, such iconoclasm now often tends to assume a pose of empty gesturing. And it may well turn out to be one of the major tasks for present-day artist æstheticians and scholars to follow pioneers such as Duncan or Ginsberg in the attempt to reformulate the new æsthetics in terms of this heritage and to rewrite literary history surrounding such major figures as Dante, Shakespeare, Goethe, or Yeats, whose works played a crucial role in rescuing the heretical wisdom from total suppression and in preparing the ground for a total redefinition of art in our century.

[1]*Poems of the Late T'ang,* ed. A. C. Graham (Harmondsworth: Penguin Books, 1970), p. 95.

[2]E. Kahler, *The Disintegration of Form in the Arts* (New York: Braziller, 1968), p. 3; C. Brooks, "My Credo," *Kenyon Review* 13 (1951), 72.

[3]See for instance D. D. Pearlman, *The Barb of Time: On the Unity of Ezra Pound's Cantos* (New York: Oxford University Press, 1969), p. 13 or B. Sankey, *A Companion to William Carlos Williams's Paterson* (Berkeley: University of California Press, 1971), p. 213.

[4]E. Faas, *Offene Formen in der modernen Kunst und Literatur* (Munich: Goldmann Verlag, 1975).

[5]Cf. H. B. Staples, *Robert Lowell: The First Twenty Years* (London: Faber and Faber, 1962), p. 45.

[6]*Tri-Quarterly* 7 (Fall, 1966), 81.

[7]*Yale Review* 41 (Autumn, 1951), 157.

[8]*The Art of Sylvia Plath,* ed. Charles Newman (Bloomington, Ind.: Indiana University Press, 1971), p. 69.

[9]R. Browning, *The Poetical Works* (London: Oxford University Press, 1962), ix. There is a more extensive discussion of these matters in my *Poesie als Psychogramm* (Munich: Fink Verlag, 1974), pp. 18f.

[10]*The Contemporary Poet as Artist and Critic: Eight Symposia,* ed. A. Ostroff (Boston: Little, Brown, 1964), p. 108.

[11]See *Athanor* 4 (Spring, 1973), 20.

[12]See below p. 239.

[13]See below pp. 125, 126.

[14]In conversation.

[15]See *Thomas Taylor, the Platonist. Selected Writings,* ed. K. Raine and G. M. Harper, Bollingen Series LXXXVIII (Princeton, N.J.: Princeton University Press, 1969), p. 35.

[16]See J. Benziger, "Organic Unity: Leibniz to Coleridge," *PMLA*, 66 (March, 1951), 24-48, 42.

Charles Olson
Robert Duncan

Photo: Gerard Malanga

# CHARLES OLSON (1910 - 1970)

"I am an archeologist of morning. And the writing and arts which I find bear on the present job are (I) from Homer back, not forward; and (II) from Melville on, particularly himself, Dostoyevsky, Rimbaud, and Lawrence. These were the modern men who projected what we are and what we are in, who broke the spell. They put men forward into the post-modern, the post-humanist, the post-historic, the going live present, the 'Beautiful Thing.' "

Born in Worcester, Mass., the son of a Swedish father and Catholic Irish-American mother, Olson was "uneducated" at Wesleyan, Yale and Harvard (B.A., 1932; M.A., 1933). He taught at Clark University in Worcester and, from 1936-39, at Harvard. His first book *Call Me Ishmael* (1947) appeared two years after the publication of his first poem at age thirty-five. From 1939-48 he worked in various jobs, from fishing-boat hand to government official in the Office of War Information. "I have had to learn the simplest things / last."In 1948, he took the place of his friend and mentor, novelist Edward Dahlberg, at Black Mountain College and as its rector (1951-56) began his influential career as teacher, æsthetician and leader of the Black Mountain movement (Creeley, Levertov, Duncan, etc.). His epoch-making essay on "Projective Verse" was published in 1950, its propositions enlarged and developed in further essays (*Human Universe,* 1965; *Selected Writings,* 1966; *Additional Prose,* 1974), letters and reading lists to friends (*Mayan Letters,* 1953; *Letters for Origin 1950-1956,* 1969; *A Bibliography on America for Ed Dorn,* 1964) and lecture series (*The Special View of History,* 1970; *Poetry and Truth,* 1971). Of his poetry (*In Cold Hell, In Thicket,* 1953; *The Distances,* 1960), *The Maximus Poems* (1-10, 1953; 11-22, 1956; combined in 1960; *Maximus IV, V, VI,* 1968; *Maximus Poems,* vol. 3, 1975) in the tradition of Pound's *Cantos* and Williams' *Paterson* are his most important legacy.

# Charles Olson

**W**hen I first entered the American literary world in 1972, I was amazed to find that Olson, a man of firmly established international reputation abroad, was at best considered a figure of ridicule in New York literary circles. Here, James Dickey's derisive comments from the early sixties still seemed to be the stock-in-trade for polite cut-throat party chatter: that Olson's poetics were largely derivative (Dickey quotes René Nelli's *Poésie ouverte, poésie fermée*) and that his "trump card" was to have discovered the influence of the typewriter on modern poetry (Di,B,136-7). Since then we have witnessed a veritable explosion of Olson research: there is an Olson journal, an Olson archive, a 367 page *boundary 2* (1973/74) Olson issue and above all an ever increasing number of Olson Ph.Ds. Another lit. crit. "industry" has started, and only eight years after his death in 1970, the poet seems to be well assured of his niche in the mausoleum of academic scholarship.

As pointed out, Olson's poetics may be considered as part of a general new æsthetics in progress in which the modern tradition seems to be gradually coming to a full understanding of itself. The ideas of the composer John Cage and the painter Jackson Pollock, for instance, were well known to Olson. Others like the novelist Robbe-Grillet or the composer Karlheinz Stockhausen have formulated comparable theories in which the American poet would have found welcome confirmation for parts of his own. Yet it may well be that no other poet or artist before him has discussed the evolving new æsthetics in more far-ranging and comprehensive terms than Olson himself.

In our world of specialized knowledge any such polyhistoric attempt is, of course, bound to fail in a strictly scholarly sense, and it would be easy to point out the errors, misconceptions and above all the eclecticism to be found in Olson's writings. But the same applies to a comparable figure such as Coleridge, whose ideas had an unceasing influence on generations of later poets. And as the desire to understand poetry in its widest implications persists, there will be people grateful for the insights these men have afforded us. They will share some of the excitement with which William Carlos Williams greeted the publication of Olson's essay on "Projective Verse." "[It] is as if the whole area lifted," he wrote Robert Creeley (O,W,6). By printing part of the essay in his autobiography Williams conceded how to him as to many others Olson's insights brought a fulfillment and clarification which their own efforts had denied them.

It has by now become a commonplace of literary history to see Olson in a continuing line of poets which includes Pound, Crane, Zukofsky and Williams; it is thus easy to forget that it was Olson himself who as early as 1953, at the height of Eliot's fame and influence, described these poets as the great and future tradition of American poetry, and the school of Eliot as a dead end in the development of modern literature. And though there is disagreement as to the "great tradition of American poetry," Eliot's reputation among poets of the 60's and 70's seems now to be more or less what Olson predicted two decades ago. On the other hand even Olson himself had reservations about the "advance in discourse which Pound & Williams, and Crane, after his lights, led the rest of us on to" (O,U,63).

Although he acknowledged Pound as the founding father of this development, he considered the philosophical understanding shown by his predecessor both wrong-headed and limited. It was Fenollosa's rather than Pound's ideas which, according to Olson, could have helped Hart Crane to a full unfolding of his poetic temperament, crippled under the dictates of the New Criticism (O,W,21). Pound's thinking was almost violently anthropocentric, whereas Olson, following philosophers such as Whorf and Whitehead, was searching for an "ALTERNATIVE TO THE EGO-POSITION" (O,W,83). Pound's major importance lay in his "methodology" ("the necessities that the execution of form involves," O,L,105), Williams' in his emphasis on the particular and concrete, his "no ideas but in things." Neither of them offered a model for what Olson called his "stance toward reality": "if i think EP gave any of us the methodological clue: the RAG-BAG; bill gave us the lead on the LOCAL . . . Neither of them: WHAT" (O,L,129).

Olson's "stance toward reality" was based on extensive studies ranging from nuclear physics, non-Euclidean geometry and modern philosophy to Primitive culture, Eastern religion and metalinguistics. There was one poet, however, whom he acknowledged to have anticipated the general drift of his theorizing: D. H. Lawrence, whom Olson considered the only "prospective" poet of that generation (O,U,102). It was one of Pound's worst mistakes to ignore Lawrence, who could have provided him with intuitive insights denied to his more strictly critical genius. Yet the American poet had an ineradicable aversion to the British novelist. "Detestable person but needs watching," he remarked in 1913 (P,L,17). As it happened, Pound didn't follow his own advice, and it was left to a later writer to combine the achievements of these two most important and influential pioneers of modern Anglo-American literature. "Pound and Lawrence more and more stand up," Olson wrote in 1951, "as the huge two of the 1st half of the 20th century" (O,L,63).

As Olson recognized, D. H. Lawrence deserves a far more eminent place in the history of the modern movement than he is granted this side of the Atlantic. A pioneer of a new kind of open form novel,[1]* he visualized, as early as 1920, an open form "poetry of this immediate present" in the tradition of Whitman; a poetry with no beginning or end, whose essence lay in "the sheer appreciation of the instant moment, life surging itself into utterance at its very well-head" (La,C,86,87). In his painting he anticipated the impulse of abstract expressionism[2] and his descriptions of the dances of the North American Indians seem to foretell the most recent developments in music, choreography and multi-media art forms.[3]

More specifically, it was Lawrence's criticism of Western civilization which exerted a direct influence on Olson. In reversal of the Christian doctrine Lawrence had described the fall of man as a fall into teleological, future oriented thinking about the beyond: "[B]y the time of Christ all religion . . . instead of being religion of *life,* here and now, became religion of postponed destiny, death, and reward *afterwards,* 'if you are good.' " For Lawrence there was no beyond and no eternity, only the timeless here and now—"there is no goal. Consciousness is an end in itself. We torture ourselves getting somewhere, and when we get there it is nowhere, for there is nowhere to get to" (La,A,32,43). As the herald of abstract thought, of the "disease of idealism" (La,F,85), Socrates, besides Christ, was the second most pernicious influence on the evolution of Western civilization. "With the coming of Socrates and the 'spirit,' the cosmos died. For two thousand years man has been living in a dead and dying cosmos, hoping for a heaven hereafter. And all the religions have been religions of the dead body and the postponed reward" (La,A,46). Lawrence spent his life in search of this living cosmos. And like Olson after him he believed he had found it among the North American Indians, the Mexicans, among the earliest, pre-Socratic cultures of the world, or even among the debris of our own civilization.

*Notes for this section on p. 51

Part of this search was for man's original language, uncorrupted by our Judæo-Christian and Greek ways of thinking. Like Fenollosa in his analysis of the "Chinese written character" (F,C,22f.), but independently, Lawrence describes it as a language of "rotary image-thought" instead of our "modern process of progressive thought"; of concrete symbols and "picturegraphs" instead of allegorical equations or abstract concepts; as a language of autonomous and open semantic entities instead of our "monolinear . . . sentence structure" (E. Pound, P,B,475), our "logical chain[s] . . . [where] every full-stop is a mile-stone that marks our 'progress' and our arrival somewhere." The *Apocalypse,* especially in its early parts, "before the birth of the Child," served him as a document for this language of the "old pagan civilisation":

> in it we have, not the modern process of progressive thought, but the old pagan process of rotary image-thought. Every image fulfils its own little circle of action and meaning, then is superseded by another image . . . Every image is a picturegraph, and the connection between the images will be made more or less differently by every reader.(La,A,43,45)

According to Lawrence there were no abstractions in this primordial language. And the concrete had a numinous and dynamic quality equal to the mutual interrelatedness of all being, or what Lawrence describes as "the rapid momentaneous association of things which meet and pass on the for ever incalculable journey of creation: everything left in its own rapid, fluid relationship with the rest of things" (La,C,86). Even to the early scientists and philosophers words like "cold" did not denote a quality, but embodied an "existing entity." The "cold," the "moist," the "hot," the "dry" "were things in themselves, realities, gods, *theoi.* And they *did things*" (La,A,46).

If Olson differed from these theories it was mainly in his definitions of the terms "symbol" and "allegory." Lawrence praised the symbol as a "complex of emotional experience" (La,C,158) and as a primary constituent of myth, whereas Olson attacked symbolism for the very qualities which Lawrence would have criticized as allegorical—that denotative character, which, ever since Plato discovered his realm of ideas, has made all signs, images and words stand for abstract ideas rather than concrete and numinous entities—"the suck of symbol which has increased and increased since the great Greeks first promoted the idea of a transcendent world of forms" (O,W,61). It was in this sense that Olson tried to refute the Eliot critic Grover Smith who had criticized Williams' poetry for its lack of symbolism. "It doesn't take much thought over Bill's proposition—'Not in ideas but in things'—to be sure that any of us intend an image as a 'thing,' never, so far as we know, such a non-animal as symbol"(O,U,65). But even Olson was aware of the fact that this use of the word was due to a corruption of its original meaning. Taken back to its radical, he wrote, it "will reveal its proper meaning: fr. Greek *symbolon,* 'a sign by which one knows or infers a thing'" (O,M,11)—a meaning even Lawrence would probably have agreed with.

Not only the symbol, our whole language, "as it [has] been since Socrates" (O,U,117), was corrupted by this process of allegorization. Our words have "suffered from the tendency . . . to acquire abstract meanings" (O,M,10,11), the syntax, originally characterized by a cumulative addition of autonomous entities, was subjected to a system of predicative logic and its *"rational patterns of discourse"* (O,U,63). Olson pointed to Havelock's *Preface to Plato* (1963) as proof of these Lawrentian speculations on a pre-Socratic language. For according to Havelock, poets such as Homer and Hesiod had used "a wholly different syntax . . . [or] *parataxis* in which the words and actions reported are set down side by side in the order of their occurrence in nature, instead of by an order of discourse, or 'grammar' " (O,R,41).

The alienation of language from nature is a result of what Olson, again echoing Lawrence, described as the "fall of man" into our scientific and teleological ways of thought. In what looks like a deliberate *mise au point* of Lawrence's notion, Socrates and Christ play the devil's role in this pseudo-Christian mystery play (O,W,146-47; O,L,33). Olson enlarged upon this notion in his critique of our Western concept of history. Originally, history was neither a search for objective facts and their causal interconnectedness, as initiated by Thucydides, nor the attempt of Christian writers to justify the ways of God amidst the suffering and meaninglessness of man's historical destiny. As shown by Herodotus, the first, greatest and last of Western historiographers, it was a "finding out for oneself " (O,V,20), an attempt to relate to the world in its here and now, where time "was not a line drawn straight ahead toward future, a logic of good and evil" (O,I,97-98), but a returning on itself. It was a pursuit circumscribed by an idea of life with no beyond, fulfilled in the "preoccupation with itself " (O,W,152). With such writers as Captain John Smith, the poet John Keats, or the early Melville, this original understanding had been preserved at isolated points in Western thought. On the whole, however, our concept of history had been a self-contradictory compound of scientific claims

and providential speculation. As Olson came to recognize in antici-
pation of recent scholarly investigation, even Hegel's dialectic (like
Marx's materialism) was but a secularized variant of this principle.
When Hegel interpreted history as a gradual unfolding of the spirit,
he merely made it fit a preconceived notion of what history ought to
be. "He takes what is condition as result, instead of leaving it, as
Keats does, *penetralium*" (O,V,43).

Olson found a similar variant of Judæo-Christian providential
thinking in what Robbe-Grillet, after the American poet, has described as the "tragic humanism" (R-G,R,71) of Existentialist
philosophy and its notion of the absurdity and meaninglessness of
life. As Olson wrote in *The Special View of History,* his most brilliant
piece of general criticism,

> a teleology of form as progressive was the hidden assumption
> of the old cosmology, and Void is what's left when the kosmos
> breaks down as the interesting evidence of order, Man falls
> when that purpose falls, and so Void is the only assumption
> left.(O,V,47-48)

To Olson, as to Robbe-Grillet, history and reality are "neither meaningful nor absurd" (R-G,R,21). There is neither progress nor tradition. "NATURE TAKES NOTHING BUT LEAPS" (O,L,11). "The
motive, then, of reality, is process not goal . . . the chance success of
the play of creative accident" (O,V,49). This is a concept of reality
reminiscent of Zen Buddhism and, like this Eastern religion, it is
contrary to what Olson describes as the "peculiar presumption by
which Western man has interposed himself between what he is as a
creature of nature . . . and those other creations of nature which we
. . . call objects," a presumption that finally resulted in suppressing
nature within and outside ourselves. To Olson "man is himself an
object" (O,W,24), his true function not a controlling of nature, but
the attempt to be one with her. And again D. H. Lawrence had been
the first to point the way out of this dilemma—through those
"primordial & phallic energies & methodologies which . . . make it
possible for man, that participant thing, to take up, straight, nature's, live nature's force" (O,U,23).

If Lawrence had upheld pre-Socratic and non-Western cultures
as models for these new concepts of man and the world, the results of
modern science, as interpreted by Olson, seem to point in the same
direction. Describing reality as "continuous" instead of "discrete"
("the old system . . . [including] discourse, language as it had been
since Socrates"), the non-Euclidean geometer Riemann, according
to one of Olson's typical sweeps of eclectic syncretism, reverted to the

Heraclitean idea of a "flow of creation" (O,U,117,119), first re-
envisioned through Keats' *"Negative Capability"* and finally reclaimed
for our modern world picture by Heisenberg's quantum theory:

> Our advantage is that a century and a half after Keats, the
> universe as seen by Heraclitus' naked eye and mind has been
> restored . . . One cannot abstract from it. One has to get it in its
> place or occurrences. And study it in place and in motion
> (what Heisenberg gave us the wonderful words for to go with
> Keats' ambiguity: The Uncertainty Principle. Right out of the
> mouth of physics one can seize the condition Keats insisted a
> man must stay in the midst of: . . . "a man is capable of being in
> uncertainties, mysteries, doubts . . ." Only thus do you have
> *both* mass and momentum, or substance & motion. (O,V,33,39)

Morever, Olson believed himself in the advantageous position
of finding the intuitive insights of a Keats, Melville or Lawrence
confirmed by recent linguistic and anthropological research. There
were Fenollosa and Whorf, guides "fr the Old Discourse to the New"
(O,P,7), there was Eric A. Havelock on pre-Socratic syntax, as well as
a host of other scholars such as Michael Ventris, C. H. Gordon, Hans
Güterbock and S. N. Kramer in the fields of Cretan, Ugaritic, Hittite
and Sumerian studies. "A tremendous moment" in the history of
Western thought, as Olson thought:

> We live in an age in which inherited literature is being hit from
> two sides, from contemporary writers who are laying bases of
> new discourse at the same time that such scholars as the above
> are making available pre-Homeric and pre-Mosaic texts which
> are themselves eye-openers. (O,U,150)

As is well known, Olson had himself carried out extensive
studies of Mayan culture and language, and it was in a similar spirit
of learning and research that he pursued his vocation as poet and
creator of a new language. He believed that this "new discourse"
could be gained by restructuring the old and that the English language, following the model of non-Western languages, could ultimately return to its pre-Socratic origins. As Fenollosa taught him,
the general changes concerning syntax and grammar would have to
be based on the potential vitality of the spoken word, the "language
as the act of the instant . . . [not] the act of thought about the instant"
(O,W,54). And it was probably Hopi language, as analyzed by
Whorf, that inspired his attempts to reorganize the tenses, to "drive
all nouns, the abstract most of all, back to process—to act" (O,U,70)
and to regain "the kinetics of words" (O,M,10) in

general. For under a thin semantic layer of abstraction there was the old dynamic potential, and the syllable, that "least logical" part of the language, offered a direct access to this latent etymological force. Our abstract "is," for example, "comes from the Aryan root, *as*, to breathe. The English 'not' equals the Sanscrit *na*, which may come from the root *na*, to be lost, to perish. 'Be' is from *bhu*, to grow" (O,W,18; also see F,C,15). In this way "both the phonetic and ideographic" elements are "still present and available for use as impetus and explosion in our alphabetic speech" (O,U,18). And for Olson it was the poet's task to reclaim them.

Naturally, the syllable and its prelogical elements, as divined by the poet's ear, become the prime element of poetry: the "king and pin of versification." It is by their syllables, not by any preconceived patterns of discourse, that words are "juxtapose[d] in beauty," by a process of physio-linguistic empathy rather than of intellectual organization. "In any given instance, because there is a choice of words, the choice, if man is in there, will be, spontaneously, the obedience of his ear to the syllables" (O,W,17,18). As hearing recovers the old vitality of human language, the poet's creativity springs from a fusion with the "flow of creation," for which man's original language had been the direct medium. Poetic creation becomes a simple release of these natural forces, in which the poet feels himself to be a part of the cosmos. Poetry is not made but happens, is not an abstraction that tries to transcend nature but a natural event that embodies it—what Lawrence describes as "life surging itself into utterance at its very well-head," and Olson as the poet's "projective act":

> if he is contained within his nature as he is participant in the larger force, he will be able to listen, and his hearing through himself will give him secrets objects share . . . It is in this sense that . . . the artist's act in the larger field of objects, leads to dimensions larger than the man. For a man's problem, the moment he takes speech up in all its fullness, is to . . . cause the thing he makes to try to take its place alongside the things of nature. (O,W,25)

The poet's "projective act" resembles the gestural autodynamics of action painting or the meditative sound releases in recent Stockhausen compositions[4]—a common impulse, perhaps antithetical to our Western concept of art, but with precedents in cultures that are equal, if not superior to our own; as in Sino-Japanese calligraphy and *Sumi-e* painting which flow from the autonomous spontaneity of the artist's bodily movements (Wa,W,174), or in Zen Buddhist flute music, in which the breath rhythm, expressing man's vital harmony with the universe, determines the sequence of sounds (G-R,W,610).

Similarly Olson declares breath—"the breathing of the man who writes, at the moment that he writes"—to be the second most important factor in poetic creativity besides our hearing. The "projective poet," he writes at the end of his famous essay,

> [goes] down through the workings of his own throat to that place where breath comes from, where breath has its beginnings . . . where . . . all act springs. (O,W,19,26)

It is here that we come to what Dickey has derided as the "trump card" (Di,B,137) of Olson's theorizing: that the poet, thanks to the typewriter, can "indicate exactly the breath, the pauses, the suspensions even of syllables, the juxtapositions even of parts of phrases" and thus mirror in print the "presentational immediacy" (Whitehead, Wh,S,21ff.) which is the poem's essence. In this way the reader will be able to "voice [the poet's] work" (O,W,22), and, given that it is successful, will be drawn into the poem rather than analyze or judge it. He will relive the process of creation and share the dance of cosmic forces that has found a voice in the poem's words and rhythms. Being a direct release of the unceasing "flow of creation," there can be neither "prior concepts of COHERENCE" (O,L,105) nor any preconceived limitations to the "projective act." The poem, like a painting by Pollock, has "a life of its own," its creator simply trying to "let it come through" (Rn,P,194). Rather than the poet writing the poem, the poem writes the poet.[5] From the moment he ventures into "FIELD COMPOSITION," as Olson calls it, "he can go by no track other than the one the poem under hand declares, for itself " (O,W,16).

Like Robbe-Grillet, Olson could have spoken of the poet's "total subjectivity" (R-G,R,148), and it is not surprising to find that Olson, several years before the French novelist, expanded upon this notion in his introduction to Robert Creeley's short stories. Olson and Robbe-Grillet share a concept of reality as "neither meaningful nor absurd." And they both know about the difficulty of describing it. Our language, or rather what Robbe-Grillet (after Roland Barthes) defines as its socio-political component ("l'écriture"), represents a dense semantic network that tends to subject reality to the "tyranny" of its cultural, religious or ideological "significations." This, however, is the very language of our traditional novels, which therefore fail to render reality in its phenomenological existence of "being there" (R-G,R,24,25). A normal description, as Olson puts it, does not come to grips with what really matters: that a thing, any thing, impinges on us by a more important fact, its self-existence, without reference to any other thing, in short, the very character of it which calls our attention to it, which wants us to know more about it, its particularity. This is what we are confronted by, not the thing's 'class,' any hierarchy, of quality or quantity, but the thing itself, and its *relevance* to ourselves who are the experience of it. (O,W,56)

Reality has to speak for itself, through a medium that is an inextricable part of its flux and change—not through the omniscient author of traditional novels, but through "a man placed in space and time, conditioned by his passions . . . [and] involved . . . in an adventure so passionate and all-engrossing that it will tend to deform his vision" (R-G,R,149). In other words, reality, as Lawrence had been one of the first to realize, must be reenacted instead of being described. And according to Olson there were two narrative techniques or "methodologies" to achieve this. One was Joyce's "exit author," "what I call DOCUMENT simply to emphasize that the events alone do the work, that the narrator stays OUT, functions as pressure not as interpreting person." The other technique, which Olson found in Creeley's stories, equals Robbe-Grillet's "total subjectivity" of the narrator: "the total IN . . . total speculation . . . the narrator taking on himself the job of making clear by way of his own person that life *is* preoccupation with itself." Although the exact opposite of the former, it "drive[s] for the same end": to let reality speak for itself, "so to re-enact experience that a story has what an object or person has: energy and instant." For the narrator may be present at every moment of his narrative, but his "total subjectivity" renders him a mere object among other objects. "And the writer, though he is the control (or art is nothing) is, still, no more than—but just as much as—another 'thing,' and as such, is in, inside or out" (O,U,127-8).

To be sure, Olson does not share the almost schizophrenic combination of hyper-empirical phenomenalism and analytical intellectuality that tends to reduce Robbe-Grillet's world to a labyrinth of geometric abstractions. For to Olson, as to Lawrence before him, the essence of reality is its life-force, and poetry as well as the other arts has to partake of this vitality in order to reenact it. Far from being intellectual, this is a concept of art reminiscent of what W. Schmalenbach defines as the foremost principle of Primitive art: the embodiment of nature's animistic forces, which turns art into an "expression of intrinsic vitality" ("Ausdruck . . . von Kraft an sich,"

(G-R,W,431). And, indeed, Olson demanded "the replacement of the Classical-representational by the *primitive abstract*," a form of art, that, within the framework of an animistic universe, becomes the only valid form of religion. "There is only one thing you can do ✓ about kinetic, reenact it. Which is why the man said, he who possesses rhythm, possesses the universe. And why art is the only twin life has—its only valid metaphysic" (O,W,61).

Olson was a professionally trained dancer, and as any reader of his criticism realizes, dance and rhythm are his most frequent and central metaphors to describe poetry and art in general. More explicitly he called "dance the base of his discipline" (i.e., of the "recognition of the kinetic as the act of life") "and its syllabary the source of any other" (O,M,12). What he meant by dance, however, was radically different from the programmed choreography of traditional dance, which he found "altogether too descriptive and so . . . of all things for dance to be!—non-active." To Olson dance is "not mimesis but kinesis." But at the time he formulated this principle in his *Apollonius of Tyana: A Dance, with Some Words, for Two Actors* (1951), he could only think of "one or two" people who were trying to recover this original form of dance. In a letter of the same year he identified Merce Cunningham as one of these (O,L,53). And indeed Cunningham (by 1951 still an unknown or at best ridiculed artist) has since fulfilled Olson's promise by becoming one of the foremost innovators of choreography in America. Olson and Cunningham collaborated at Black Mountain where they performed what is regarded as the first happening in the history of modern art. In their ideas about dance they were both inspired by Primitive culture, a model Olson's Apollonius finds among a fictive tribe of the Upper Nile. These GUMNOI or "NAKEDS" "have taken up direct from energy . . .[from] the dæmonial nature in anything, including ourselves," so that their dances are a spontaneous reenactment of cosmic forces, uncontrolled by any mental principles or preconceived patterns; where each dancer is "allowed to be himself alone in the midst of the phenomenal world raging and yet apart" (O,W,152).

Again, Olson seems to draw upon the prophetic insights of his greatest and most important predecessor. In 1922 D. H. Lawrence visited the North American Indians, and although at first repelled by the tourist industry surrounding them, he finally seems to have found in their dances an embodiment of the original and future ideal of art as he conceived it. What he describes is a kind of Primitive happening in which dance is a spontaneous release of cosmic energy, a segment of the "untellable flood of creation," with "no beginning and no end," with "no division between actor and audience" and consequently "no judgement: absolutely no judgement . . . because there is nothing outside it, to judge it" (La,M,62-3).

"Lawrence . . . alone," Olson writes, "had the true mask, he lacked the critical intelligence, and was prospective" (O,U,102). This equally paradoxical and insightful remark could stand as an appropriate epitaph for Olson's own achievement. More than any American poet of his generation he gave his successors a goal towards which to direct their own endeavors. But his message is destined to remain a goal rather than become accepted doctrine. Like Lawrence before him, Olson lacked the "critical intelligence" and erudition to relate his insights to the mainstream of Western thought of which they remain a product, however much they tend to reverse it. And there are more than half a dozen figures besides Melville, Rimbaud or Keats who are part of this mainstream. But one should not forget the debt modern poetry owes to Olson as to Lawrence, even for their very lack of "critical intelligence" which gave them part of the courage needed to discard the dead weight of a tradition that frequently stifled the insights of men more learned and prudent than themselves. And there have been poets younger than Olson, both amongst his followers and enemies, who, as we shall see, have since tried to remedy these deficiencies.

[1]See Alan Friedman, *The Turn of the Novel: The Transition to Modern Fiction* (London: Oxford University Press, 1970), pp. 130ff.

[2]Compare Pollock's statement quoted above, p. 12, with Lawrence's "Making Pictures" (La,E,301): "It is to me the most exciting moment—when you have a blank canvas and a big brush full of wet colour, and you plunge. It is just like diving into a pond—then you start frantically to swim. So far as I am concerned, it is like swimming in a baffling current and being rather frightened and very thrilled, gasping and striking out for all you're worth. The knowing eye watches sharp as a needle; but the picture comes clean out of instinct, intuition and sheer physical action. Once the instinct and intuition gets into the brush-tip, the picture *happens*, if it is to be a picture at all."

[3]See pp. 49f.

[4]See *Texte*, 3 vol. (Cologne: Verlag DuMont Schauberg, 1963-71), III, 108 f., 313 f.

[5]Alain Bosquet's phrase; in his *Verbe et Vertige: Situations de la poésie* (Paris: Hachette, 1961), pp. 89f., he describes a similar phenomenon in modern French poetry.

# Robert Duncan (1919-      )

> "What released my sense of a new generation in poetry was first a poem ("The Shifting" by Denise Levertov) in *Origin* VI, 1952; then in 1954 thru *The Gold Diggers* a grasp of the art of Robert Creeley, where such minute attentions and cares moved in the line; and third, but from the first, the break-thru to a meaningful reading of Olson's *Maximus*, from which his *Projective Verse* and *In Cold Hell, In Thicket* took on new meaning: that, for one thing, the task in poetry can be promethean. In Whitman's words: 'The theme is creative and has vista.' "

Born in Oakland, California, Robert Duncan never knew his mother, who died shortly after his birth, or his father, who gave him up for adoption at the age of six months. His foster parents' association with the local Hermetic Brotherhood prompted the poet's life-long, but not uncritical, fascination with the occult, Hermeticism, Gnosticism, neo-Platonism and Christian religion. Such interests fused with others in psychiatry, field psychology and modern art during his post-1938 period of travel between West and East coast as a 20th century vagantes scholar poet: first in close proximity with Anaïs Nin and her New York circle, then as a pivotal figure in various groups (around Robin Blaser, Jack Spicer, Philip Lamantia, Kenneth Rexroth, Helen Adam, James Broughton and others) that led to the San Francisco Renaissance of the 50's. After a first meeting with Olson in 1947, he became an important member of the movement associated with Black Mountain College where he taught in 1956. Though recognized by Anaïs Nin and others as a poetic genius in his late teens, Duncan was a late developer like his friend Olson. Aside from *The Venice Poem* (1948), which marked his transition "from the concept of a dramatic form to a concept of musical form," most of his major poetry is contained in three collections: *The Opening of the Field* (1960), *Roots and Branches* (1964) and *Bending the Bow* (1968). He has vowed not to publish another volume before 1983. A one-time disciple of Ernst Kantorowicz at Berkeley as well as a scholar of life-long dedication, Duncan never took an academic degree. For all that, his critical prose (including his semi-autobiographical H. D. book in progress) published in avant-garde journals and booklets (*The Sweetness and Greatness of Dante's "Divine Comedy," 1265-1965*, 1965; *The Truth and Life of Myth: An Essay in Essential Autobiography*, 1968) represents a unique achievement, both for its theoretical originality and erudite comprehensiveness. It badly needs collecting.

# Robert Duncan

I

*Faas*: On January 1, 1970 you flew from San Francisco to New York to pay a last visit to Olson shortly before he died. What did you talk about while you were with him?

DUNCAN: Charles was trying to work something out around the notion of liver. Being a devout Jungian, he was trying to figure out what the meaning of that cancer taking place in his body was. And an analyst had told him that liver was feminine. So one of the things he was writing on a piece of paper while I was with him was "live-her," as a kind of formula of liv-er. So off and on we were talking about that "her." You have seen the letter I wrote Jess the following day. It was published in the first Olson journal. That gives my own account right on top of that session.

last session with Olson

Charles opened our conversation by saying: It's been twenty-five years of adventure. And my first flash was, of course: Oh, no. But then I realized that, indeed, I had first met him in 1947. I have always had a feeling of panic that those people I knew before I knew Jess would feel some prior claim. And it was as if Charles at that point was making that prior claim. Of course, he was like this with everyone. He had the special message for everyone that was with him. But certainly, I had been on an adventure with him. Although my age of Olson was really between 1950 and 1972.

*Faas*: You first read Olson's essay on "Projective Verse" in 1950, I remember.

DUNCAN: Yes, it was by 1950 that I was beginning to read it. From 1950 onwards I began to answer Olson's call and to step into that arena and to take my place there. But not before 1952 did I really absorb his essay.

*Faas*: Obviously, Olson knew that he was dying.

DUNCAN: Oh, yes. He had terminal cancer. We couldn't have any doubt about his dying. As a matter of fact, at that point, he only had about three weeks left to live. The cancer was in his liver so they really couldn't give him pain killers and he was just out of his mind by that afternoon. But during our morning session, he was talking all

55

the time, and I felt: Gee, he's going to exhaust himself. But he wanted to go on. It's only when he lapsed into sleep that we finished talking.

*Faas*: Was he in pain all the time while he was talking?

DUNCAN: No. I think he was so keyed up in talking and working that he didn't feel it. So he worked on that "live-her" thing. And the one thing I wanted to say to him right away was: Isn't it remarkable, Charles, maybe you and I are the only ones, as it looks like, who are concerned about composition by field. Of course, Creeley's *Pieces* is composed by field. But only Charles and I seem to have had field theory. And we are the only ones after all from the thirties when Koehler's field theory was very exciting. Koehler's field theory of the æsthetics of painting and his attempt to read music that way. That was the important thing before Freud completely took over riding high in certain American circles.

composition by field

*Faas*: What was Olson's reaction?

DUNCAN: Well, he grinned, and I added: To think that at the end of it we each just have our own actual duties to do and that we aren't leaders, and that it wasn't part of history. And he entirely concurred with that. But he said: Well, we've been on a great twenty-five year long adventure together.

*Faas*: What was his sense of his own life at that time?

DUNCAN: He told me that he had completed *Maximus* which shocked me. Although I had already seen that *Maximus* was a poem which wasn't open. I mean, in my sense of open. Because Olson had never observed that open would mean that you wouldn't begin or end. He always remained a good Roman Catholic who does begin and end.

*Faas*: Was Olson afraid of death?

DUNCAN: Well, the second thing I said was: I came to see you die. You've always been an older poet adventuring ahead of me, and I have come to see you die in order to practise, in order to see how appropriately a man would die. And he said: Well, no it's that "live-her" thing, I am not doing that. And by the time he died he was completely out of it. Although I saw him die almost as if he was going to unlock "live-her." And he had quite a number of jokes about "her" and "she," meaning the *anima*.

unlocking "live-her"

He had no clothes on and he was naked entirely except for a sort of sheet which he wore a little as if he were some huge Socrates. And he had lost all his flesh, so that he seemed like a truly magnificent and very Nordic looking creature. He really looked like some kind of Wotan. And his skeleton was much more appropriate to his size than his flesh had ever been. He really looked like his Oceanus. And he said to me: Come and hold me. And I went to the bed and held him. At that point the nurse came in and was very upset. And Charles said: I asked this man to hold me in his arms. Do you want to do something about it? And the nurse let out a scream and ran out of the room.

And yes, he did talk about dying. They had taken him to a special cancer hospital and at that point he was unwilling to admit that he was in terminal cancer. But after a couple of days they took the liver puncture and found that they couldn't operate because the cancer had reached the liver and he would never have been able to survive the anæsthetics. So then they threw him away. I mean, they were just a repair factory.

At one point he said: I want some doctor and you know what I mean, Duncan, your dream. He meant the dream that I brought into print in Charles's lifetime, the dream in which Charles and I are at the springs and we are releasing the springs. As a matter of fact, Robin Blaser is on the horizon in the far West in that dream. So while I had come to get my instructions on how to die he was concerned with the fact that he didn't have a doctor to attend him. Meanwhile, I was shocked that he didn't have a priest and that he didn't receive the Extreme Unction which he didn't.

*Faas:* A priest for Olson?

DUNCAN: Well, you see, my idea of death is ritualistic. And Charles himself insisted upon the Catholicism throughout. When Betty, his common-law wife, died, he wanted to put Charles Peter into a very strict convent school. Only his friends prevented that. But his first impulse was to do that. And he had a Catholic funeral service read over Betty and was very upset because they now read it in English. He said: I didn't know that they would read it in English.

Olson's<br>Catholicism

*Faas:* Betty was the woman who died in the car accident?

DUNCAN: Yes. So Charles wanted to keep the Catholic origins somewhat in the same way that I kept my Hermeticism. Although Charles didn't go to Church. So finally he didn't ask for a priest either, but he asked for a doctor. So he is Jungian and that was a better place for him. He didn't have an analyst, of course, any more than, I mean, who? And at death he wanted a doctor, a kind of mystery doctor to take him through the mystery of death, preparing him for that mystery. But as a poet, of course, he had to do it all on his own. I am sure I will have to do it on my own, too. Since we have hugged all those moments ourselves and had only language to do it, we have to do it in language. And he must have been doing it with "live-her." You know, "live-her," once it was divided and he was staring at it, he may have been staring not at the *anima,* but at Persephone herself in her awful character as Queen of the Dead. So "live-her" may be "life-death." He was unable to unlock it and he kept on looking at it and trying to see what it was that was happening there, and that went back and forth on his mind.

*Letters for Origin* had just arrived and he inscribed a copy for me and that is the last piece of his writing. And there he addresses the fact that I was the poet that had been writing before his age began. Of course, at the same time he was very questioning of the fact that I might not be the person properly active in the new poetry and that I might be the person rather to disgrace it. But still, from his whole sense of continuity and tradition, he needed a key that before he started to write there had been a poet preceding him. And that identity I came in some way to occupy. It was a little like Anaïs Nin trying to find a poet when I hadn't written any poems yet. So he was excited about my poetry, but it was not the new poetry. The new poetry of that age was to be worked out entirely between Creeley and Olson. I was always then an intermediate between that and the poetry of the generation of the masters.

*Faas:* Could I see that last inscription?

DUNCAN: Of course. Let's go up to the attic and have a look at it. [After walking up to the attic.] This is it. [Handing me the book.]

*Faas:* It's quite illegible.

DUNCAN: [reads]: "To Duncan who taught me first the way," signed "from Charles, New York Hospital."

*Faas:* What does the rest say?

DUNCAN: [reads]: "To Duncan who taught me first the way and thought which I now" . . . The rest I can't decipher . . . "carry"? And then: "I am told"? No, I think, it's "I am tired."

*Faas:* And it's in *Letters for Origin* that Olson expressed the suspicion that you may not be quite reliable after all!

## II

DUNCAN: Even Creeley, I think, at first thought I was going to be a little bit like the characters he had known at Harvard. Something like *The Venice Poem* must have spoken to him of some precious scenes at Harvard that none of us would exactly want to resurrect. Remember that I was quite an old person in relation to the Black Mountain generation. Although Olson was ten years older than I was, I had already begun to write

*[margin note: last inscription]*

*[margin note: the Black Mountain poets]*

long before him and all the others, of course. So in a way it is an odd thing that I ended up with that group of writers. Yet not before they appeared on the scene did I find home ground. And home ground is very hard to find. Even if we had thrown in a university education, I would have found it very difficult to find a home ground with the poets of my own generation. I mean, the generation of Lowell, Jarrell or Berryman in which I would have just been the youngest. All these were published in the magazines at the time when I was. In *View*, for instance, there was Jarrell's poem along with a poem of mine. All of them, as we know, were very sick boys who drank themselves to death or committed suicide except for Lowell, who, if it's a death, is one that has taken the longest time going around. But that was not the kind of person I was. So I was really incommunicado with whatever they were.

*Faas*: Your discovery of Denise Levertov's poem "The Shifting" seems to have been the decisive turning point in your relation to the Black Mountain poets.

DUNCAN: Yes, I was reading *Origin*, trying to figure out what was going on. And I had been seeing poems that had been doing things. But that poem I understood completely. I mean, how and why the lines were moving in such and such a way. What puzzled me at first was the typography. So I concluded that this was a notation and that the lines stood for possibilities of feeling that would have no fillers. And more than that, there was not just an absence of fillers, but she seemed to recognize that there were breaks and junctures that are part of the utterance. Of course, I wouldn't have analyzed it like that at that time. And the poem I wrote right afterwards was for an amusement and I sent it off to Corman. He did not accept the poem but sent it to Olson instead, asking why I was making fun of Olson. And he sent it to Denise asking why I was making fun of her. And the lead to Denise may have come from the fact that I had written to Corman saying her poem, "The Shifting," was terrific and here was a poem of mine. So she wrote to me saying in great distress: Can you write this about me and so forth if you are the same Duncan who has written *Heavenly City, Earthly City*. Because Rexroth had sent her *Heavenly City, Earthly City* which wasn't too far from her first books of poetry.

*Faas*: You mean the poetry written in England?

DUNCAN: Right. So I got into a correspondence with her and it was a very intensive correspondence.

*Faas*: How did you react to her letter?

DUNCAN: Well, I wrote back that I hadn't intended a satire. But otherwise I don't remember, because I don't keep copies of letters and this

is a long time ago. But then we were corresponding very heavily. So
she was one of the first people I wanted to meet when I was on my
way to Europe in 1955. We left for Europe from New York so I did
meet Denise finally. And I absolutely loved her. And then for a
matter of almost ten years, we had a very constant correspondence.
Now often that correspondence was on poetry. And she found it
intolerable when I would get over into the Sitwell area and would
reprove me right away. So it was really Denise who determined my
returning to a rhetoric of Stevens and Sitwell as I do in the poem at
that point. She was very worried about my retrograding in that
direction.

*Faas*: You mean in reaction to her.

DUNCAN: Yes, in answer to her. Remember that I was determined to
go back to that rhetoric.

*Faas*: So it would be like your reaction to Williams when *he* told you
off.

DUNCAN: Yes, if he scolds me, then I'll go and do medieval things. As
a matter of general principle I don't understand that anything in
writing is prohibited. Like what if it *were* sloppy! Meanwhile, I would
be very disturbed by certain things in Denise's poetry and it would go
back and forth.

*Faas*: You once told me how you had interpreted one of her poems
by drawing attention to sexual puns which she hadn't been aware of.

DUNCAN: She was always infuriated by my tendency to read things
first in a Freudian systematic way. Also, when the interview with
Hogg and Bowering came out, I realized that it wasn't that recent
that I had been disturbed with Denise's poetry.

*Faas*: The interview was in 1969.

DUNCAN: Yes, already at that time I was very vocal about my troubles
and disappointments and mistrusts about what was going on in her
poetry.

break with
Levertov

It had been awfully important to me to feel that
Denise Levertov and Robert Creeley and Charles Olson
and myself were a kind of movement and that they took
care of a lot of areas that I even by temperament wouldn't
be likely to cover. One important aspect of my work is the difficulty
of getting a picture of experience. And in a group, of course, you can
assume that your reader is also going to read Olson. So you can save a
lot of time, because all you have to do is take a potshot that hits off
against a facet of Charles Olson and he covers miles of territory of
what you are. Of course, you don't do it by agreement. But you only
have to make the slightest distinctions and your reader will realize
how a lot of things are disposed. And then in the composition of a

poem you don't have to do lots of explication. There is a difficulty about truth in relation to the fact that it is always being created and hence cannot be located. This was evident to Charles Olson who immediately grabbed the whole of Heisenberg's Uncertainty Principle. The other thing is : if I have an anxiety it is not because I am afraid I might die tomorrow, or some work won't be completed. It is rather my concern with fitting in the mosaic of the accounts so that there are enough hints that it might be an adjusted picture. This is the only way in which I can understand what it means to do justice to an event as being. I keep worrying about the fact that I have not yet given account of something or that I have not yet given another account of it. And in that respect, I felt that I had lost an ally in Denise. And yet I knew that sooner or later Denise was going to be a lost ally in some very important areas.

*Faas*: At various points you have emphasized your "entirely differentness" from Olson, once stating that to you poetry was a revelation of language, not of personality.

DUNCAN: Where was that?

*Faas*: That was in an open letter published in *Origin*. And then there is a statement concerning your "radical disagreement" with Olson published in the *Black Mountain Review* in 1955.

DUNCAN: These were very much directed at "Against Wisdom as Such." You remember we were just beginning writing and we had to sort out all sorts of things, to make these opposites, pose them as possibly being there. So I wouldn't put that forward at this point.

*Faas*: And yet in your 1969 interview with George Bowering you stated that what you had made of composition by field was very different from Olson's practice, adding that you didn't want any dichotomy of closed versus open. Instead you would make poems which are open, but which also contain closed elements.

DUNCAN: Of course. If we have a field, how can we throw out closed forms? They are only forms within a field. In the early *Passages* there is a proposition that the universe has only the boundaries we imagine. Every step in science is the imagination of a new boundary and every boundary gives us a new figure of the universe. And all of them are imagined. Of course, there are boundaries that don't fit any more, and they are let go. And that's all right. Some boundaries prove to be fitting but then a new factor enters and the boundary proves not to be a boundary any more. This would suggest exactly what an open field or an open mind is. And it may actually be an intuition about the nature of the universe. On the other hand, I find myself in great emotional conflict when I read that there is no reason to believe that the

boundaries of the universe

universe is integral. That there is no rationale to the universe being integral. Well, I find myself emotionally incapable of entertaining the notion of a non-integral universe. You see, there are no trivial events for me. This is really the question raised by Williams' famous "so much depends / upon / a red wheel / barrow." The real point of that question is: Are there any trivial events, are there any trivial people or trivial anythings, trivial beings or propositions? And for me, everything happening in the poem is properly apprehended and therefore not trivial.

*Faas:* You mean this is an emotional need.

DUNCAN: No, it is really that I can't feel it any other way. So I have a closed form at this point.

*Faas:* When you talked about changing models for the universe right now, you almost sounded like a Buddhist.

DUNCAN: No, I think what I meant was something really more scientific. Where boundaries are replaced by new scientific facts found in actual scientific discovery. That is something different isn't it, from ever-changing models of the universe. On the other hand, of course, I do agree that Gary's poetry and mine, for instance, look remarkably similar except for the fact that

Snyder's poetry

my verbal events are primary events and none of his are. His verbal events all convey an idea which stands at the back of them. My ideas are thematic and they operate like themes in music. That is to say, they are like themes in music and the music themes are just one thing and we know that everything else also counts. For Creeley, too, everything is in the verbal event. So in that sense, Gary to Robert seems to be very much out of order. I tend not to read Gary, like I don't read Rexroth. Because their sense of language is not what I use and yet when I read Gary and hear his poetry, I find that his actual picture of the universe is very much like mine. There is one big exception, of course, which is that his picture of the universe excludes Christ. Rexroth, for instance, who is also a kind of Western Buddhist, has Christ in his poetry. For there is nothing in the Buddhist universe which disallows the presence of any divinity, and you can also have an order of creation going on.

*Faas:* In this specific sense of language you are talking about, Creeley seems to be very close to people like Robbe-Grillet.

DUNCAN: He sees that himself, by the way. When we went to Majorca in 1955 he was excited by Beckett, and he gave me *Waiting for Godot* in French. So he must have read it in French. He

French influences

also gave me Cocteau's *La difficulté d'être* and then I remember having discussions with him about these books.

*Faas:* Does he know Roland Barthes' *Le degré zéro de l'écriture*?

DUNCAN: No, he has never mentioned that book to me. The people in the next generation who stem from Creeley are very close to Barthes. But I have never heard Creeley himself talk about it, whereas I myself have taken a whole bunch of things from Barthes. I get the impression that Creeley deliberately avoids him. It's too close for comfort, as it were. But he definitely stems from Existentialism and then seems to keep his distance from allying himself with those things which like him have developed away from Existentialism. The same thing happened to me when one of the first people to write a Ph.D. on my work started sending Merleau-Ponty and Barthes to me. I had previously consumed Piaget and I had read everything of Gestalt psychology which I was able to put my hands on. So Merleau-Ponty sounded to me like some sections of my journals. So I wrote back to that Ph.D. student saying all this makes me a little ill. I do enjoy Merleau-Ponty, but I find him almost impossible to read. He seems too redundant and robbing of my own thoughts. This may be the reason why I became acquainted with his work relatively late. Younger people had been reading him, but I didn't. So Creeley may have had a similar intuition. Like this is too close for me, I've got to look at something that will challenge that.

*Faas*: Yes, he never mentioned either Robbe-Grillet or Barthes in his writing.

How did you get to teach at Black Mountain?

DUNCAN: When we were in Majorca early in 1956, Ruth Witt had a grant for The Poetry Center in San Francisco. So there would be a salary for me to come home to if I would be Assistant Director to The Poetry Center. And I accepted, saying I would come back the following September. So, when Charles heard that, he wrote: If you are going to come back anyway, will you come in April and take two terms at Black Mountain before you return to San Francisco? So I went there.

*Faas*: What did you teach at Black Mountain?

DUNCAN: I taught basic techniques.

*Faas*: Of writing?

DUNCAN: Of poetry. A three hour course every day which was vowels and consonants and syllables and stress, interestingly enough. And we were getting somewhat sketchy although we were meeting three hours a day. It wasn't lecture courses, we were practising. We would sit at a long table and do exercises like write thirteen syllable lines as fast as you can and then see how many syllables come out, when you think you are going to do thirteen. And also exercises of line to stanza, not much more.

*Faas*: And the other courses?

DUNCAN: Then there was a lecture course I gave in the evenings three times a week. The first time a student gave a talk on what was then going to be my lecture the following Wednesday. Then on Friday, we would meet and talk about the whole thing. In that, the question of the law came up. The first one was genesis, the second one was law, and then tragedy and comedy. It was still revolving around the proposition that one could take approaches to the meaning of form. The kind of questions like what is the meaning of law.

*Faas*: What do you mean by law?

DUNCAN: Well, that was exactly the question they were to address. And that poem, *The Law I Love Is Major Mover,* came because Joe Dunn who had that project felt that the law was just the law, you know, cops and robbers. I remember one day going into the library at the school there and he was pouring over everything trying to get it into his head. And nothing could have been more garbled than the account he finally gave. And when he finished I said to him: Well, Joe, when you write a sentence beginning with the word "the," aren't you already under the law of "the"? No matter what you do from here on, you are under its law. And I think that's part of what a law is. In other words, lawful action to me is total responsibility to what is present. So I began to realize that at the time.

*Faas*: And during the summer you produced your *Medea?*

DUNCAN: Yes, and besides the *Medea* I gave a course on the *Illuminations* by Rimbaud.

teaching
Rimbaud

*Faas*: Rimbaud is an interest of yours which had begun much earlier. You did "A Derivation from Rimbaud" in '48.

DUNCAN: Right. Also, my quarrel with Verlaine starts fairly early. I know, Verlaine shot Rimbaud, but I would have shot *him* first. [Laughing] I can never translate a Verlaine poem without correcting it. Which is the most atrocious thing you can do to a poet—change the ending or something.

By contrast, Rimbaud is a real challenge. Two of the students in my group really knew some French, so they were way ahead of me. But we proceeded as if we didn't know a thing, no matter what. We had all the translations and all the dictionaries and all the guesses and we filled the board with them. So there were huge maps of what was going on in any sentence. It got to be a demonstration. I had started writing *The Structures of Rime* at Black Mountain and I knew about the Rimbaud prose poem. That's why I took the *Illuminations* that summer. I wanted to find out to what extent Rimbaud was a part of this, and I was sure that he was.

*Faas*: And then Olson came to San Francisco to give his Whitehead lectures at your house.

DUNCAN: Yes, and Whitehead comes immediately into action while I am working on *The Opening of the Field.* Charles is there giving his lectures and I am scribbling poems while he is lecturing.

Whitehead's "presentational immediacy"

*Faas*: Really.

DUNCAN: Yes, the minute he started, I also started reading *Process and Reality.* But of course, I was reading the book with an entirely different mind. So his Whitehead was turning into mine before I could turn around. I saw all sorts of things in Whitehead that would probably never have dawned on him. I remember the moment in Whitehead where he talks about "presentational immediacy" as being analogous to being cross-eyed. Wow! These are times when I identify as being the very center of the kind of consciousness that's talked about. Because being cross-eyed, I have been subject all my life, except for the first three years, to one of the states of presentational immediacy. While all the kiddies were going out taking drugs and getting hallucinations, I was subject to one which was much more mysterious. When I look at something, I see it double and I can never tell which one is the real one—the one which I see with my left eye or the one that I see with my right eye. As a child I used to go forward and touch it. But even then I was still the victim of the reduplication. So ever since my third year, I have been steadily in a quandary of presentational immediacy.

### III

*Faas:* You first met Ginsberg around '54. What was your reaction when *Howl* came out?

DUNCAN: Well, I started to write a poem like it the day it arrived.

*Faas*: When it arrived?

Ginsberg's *Howl*

DUNCAN: Yes, I sat down and read it aloud to myself.

*Faas*: Was that in Europe?

DUNCAN: No, at Black Mountain. Allen himself had sent it to me. Then when I stared at what I wrote, I noticed that it was simply inappropriate. I couldn't do it. Because I was going in a completely different direction.

At that time whenever I was invited to give readings, people used to ask me what I thought of *Howl*. And I had no proper thoughts on *Howl*. My thoughts on *Howl* were very much colored by my wanting it out of my way. And I think that was true of people from Daddy Rexroth to anybody that had to ride that same period. Though I wanted to do something like it the day or night that it arrived. The other thing about it was that the pan-sexuality directly came in conflict with my very strong Apollonian dedications. I mean, strong enough for a householder. Allen himself, of course, wants to be a householder, so it goes in other directions. What I did not at all like was its wanting to break down the high demands for mutuality. And I also mean mutuality in relation to the poem. As you know, it became an enormously popular poem. And that's a phenomenon, because it's not like Ferlinghetti. It is not an easy poem. It is filled with trouble, and it is a poem that daringly brings together the Orient and the Occident which is an enormously productive and always fecund level for the poem. But in Ginsberg you have the Oriental or rather Hindu promise that the poetic furor would be sustained which in fact is sustained remarkably throughout *Howl*. And in the sexual sense there is the promise that if we would just respond immediately everything would be all right. But that to me is kind of a fantasy from high school. I can only see it as a kind of agony which in fact it has been for me. And it has been agony for Ginsberg as a matter of fact. But whatever it was to him personally, I found it very threatening.

My own poetry was going so much for a higher and higher demand for a kind of *areté*. And while I may be multiphasic there *will* be phases. That is to say, there will be boundaries. And I am very much concerned with the boundaries and various centers. The whole thing has to have an architecture. It's got a character armor, to use the Reichian term, and in that I am identifiably Protestant. Ginsberg's melting down, or breaking down, and wanting to disappear, or Burroughs' tendency to the same effect, was very disturbing to me. Are we really going to dissolve all the boundaries? So I was in direct conflict. When we came to our poetry conference at Vancouver in 1963, I was frequently on the floor challenging Ginsberg's position. And a lot of it was concerning his position on the poem. Mine would be the Constructivist poem, the poem as a work of art, and I very well understood where Ginsberg was in that. I knew about the prohibition that you shouldn't *make* a poem from the *Zohar*. You should pour forth God's voices, and that I went exactly against. Fine, go ahead and pour forth that God voice, but let's distinguish that from the poem. A poem, to me, is a mystery in making. Always, of course, with tutelary address. Often with the address of a lure.

*Faas*: Of another poet?

disagreements with Ginsberg

poetry a mystery in making

DUNCAN: Yes, a presence of a poet which would be comparable to falling in love. And frequently the presence of a God, Helios or Apollo. *The Venice Poem* is the first model of those presences. Although "Toward the Shaman" is already an exercise in presences.

*Faas*: Your own rediscovery of Whitman seems to coincide with the point at which Whitman was finally integrated into the mainstream of American poetry through the influence of *Howl*. Whitman

DUNCAN: Well, I started going to Whitman a little earlier than that.

*Faas*: You mentioned that *Leaves of Grass* became a kind of bedside book for you around 1956 when you were writing *The Opening of the Field*.

DUNCAN: Of course, I had read Whitman in high school. I was reading Whitman and Crane in order to assert the nature of homosexuality. And at that time everybody in college considered Whitman's poetry as very poor stuff. People would be embarrassed about it all. Of course, it was poor poetry to them mainly because they were embarrassed by the content.

So I did have some returns to Whitman before the '56 point. I think, I even took Whitman with me to Majorca. Anyway, when I started *The Opening of the Field*, I knew very well that *Leaves of Grass* were the field. That's why I am reading it from there on. And I still read it.

*Faas*: Did you discuss Whitman with Olson?

DUNCAN: Not very far. One wouldn't have gotten very far in trying to explain to Olson what was going on in a Whitman line. As a matter of fact, it is not that easy to explain. I have Whitman and Olson done some analyses of sections of the *Cantos*. But I haven't analyzed the kind of lines in which I find Whitman astounding, I mean literally within single lines.

*Faas*: Did Olson ever see your essay on Whitman?

DUNCAN: He may have, but it sure didn't strike him.

*Faas*: At first it puzzled me that you place Whitman above and beyond Olson, Pound and Williams. But literary history seems to prove you right.

DUNCAN: Well, if you think about how large Whitman's vision is: he completely expands his concept of man so it goes far beyond questions of European man, or modern man, or man of some period. And that I do think of as largeness. Shakespeare does the same thing, although even more amazingly. Because he is able to invent personality.

But that largeness also seems to me to have an immediate hinge in the understanding of how a cadence is built in a line. In other words, I think of Whitman as having melodic intelligence the way Beethoven has. And we know now that Whitman's lines derive from the fact that he was listening to arias in which melody opens up so it can pour forth while still remaining melody. I mean, it can still have all its elements properly intoned, so to speak, so they remain significant.

Of course, the lines in *Howl* are not at all Whitmanic lines. In fact, Ginsberg himself never lost track of the fact that it was Christopher Smart who gave him one of the hints as to what that line was going to be. And the lines in *Howl* are very much Christopher Smart lines.

Whitman and *Howl*

*Faas*: Ginsberg actually denies the direct influence of Whitman on *Howl*. He told me that Whitman's influence on his poetry came much later.

DUNCAN: Ginsberg's long lines tend to sprawl, something I don't find at all in *Leaves*. You remember when Whitman talks about line or rhyme, he talks about a tree or vine growing, or simply about an organism. And Whitman had the true feeling of organisms where every part is actually growing out of another and having a role throughout. No wonder his world doesn't look too different from Whitehead's who is talking about a philosophy of organism. Of course, Whitman is no philosopher, so he doesn't develop a philosophy of organism but simply rides the wave of philosophies that feed his feeling of organism in the poem. Organism also means that any part can function in coordination with any other part, so you aren't building perfect bodies, for instance. Whitman doesn't have the superstition of perfection which life itself doesn't have, of course. My Whitman is a Random House Whitman which I acquired when I was a freshman in college. And that edition has Whitman's little essay on Darwin, and he right away sees that Darwin is his man. And he doesn't have Darwin wrong. He doesn't believe that evolution produced the marvellous thing called man. He takes Darwin right straight and sees that the local, immediate event is evolving and that that doesn't mean the event perfecting itself and climbing up a ladder.

*Faas*: It seems to me that your own and Ginsberg's return to Whitman represents a major reorientation of the Pound-Williams-Olson tradition.

a major poetic reorientation

DUNCAN: Well, the æsthetics of Pound and Williams in their negative response to Whitman seem to me a regression in poetics. Especially for me because it puts me in a threatened position. It was a regression from the kind of confidence that Whitman had. *Personæ* by Pound still had that kind of confidence and freedom. And so did *Spring and All* by Williams. Lawrence has it all the way through, of course,—the freedom which is essentially the freedom of a created "I" that can do anything in a poem. In that way, I thought Whitman and Lawrence remarkably resembled my own poetry.

*Faas*: O'Hara seems to have been another major force behind the recent Whitman renaissance.

DUNCAN: What was so striking about O'Hara was the tremendous emotional power of the early poems. He must have felt that he was on an entirely different level than anyone around him. It's amazing how O'Hara has widened the common language of Whitman. And that is something that I do believe in myself. I am not interested, and increasingly not interested, in my poetry, in any uncommon language, any specifically poetic language. I think that when mastery increases poetry gets much much simpler word-wise.

Frank O'Hara

*Faas*: To me it has never made sense to lump Ashbery and O'Hara together.

DUNCAN: But you see they grew up together. Temperamentally they are quite different. John never had to make any step of this kind of democratization of the poem. But Frank did it because I think he is Whitmanesque. In many ways Frank is more Whitman than Allen is. Allen's stepping in front of these huge audiences and commanding them is very non-Whitmanic. So they are like a funny split of the Whitman tradition really, aren't they? But my critique of O'Hara would be that in his democratization the poem becomes almost simple-minded. I can see no difference between our admiration and thrill when an athlete clears the eight foot bar when we couldn't even jump over a table, and our thrill at an intellectual performance. So what I admire in Shakespeare is simply what I could never do, not what is "simple."

*Faas*: So many parallels have been drawn between O'Hara's work and action painting.

DUNCAN: But the painters he was interested in really were not action painters. I mean, he wrote about Pollock, but his actual contemporaries among painters were an entirely different group.

*Faas*: Exactly. In fact, his kind of poetry strikes me as a kind of equivalent of pop art.

DUNCAN: Quite. And Rivers becomes a really trivial painter under the O'Hara course. The trivialisation of the painters that he was close to is very obvious.

IV

*Faas*: Robert Bly claims that American poetry has missed out on Surrealism. I am sure you wouldn't agree with that.

DUNCAN: Those remarks of his I simply find humorous. Or his remark that I stem from French Surrealism and not from Spanish. I mean, he just doesn't know. We read our Lorca over and over again. The impact of Lorca and Rilke was what made the big jolt from Pound, and that was in the late thirties.

Lorca and Rilke, the big jolt from Pound

*Faas*: So you feel that you have absorbed the influence of Surrealism.

DUNCAN: Yes, although not of South American Surrealism. Neruda was translated but somehow we didn't read him. Maybe because as Anarchists we were anti-Neruda. Because he was Stalinist and we were violently anti-Stalinist, Neruda was reactionary to us as kids when we were in our teens. At that time, Neruda was for the Moscow trials. So while I could stand Pound's Fascism because I didn't even have such a tendency, I felt that people like Zukofsky and Neruda had betrayed the Socialist Communist Revolution.

*Faas:* You once stated that an image could be close to the psychological archetype of Jungian analysis, or that images should be an evocation of depth. One could compare these definitions with similar ones by Robert Bly and other poets of the deep image school of poetry.

the "deep image"

DUNCAN: What interested me more at the time was Robert Kelly's remark about a melody of images, and that formula remains interesting to me. It is a more suggestive possibility than my sense of themes. A melody is a little different from a theme, a much freer invention. Concerning deep image our critique and my witticism right away was: one inch deep, two feet deep, how deep? It's like, what is important and what trivial? In my sense of things, there is nothing trivial, so that everything has to have depth since it relates throughout. And what we can do is recognize the depth which is going on.

Bly's attack

Then when Bly started out with his magazine *The Fifties*, there was not only an open attack on us as a group, but an attack on the techniques of the poem. He is all in favor of primary intuition, but I don't think that there is any division between techniques of the poem and primary intuition. Olson's great contribution which Bly overlooks is that he relates technique to the body. The most important contribution Olson made is that he studies poetry almost at the medical level, at the morphological level.

His understanding of poetry along those lines is much vaster than mine today. I had studied the ear and the development of the eye whereas Olson was really studying embryonic development. When I first met him, he hadn't related that to the poem yet. But he said that the understanding of man had to proceed from that.

I have to add that my discussion of Bly is rather uninformed because I have hardly read him.

*Faas*: Didn't you have direct contact with Bly at an early point?

DUNCAN: Yes, I had a little correspondence with him after he had announced that his magazine was going to be Surrealist. So I wanted to find out whether that meant Breton and Romantic Surrealism. And I also wanted to find out if he knew that Surrealism involved magic. What I got back was a somewhat angry letter in which he stated that he didn't believe that Surrealism involved magic, but that instead it involved depth-psychology. And that depth-psychology was an antithesis to magic. From then on, I had not much interest in him, finding that Bly had no concept of magic at all.

*Surrealism and magic*

*Faas*: What would be the difference between depth-psychology and magic?

DUNCAN: Well, magic would mean that you are not only dealing with some archetypes in your psyche but with some real entities like angels. I mean, angels in a poem are real and literal and not fancy.

*Faas*: That, I guess, would also account for your dissent from Jung.

DUNCAN: Well, I must have been extremely attracted to the archetype initially. But then I took Mescalin and I burst into tears when I realized I was seeing something I hadn't made, that I hadn't drawn. And that somebody else hadn't made. So the presence of an image in my mind put me into a total quandary. Because it was difficult for me to accept that there was such an image in my mind. So a poem must be very reassuring to me. You see, in a dream there is a process in which things are put together. So it is a kind of creative process in the mind. I am not so angry with Jungianism because of the fact that it refuses to recognize that there are externals but because it insists that they are internals. During the period that I took the Mescalin, my sense of the external was so acute that I raised the question, as I still often do, whether there is any possible being in me which can be called my ego. Because I recompose what I call myself from a world. So for me there is a question: Is there a me? I? What I do is that I pose a creative process in which I assemble me from surrounding facts including the body and so forth.

*dissent from Jung*

*Faas*: Are you referring to any specific drug experiment?

DUNCAN: Yes, the only time that I ever took a hallucinogenic drug was in 1952 in an experiment run by Stanford University. It was Mescalin. What I saw was the world tree. It was also, however, a tree realized in jewels as well as being cosmic with lights. It was like a huge mosaic and I felt it as the existence of an archetype, like what Plato is talking about. It was then that I also had my first experience of dissent from the archetype. I burst into tears, and I also did not accept seeing what I had not made. Later in 1963, at the University of British Columbia, I gave a lecture which was about my refusal to have any mystical experiences because I wanted to be made out of thousands of threads that I myself have tied. My figure is the Muslim rug which one spends a whole lifetime in tying, simply thread by thread. Of course, you know the figure. Everybody knows the figure. So I do not disavow the knowledge of the figure. But I will not let that figure in any way substitute for the work. There we are back with the concept of the poet as maker.

*taking Mescalin*

*Faas*: So a symbol or poetic image would hardly be an archetype.

DUNCAN: Well, I wonder how any poet could be attracted to Jungianism. To me poets use symbols to be initial and in the universe. Jung uses them to be in a psyche and around a center. When we, from my generation, were looking into the universe, there wasn't that apparent a center in time or in space. Charles had the same observation. But the distinction between a centered universe and a non-centered one never bothered him. He took the center to be wherever you are. Anyway, I am not a creature of the center. I am a creature of outside.

*Faas*: You have often criticized Jung's *maṇḍala* concept.

DUNCAN: Exactly. That's the area I am critical of. I don't disbelieve in the existence of archetypes, but I wouldn't posit their importance in the way Jung does. Where I don't join Eastern philosophy at all, is that I think that everything we see is posited in the material world. So that an archetype doesn't get to be very arche. Instead of looking at an archetype, we'd better look at a tree or a particular individual.

*Faas*: You have compared the poem with dream-work. On the other hand, you say that the poet in the act of creation must wrestle against sleep, using all his watchful craft and learned art. You also said that the entire area of poetry is consciousness.

DUNCAN: Yes, but what dream do we know that is not consciousness? And now that we have got the map of it, it seems evident that we have not yet gotten to sleep when we are dreaming. By the way, that thing about wrestling with sleep is an instruction that came to me in a poem. So I wouldn't say that I am voluntary in that, although I will take it once I am given the instructions. When I was in my early twenties we read Kafka and we thought he was an expert reporter of dreams. And I kept extensive notebooks which are now at the University of California and they contain descriptions of dreams. I even recorded conversations and verbal happenings in dreams. So, dream was evidence that you had a primary conscious activity of composition that was tremendous, absolutely tremendous. But I would still call that consciousness, *poetry and dream* bringing consciousness together. My objection to the Jungian concept, that the unconscious has anything in it, is that I take the unconscious to be *un*conscious. What Jung is talking about is the subconscious, not the unconscious. James already makes such a distinction. And while Yoga observes that there is very little in the body that our consciousness can not inhabit, I personally would allow that there is an unconscious and that it actually is an enormous area. But if it is truly *un*conscious, then there are no images. Because the minute there is an image, it is consciousness. By the time a dream is in our mind, its entire event is in consciousness. And when I am talking about the unconscious, then I am not talking about the dream we don't remember. As Freud found out, there is a subconscious which is a kind of reservoir held by consciousness. But that is not the unconscious. The unconscious must mean a sense of void or blankness or unavailable information or otherness. And this the consciousness doesn't dream about. But the conscious mind imagines what is in it, and fills it with imaginings and in that, it is creating. In my picture then, of God, He is imagining Himself. And the world is the current image of that Self. So we do have an Otherness that is imagining.

*Faas*: Would you approve of automatic writing as a viable mode of composition?

DUNCAN: I don't understand what automatic writing is. A requirement for automatic writing or any autistic activity to take place, is a split personality where there is no connection between the two. Now in a multiphasic personality, we don't have *automatic versus* such a split. Because if your personality is a field, then the *autistic writing* co-existence of multiple personalities is not carried on as a split. The minute you have a split, then you have another kind of Other, so to speak. And speaking for myself, I call the unconscious the Other. All the other others are integrated. They form some kind of texture and that we can't pose in automatic writing. So that is what is puzzling to me in automatic writing. By the way, the thing that Breton and Éluard are doing is imitating automatic writing. They simulate states of madness. They simulate automatic writing.

But a good deal of *The Structures of Rime,* of course, is presumed to be autistic. And *Passages* when it arrives, arrives. So I've got autistic elements that are felt to come from outside, or that I go into. So at that psychological level, much of *Passages* I can't view as anything other than being received. So it obviously has a good area of Other.

## V

*Faas*: To James Dickey the subject matter of poetry seems to be a kind of given which he then proceeds to write poems about. I guess you wouldn't share this approach.

the subject matter
of poetry

DUNCAN: Of course, he is a narrative poet and then psychologically he is upset.

*Faas*: Creeley takes the exactly opposite approach.

DUNCAN: Yes, because he is working with the same material over and over again. And I would also take the Creeley position. A subject doesn't give me a poem. The beginning of a line does. But, of course, Creeley has demonstrable subjects.

*Faas*: But then he always stresses that his poems don't have any referential meaning.

DUNCAN: Well, but then that's balderdash. His subject seems to be a very special kind of Creeley predicament. So that when that predicament rises in his mind, he produces certain poems. One of its features, of course, is stumbling and proceeding in some fashion in which clumsiness is imperative. It's a mysteri-

Creeley

ous predicament to me since I still read the poems. But some of its solutions have been very, very simple. I mean, he proposes subjects I would never dream of being subjects. At some point, he proposed minimal subjects. But that still is a subject proposition, not one that arises from a line.

*Faas*: None of all that would apply to Dickey, of course.

DUNCAN: No, with Dickey the case is entirely different. Dickey's weakness shows up in the fact that he is quite dependent upon an adequate relation to his *one* subject which is recharging his sense of being alive by the panic of something he is killing and which is suffering pain. And since he can't revivify that by actually shooting and chopping and burning people all the time, his poems often become fantasies of doing this. And they are considerably weakened on account of it. At first I was misled, although not entirely misled. I found the first poems by Dickey

Dickey

which I saw very curious, especially the one about the battlefield with the dead stirring underground. Having grown up in a family that was also Southern and that also had a cult of spiritualism of the dead, I was intrigued. I thought: Gee, there is somebody from the South with a cult of the dead who is involved in spiritualism again. That seemed to me significant. After all, they had lost the Civil War and they had all these ancestors killed in it. So I wrote to him and corresponded with him briefly and asked him to come and visit. And one couldn't imagine a less fortunate meeting, of course. But "Drinking from a Helmet" is a remarkable poem. And the poem of the shooting of the deer and beginning to feast is also remarkable. But by the time he begins to feast on the panic in the deer, I began to see some of the tangles of what it was. Then I felt: My God, this is really a very strange, murderous cult. And I asked for a book of Dickey's to review and they gave me the volume which has "The Firebombing" in it. Now, that poem already has the deterioration which marks his later work. He, of course, had been in actual missions of firebombing, but that was "The Firebombing" some time ago. So he was now trying to find expression for this terrible nostalgia. He was trying to charge the poem by gloating back to the feeling of the murder. And the poem has some remarkable clues. It seems to expand around a remarkable hostility against everything around the poet. So finally, he firebombs the world which he is actually in, the American suburbs. So in "Up Rising," I took some parts out of that poem, and more than that, I located it in myself in the period when we did our little crayon drawings and burned our whole families. Of course, by locating it back in myself, I wasn't talking about Dickey.

But, gee, by the time you come to Dickey's poem "Falling" about the stewardess falling out of a plane, you have something he read in the newspapers and cannot resurrect in his imagination. Because it still won't be something which he can actually see. So the whole thing becomes ludicrous. He can't connect with her panic. Psychologically, of course, he has to connect with panic in order to write his poems. You've got the same thing in *Deliverance*. The end of the thing is absolutely phoney. Because he has to invent all sorts of pains. And then suddenly on walks James Dickey acting as a sheriff, and it is a better sheriff than you ever saw in a million movies. Dickey also has a split personality, quite apart from the artistic problem. He was once an advertising agent, and when he writes criticism you wouldn't dream he was a poet. He is a Madison Avenue career-maker. And very successful at it. We have had a lot of Madison Avenue career-makers. Yet this is the first one who is actually a poet at times. But he is not a poet who makes me feel happy. I realize there is no conversation I could have with Dickey. Not only did I not have one, but I couldn't even have one in my imagination. But still, his work is very significant. I think it is more significant than he realizes.

*Faas*: It is interesting how the Black Mountain ideas which he fought more than anybody else have recently caught on with him.

Dickey and open form

DUNCAN: My God, yes. Just look at the structure of his line. I mean, do you think he can rip off those lines and not get into trouble? [Laughing]

*Faas*: At some point Dickey wrote an essay where all of a sudden he discovered his predilection for open form poetry and "presentational immediacy."

DUNCAN: But then, I guess, that was a little bit like *Naked Poetry* who also thought that they were open form and presentational immediacy. But, gee, did he get that term "presentational immediacy" from Whitehead?

*Faas*: Yes.

DUNCAN: Oh, great. I, of course, fell in love with that term "presentational immediacy."

*Faas*: Would you share Dickey's prognostication that open form poetry is going to be the predominant mode in America?

DUNCAN: Yes, just remember how suggestive open form is to us in America. I mean, there are our open spaces, our open minds, our everything. And Dickey is very much of that era. His opposition to Black Mountain, in fact, was that he felt we were closing down the open possibilities in the poem. He saw us as quite the contrary to what we were proposing.

*Faas*: Do you think that open form is an American phenomenon?

DUNCAN: Oh, no. It's only of special significance in America. It's the whole modern thing.

*Faas*: So it would be something common to the whole Western world.

DUNCAN: Yes, and then you have Japan, for instance, opening itself up to the West. In a way, there are no more crucial openings. Everything has been opened up. Nobody is hiding away in a closet today—some poor Eskimos or something.

*Faas*: You just suggested that the beginning of a line may give you a poem. Do you have a definite feeling about when and how a poem begins?

beginning of a poem

DUNCAN: Yes.

*Faas*: What does it feel like?

DUNCAN: It is like a musical feeling. Yes, you do have a primary feeling about fittingness. Naturally it seems to me the criterion of truth in a poem. Its fittingness is pre-Gestalt. That is the notion which interested James.

*Faas*: William James?

DUNCAN: Right. William James. So when I find that certain parts are not fitting or true, they are never not fitting or true in themselves, but in the way that they are assembled. I was annoyed when Rosenthal said that I was an æsthete or something, because largely I feel that a thing is beautiful when it is fitting. That's not a purely æsthetic intuition.

*Faas*: Do you have any other criteria for evaluating poetry? The critics writing about *Paterson*, for instance, still remain largely concerned with the question of whether or not the poem has a unity.

DUNCAN: Well, I'm not worried about unity. But let's ask: Where do I have my troubles? Well, *Paterson* was one of the places where we really took hold and where we saw something to be done in the poem. But I'm still wondering: How come he lifted it out of *Finnegans Wake* that it was going to go in a circle and evaluating poetry that the man was going to be the city and the woman the river. All that I think of as the superstition of the poem. All right, I think there are superstitions in my poems. There are configurations that are entirely idiosyncratic. That is, they are not pertinent to the immediate poem. They are not structurally important at all in any conceivable community of meaning. I mean, that whole thing about the man, the city, the woman and the river is essential to *Finnegans Wake* because it was so conceived. And that they get confused, is also part of the process of the poem. But in the case of Williams it was simply borrowed as a superstition. So I am criticizing *Paterson* for introducing ideas as if they were as incidental as rhyme at the end of a line. However, there was no harm done. Because when he finished book IV, he had this marvellous example of a coda. Williams realized that after his conclusion he had another book. And his initial real daring is way back in the early twenties in *Spring and All*. When I first began to read those poems, I couldn't even grasp them. *Spring and All* is far beyond all the stuff we are talking about. So I do have some evaluations when I find those superstitions. And I find *Spring and All* to be a poem totally written without any superstitions.

*Faas*: You rarely comment on your practises as a poet. Do you revise a lot?

DUNCAN: Well, when I was 19 or 20, I was absolutely bowled over by Rilke's *Duino Elegies*. And then in Rilke's letters about the elegies I came across a doctrine that the poet should not rewrite and correct. So I sort of came to feel guilty about any kind of rewriting and correcting. If the poem was received, how could you rewrite it? But

then, of course, there is the evidence of *Medieval Scenes*. I considered
those poems as absolutely received. But then I wrote
revising    another version of them which was the one that got
printed. And I wrote that second version for public deliv-
ery. I introduced a series of thematic bridges exactly in
the way the Middle Ages proposes: themes which are absolutely
separate and which don't even form a sequence except that they are
together, 12 in number. That's the version which appeared in the
*Selected Poems* that City Lights put out. In the other version, of
course, there were no bridges at all. So there is an example of
rewriting.

*Faas*: But more in the sense that Lawrence proposes, that is to say, of
giving your creative impulse another chance to realize itself.

DUNCAN: Yes, and I have become more and more aware of this
phenomenon of different versions. *Passages* I write in notebooks
which I can show you. [Fetches notebook from the shelf] When they
did the N.E.T. film on me, I was photographed writing this poem.

*Faas*: This is the first draft?

DUNCAN: Yes. I think of this as of a cartoon as you have a cartoon for
a painting. Then on the typewriter, this has to be reinterpreted. So
these people doing the film asked me to show them how I would
write the poem at the typewriter and I realized something I would
not have imagined. I was certain that I would not mouth a poem
while I was writing it. When I write by hand, I can feel the poem in
my hand. Yes, I know what that means. The typewriter doesn't give
me this kinæsthetic feeling of the line: the kind of disequilibrium
which you feel in the hand—the disequilibrium which produces the
new line. So what I mean is that there is a sound which you don't
consciously hear, a pitch which is not in the range of hearing and
which yet enters the range of equilibrations, like somebody adjusting
a horizontal. So no wonder I feel the line in this way. I am a writer in
the original sense of writing with my hand.

*Faas*: When do you end a poem? Stafford once said that he usually
concludes a poem when his powers to homogenize an experience
come to an end.

DUNCAN: Well, we are not homogenizing. So that can't be
poetic closure    it. Very frequently, the end of a poem is a close. Analogous to Stravinsky's invention of closes for series. It's sort
of very simplistic. Just making a coda. You find that in *The
Venice Poem* I do such a coda. And in *Passages* I very often do that. But
by no means is that a form of homogenizing.

*Faas*: So you don't just leave off when your creative impulse has
exhausted itself.

DUNCAN: Oh yes, I do that all the time.

*Faas*: No, I mean in a printed poem.

DUNCAN: Oh, no, in print the end of the poem is when the content of the poem is completely present. And that content of the poem is demonstrably the working out of certain rhymes. The sound level and the significant thing about the sound level I got from Pound who once wrote me about the tone leading of the vowels. That expands the elements of the poem with which you are composing. And I, of course, wanted an expansive content for the poem. If you just take a rhyme, it would give us time and dime and mime and so forth. And that is a very limited series. But if we take the vowel and take the tone lead from that, we expand the vocabulary and thus expand the possible content. So I am working with sound all the time.

If you consider the poem as an object, you can think of it as completed in the area that it is in. But, of course, that doesn't mean that it is really completed. There are several bold decisions one could make at any time, by which one could give an entirely different significance to everything that is going on in there. And there are millions of decisions one could make. I am considerably less skilled as a visual artist than as a poet. So almost any interior form in my drawings, for instance, is schematic.

*Faas*: So when you finish a poem, you really feel that that's the end of it?

DUNCAN: Oh, sure.

*Faas*: And it is not open in the sense that it could go on indefinitely?

DUNCAN: But remember that the form is always local. So when we talk about finishing we talk about finishing the poem and not finishing the form. The poem is as specific as when you know how to write a play. You know when you are in act one. So the end is a kind of decision. It is an absolute decision and if I would add two more words, then it would be an entirely different poem. It is not a homogenization. It's like a decision. That's it. In this way, I absolutely feel the end of a poem.

## VI

*Faas*: Often when you talk about the universe as a meaningful creation you almost seem to strike a neo-Platonic or teleological note.

DUNCAN: Well, no. Meaningfulness is intent. But let's look at it from a different angle. I am a Darwinian, not a Lamarckian. Unlike John Cage, I don't believe there is any chance at all. Intent and creation is fundamentally mysterious. It is actually going on. I don't think of creation as something redundant, as God making up something.

It delighted me to come across the Greek criticism of Heraclitus.
They couldn't take it that Heraclitus believed that the
a "meaningful" universe created itself and that the process of creation
universe was actually going on. That scandalized the neo-
Platonists, and it scandalizes the Buddhists. In neo-
Platonism, the universe emanates. There is a source that's more
intent than the actual process of creation. In Olson, the universe has
a beginning and it has declined. It has had a Golden Age and it has
declined. And it is in a state of recovery. So, of course, there you can
have a cycle. For me, what is is what is. And it's creating itself. No
wonder I have the work to do.

*Faas:* And there is no chance in that creative process?

DUNCAN: Well, no. I mean, we have got testimony about chance,
don't we? But personally I find myself deficient in any sense of
chance.

*Faas:* You once stated: I do not believe in creation by chance or by
predestined form.

DUNCAN: Yes, right. Like in Darwin, there is no predestination.
Everything is so much cooperation. Creation is everywhere intending, but only in a cooperation you have
chance particulars emerging. So there is no paradigm. What was
interesting to me as it was to Charles, is that Whitehead
pointed out that the primordial is ahead of us. That the past is
actually the thing we keep posing as if it came after the primordial
which it can't possibly have done. So we are always emerging in the
primordial. And resurrection for me really would be a figure of any
definition of the present.

Where I saw all that first was in the post-Martha Graham development in dance. We had a high Fascism of the dance
modern music which dominated the thirties. I mean, Martha Graham
and dance didn't have ovens, but she did resemble Hitler remarkably as a kind of female version. There was an absolute
tyranny in the dance. And some of the people moving away from her
introduced chance operations. But then, chance operations seem to
me more and more the very opposite of chance. I mean, they show a
higher order, not a lesser order. So what was interesting to me was
that a dance was beginning to emerge in which all the dancers
cooperate. That is to say, they had to be attentive to where they were.
Similarly, in Cage's music, you cannot presume a melody. So if you
aren't hearing it, then you simply aren't. If you miss something in
Cage, you really miss it because you missed what's going on, whereas
if you miss something in Mozart you can kind of fill it in in your
mind. So we have come to a completely different kind of music. Of

course, I am referring to Cage's early aleatoric music. Now Cage, of course, claims that he is not in music any longer. But what attracted me to this aleatoric music was a potential recognition that there was something else than the neo-Platonic scale out of which we get all our sense of harmony that has dominated music for so long. Instead of that, we get a larger picture in which every conceivable sound is present. And now we find that our original harmonies don't disappear as being present, but they are co-present with all the other elements, and we have to be attentive throughout. We have to recognize that they are there. But that is only coincident to our recognizing the actual sounds that are there.

*Faas:* You have often stated that the language of poetry should be an echo of the greater language in which the universe is written.

DUNCAN: Yes, right. I think in human language we turn the sounds of our mouths into a language of things in order to imitate the way we experience. I think there is a primal    concept of intuition in our expression: The mountain speaks to me.    language So we try to speak back. What Piaget says makes sense to me. We speak back to something that speaks to us. So in speaking, there is a cooperation going on between world and person. Our engagement in language is active only as long as we are finding the universe. When we cease to find the universe, then actually we cease to have the occasion of language. That great proportion of modern poets who have suffered shipwreck in language are really no longer engaged in finding the universe. Language has in a way grown sufficient to them. But we have to have a searching psyche, a searching mind or simply a longing or a need for language to continue in the universe. Language for me is an engagement in which we are finding the universe. So, seeing is very closely related to language in a way. We imitate seeing in language. But reading of course far precedes language. For instance, we can read the tracks of the dinosaurs and we can understand them. That is their language. So, we read the universe as long as we are interested in it.

*Faas:* Wendy MacIntyre has called an Orphic concept of language the "quintessence of your poetics." How does Wittgenstein relate to that?

DUNCAN: As compared with Zukofsky's romance with Wittgenstein, my reading of him has been rather peripheral. I find him fascinating, of course. Because like Whitehead he is a poet. But he is never keyed in directly into my work. I    Wittgenstein have read some of his works here and there, but not extensively. Whitehead, I think, is the most recent philosopher which gave me the illusion that I was reading real news from the real universe. Games, I mean, yes. I played my own games even in language when I was little. It turned me on quite a bit. I mean, I am and was a very bad tempered boy. [Laughing]

*Faas:* You seem to be equally distanced from Fenollosa's, Pound's and Williams' experiments in fragmentation. I mean their endeavors to break up Aristotelian grammar and logic.

fragmentation

DUNCAN: But I ain't got any Aristotelian grammar or logic. I mean, they had to break up a very strong, presiding, simple construct. And Gary, in a way, still stems from that development. Although he organizes or reorganizes the fragments into intelligible, simple constructs again. But I have got to have a rhetoric because I have got to have something for the flow of the poem. I am not bothered about interrupting things. I mean, I can hardly start something without interrupting right away. And yet, I am still fascinated by melody. Cage once told me: As long as you are concerned with melody you are just not going to get there. But I am concerned with melody and I am just not going to worry about it. I mean, I don't need melody when I am listening to something. Although, on the other hand, my 19th century collection of music seems to be growing, growing and growing.

*Faas:* A poet like Antin traces post-Modernism to the *Cantos* and *The Waste Land.*

DUNCAN: Well, I'm not a Modernist. He can do that. I read Modernism as Romanticism; and I finally begin to feel myself pretty much a 19th century mind.

"I'm not a Modernist"

*Faas:* Really!

DUNCAN: I don't feel out of my century, I like this century immensely. But my ties to Pound, Stein, Surrealism and so forth all seem to me entirely consequent to their unbroken continuity from the Romantic period.

*Faas:* Antin talks of the poetry of collage.

DUNCAN: Well, I use collage and I fragment things.

*Faas:* But you also use the rhetoric.

DUNCAN: Oh, sure. And I would even refuse to interrupt it.

*Faas:* It seems to be one of the most important characteristics of your open form poetry and poetics that you try to integrate everything. You integrate rhetoric and you integrate closed form.

DUNCAN: Right. You see, if open form were a correction of closed form, okay. And in Olson's proposition it sounds like that. But I find that superfluous. Would you want to go back and correct, let's say, Housman? What do you think you would arrive at? Actually the open thing is really to contain any closed form. Any passage or anything else can be contained as part of a large open form. The essential recognition in open form is that every event in poetry has its form in reference to the total feeling of the formality of the language. That's the way I put it. Once you recognize that the language is through and through as formal as it is, you realize that every poem is participating in a form.

For one thing, it's our experience of the universe really which makes open form seem appropriate. If we only take the local fact of our life. We don't really have much of a memory of being born. We come out of a darkness and we cannot account for the first years of our life. And one thing we really don't get to catch up with is how we die. But if we have even a rudimentary imagination and if we then write a poem, it has more meanings, more lives than we ourselves in any way posited by way of actual experience. Even if we posit a closed form its readings aren't closed, and never have been. And when we have an open form we let the poem ride the vitality that language always has, and we ourselves adventure into that.

*Faas:* What exact role does language play in that?

DUNCAN: Language, first just at the level of names, is our agency whereby things come close to us and enter our psychic world. I mean, without any name for table, I have a suspicion that we don't really know what happens. I think the name comes along with the focus, it's a reification of the universe. Each name is a reification of things. As long as a person

is in love with and curious about and searching for the universe, he is engaged in language. And language has to increase for him to get anywhere in the universe. The symptom of ceasing to be in language, of ceasing to read a poem, of ceasing to be active in your science, of ceasing to read and of ceasing to wander and talk is a de-reification of the universe and a letting go of everything around you. Now that's what I think is the significance of the openness. All real instincts in language go toward an openness. This is why Eliot would be closed and why his religion is closed. When you want to be conclusive about that universe you do not want a new fact to come into reification. You do not want to realize some new thing.

*Faas:* There seems to be no language crisis in your poetry. By contrast, many European poets have given up writing poetry completely when they lost their belief in the Orphic powers of language. And some of them through reading Wittgenstein.

DUNCAN: And yet, as Zukofsky shows, there is no reason why Wittgenstein would lead to a poverty of the poem. And personally I'm not drawn to the different forms of Positivism. Wittgenstein I read with a great deal of pleasure because he seems to me like poetry. Like Barthes does. I mean the language itself is like a whole series of poetic events. And it does not engage my speculations about the universe, it doesn't even pose that. You see, in order to pose Wittgensteinian positive language formulas one has to have a very heavy exclusion of any possibility that language has mysterious presences. When I say, a woman comes into the room, I see one come into the room. He poses that as a game, but I don't experience it as a game. I don't play that I see a woman come into the room, although one of its analogies is that when as a child you played, the things were immediately present. The place where I go entirely with Lawrence is that they are immediately present and I'm not going to pretend they are not. I wouldn't have Christ present in a poem if he weren't really present. It's not a proposition of mine. And that's what makes it true or false. I don't mean that the truth means I've got the true Christ. But it's truly present.

*Faas:* In the poem.

DUNCAN: Right. And then I'm not bothered at all that I've got absolutely no system of logic. I'm not bothered that the truly present at one time will be entirely different from the truly present at another time. If at one time Christ is a woman, I don't turn that into a dogma so that at another time Christ won't be a man. I'm intrigued by the fact: Do I make it up? Those are not levels that I answer, can answer, so I turn them over and over. When I find that a figure like Christ or the figure of boundaries, that we were talking about, is unsettled in my poetry, then it makes sense to me that it comes again and again in the poem. And I think of it as being turned and turned and turned. And I'm really seeing and feeling myself turning a stone. And clearly my deepest feeling is that I've not come to know this enough yet. Because I'm not going to put a logic on any thing, I'm seeking to come to such a thorough knowledge that I suddenly realize—again in the process of turning into a thing—that it's all together. So I'm seeking altogetherness and not that it checks out in dictions and contradictions. I see it's there and that it often comes to live with you forever. It's the same thing in my relation to Jess. Our emotions developed over 20 years of living together. And I don't mean to say that it's a virtue to live a long time. But in my temperament there is a lot of that slow development. People often don't realize that. Because I talk so fast and grab things in a million different ways within five minutes. But what one might observe is that while I grab things in twenty different ways or go into a great manic spiel in which it is reposed and reformulated twenty different ways in five minutes, I've been doing it for nearly fifty years. I've been doing it since I was a child in

*[margin note:]* language not a game

*[margin note:]* a great manic spiel

stockings at the age of about four or five. And I haven't arrived in all that at greater certainty. It's simply a continuous process of reification.

# Gary Snyder

Photo: Layle Silbert

# Gary Snyder (1930 -       )

"As a poet, I hold the most archaic values on earth. They go back to the late Paleolithic; the fertility of the soil, the magic of animals, the power-vision in solitude, the terrifying initiation and rebirth, the love and ecstasy of the dance, the common work of the tribe . . . Whatever is or ever was in any other culture can be reconstructed from the unconscious through meditation . . . the coming revolution will close the circle and link us in many ways with the most creative aspects of our archaic past."

Born in San Francisco, Gary Snyder was "raised up on a feeble sort of farm just north of Seattle," received his B.A. in anthropology from Reed College in 1951, "studied linguistics one term at Indiana University, & after that sort of bummed around working at logging & forestry work alternate with classical Chinese study at Berkeley." Here he met Allen Ginsberg and Jack Kerouac (who made him the protagonist of his *Dharma Bums,* 1958) and became associated with the Beat movement. *Riprap* (1959), his first collection of poems, and one of the movement's key works besides Ginsberg's *Howl* (1956), Kerouac's *On The Road* (1957) and Burroughs' *The Naked Lunch* (1959), already bears the mark of his formal Zen training in Japan, embarked on in May, 1956. Besides offering "Technical Notes & Queries to Fellow Dharma Revolutionaries," as its subtitle indicates, *Earth House Hold* (1969) contains a poetic travel journal of Snyder's life in Japan and of intermittent journeys through India or "visiting Mediterranean & Pacific oil ports" as a hand on a tanker. In recent years, Snyder, his Japanese wife, and their two children, have lived in a self-made block house on the edge of a gold diggers desert in Nevada County, California. Snyder's major collections of poetry to date *(Myths and Texts,* 1960; *The Back Country,* 1968; *Regarding Wave,* 1971; *Turtle Island,* 1974)* as well as *Mountains and Rivers without End (Six Sections,* 1965), his *No* play-inspired long poem in progress, give a firm sense of his life, personality and numerous commitments.

# Gary Snyder

As T. S. Eliot, one time student of Sanskrit and Patanjali Yoga, declared after his self-proclaimed 1927 conversion to classicism, royalism and Anglo-Catholicism: "It is because of our common background in the literatures of Greece, Rome and Israel, that we can speak of 'European literature' at all: and the survival of European literature . . . depends on our continued veneration of our ancestors" (E,P,211). Charles Olson, following Pound and Lawrence, had tried to extend this restricting concept by drawing on non-Western, Primitive and pre-Judæo-Christian civilizations like the Sumerian. Yet for Gary Snyder, who claims "the most archaic values on earth," even Olson's far-ranging cultural internationalism fails to provide us with a satisfactory alternative to the accepted norm of a living tradition. Olson, he feels, was ultimately "an apologist for Western culture; the trip from Sumeria to Gloucester a sort of justification for White-America" (S,IA,111).[1]* What Snyder proposes instead is a complete break with civilization in its present form. To him, civilization is "ultimately the enemy. The very order of the society that we have lived in for the last 4000 years has outlived its usefulness"(S,IG,22). "Judæo-Capitalist-Christian-Marxist" civilization in particular, our "whole Western Tradition, of which Marxism is but a (Millennial Protestant) part, is off the track"(S,E,92,114).

Paradoxically, Snyder believes that it is neither the East nor the underdeveloped nations, but his own country which offers the only prospect for a future society. For America, as Snyder observed in 1967, "is the only culture in which a number of people" have recognized the life-destroying potential of Western civilization "and are able to go beyond it"(Ko,N,167). It is here that in literature, music and art, as well as in countless neo-tribal communities, we witness the surfacing of "the Great Subculture which goes back as far perhaps as the late Paleolithic" and which, although suppressed and persecuted by ruling establishments and institutionalized religions all over the world, has formed a powerful and ineradicable "undercurrent in all higher civilizations":

*Notes to this section on p. 104.

> In China it is manifested as Taoism, not only Lao-tzu but the
> later Yellow Turban revolt and medieval Taoist secret societies;
> and the Zen Buddhists up till early Sung. Within Islam the
> Sufis; in India the various threads converged to produce Tan-
> trism. In the West it has been represented largely by a string of
> heresies starting with the Gnostics, and on the folk level by
> "witchcraft" . . . astronomers, ritualists, alchemists . . . Al-
> bigensians . . . and vagantes, right down to the Golden Gate
> Park.   (S,E,104-5,115)

In this way America may harbor the only hope for mankind. "If we
change America we are changing the planet," and that in dimensions
far larger than Olson's or Lawrence's return to a pre-Christian or
pre-Socratic consciousness and world picture. "We've turned a
corner . . . on the order of the change between Paleolithic and
Neolithic. It's like one of the three or four major turns in the history
of man—not just culture—but man" (Ko,N,168,170).

How is this transformation to come about? Though he re-
pudiates the "Judæo-Capitalist-Christian-Marxist" view of history in
favor of Buddhism, Snyder remains deeply committed to Western
pragmatism, humanitarian optimism, and belief in progress.
Granted, life is "a great mutual sacrifice where we have to eat one
another" (S,IG,24), yet man, through meditation, art and ritual, is
capable of "intuitive knowledge of the mind of love and clarity that
lies beneath one's ego-driven anxieties and aggressions." In this way
even the horrific "Universal Form of the Lord" as depicted in the
*Bhagavad Gita*—"all created things rushing into Krishna's devouring
mouth"—ultimately points to a "loving, simple awareness of the
absolute beauty and preciousness of mice and weeds." Snyder
acknowledges "the negative and demonic potentials of the Unconsciousness" and in fact feels that art (like the "archaic and primitive
ritual dramas") should symbolically act them out and thereby free us
from their power. But, generally speaking, "man's natural being is to
be trusted and followed . . . and . . . in following the grain, one is
being truly 'moral'" (S,E,92,115,122,128).

Yet Snyder is no mere Romantic, unaware of the influence
which sociological and historical factors have on human morality.
Thus he takes a distinctly hostile view of the political apathy and
conformism of most Eastern religions. "Institutional Buddhism,"
for instance, has in his opinion "been conspicuously ready to accept
or ignore the inequalities and tyrannies of whatever political system
it found itself under." By contrast, his own conviction that no one

today "can afford to be innocent, or indulge himself in ignorance of the nature of contemporary governments, politics and social orders" (S,E,90), would do honor to any hard-core Marxist revolutionary in the severity of its phrasing. Snyder's formula for the future destiny of mankind—

> a totally integrated world culture with matrilineal descent, free-form marriage, natural-credit communist economy, less industry, far less population and lots more national parks—

may differ in aim, but not in spirit from any of the pre- or post-Marxist versions of a secularized theodicy. "The mercy of the West," he sums up in "Buddhism and the Coming Revolution," "has been social revolution; the mercy of the East has been individual insight into the basic self/void. We need both" (S,E,92-3).

While the Beat movement was at its height, this goal seemed almost to be in sight. Within about three generations, Snyder speculated, "automation . . . plus psychedelics, plus . . . a whole catalytic, spiritual change or bend of mind that seems to be taking place in the West" would produce "a vast leisure society . . . [with] a very complex and sophisticated cybernetic technology surrounded by thick hedges of trees" (Ko,N,139-40). More recently, these Fullerian dreams of a paradisaic utopia have been replaced by a nightmare vision of civilization engulfed by an apocalyptic collapse before nature has a chance to restore its ecological balance. "At the moment," Snyder said in 1970, "a breakdown would be better than over-organization . . . There will probably be a transitional period in which there will be predatory tribes living off the remnants of civilization" (S,IG,22-3). Snyder, by now, is as well aware as others of how the pristine impulse of the Beat movement has to a large extent been absorbed by the very mainstream society it opposed ("Japanese-American animal nutrition experts/from Kansas,/with Buddhist beads," S,T,10) or been miscast into yet another variant of life-negating puritanism:

> The ex acid-heads from the cities
> Converted to Guru or Swami,
> Do penance with shiny
> Dopey eyes, and quit eating meat.
> In the forests of North America,
> The land of Coyote and Eagle,
> They dream of India, of
> > forever blissful sexless highs.
>
> .    .    .    .    .    .    .
>
> And the Coyote singing

is shut away
for they fear
the call
of the wild.

(S,T,21-2)

Despite all this, Snyder seems as determined as ever to practise
the ideas he believes in. The "true heir of Thoreau," as Richard
Howard calls him, he has withdrawn from civilization into a blockhouse he built himself in the foothills of the sierra in Nevada County,
California, though as a "modern Tribesman" (S,E,116) he re-
pudiates the isolationist individualism of his 19th century forerun-
ner, and shares his life with his Japanese wife Masa and their children as well as with sympathetic neighbors, visitors and friends such
as Allen Ginsberg and Michael McClure. His childhood on a "feeble
sort of farm just north of Seattle" (A,P,444) had prepared him well
for such an existence. As Kerouac wrote of Snyder (alias Japhy
Rider), the protagonist of *The Dharma Bums* (1958), he was, from his
beginnings, a "woods boy, an axman, farmer, interested in animals
and Indian lore so that when he finally got to college . . . he was
already well equipped for his early studies in anthropology and later
in Indian myth" (Ke,B,9). After graduating in 1951, with an impressive thesis on a specific North American Indian myth, he at first
planned a career in the University. But faced with the stultifying
ordeal of having to write a Ph.D., he finally decided to set himself
"loose in the world to sink or swim as a poet" (Kh,S,9).

What put an end to his formal academic curriculum marked the
beginning not only of his life as a poet but of his amazing career as
autodidact scholar and oriental sage. From 1953 onwards, he began
to teach himself Chinese and Japanese, and in the fall of that year
decided to go to Japan. In preparation, he temporarily resumed his
studies, this time at the graduate school of Oriental languages in
Berkeley. Then, in May 1956, a grant from the newly founded Zen
Institute of America in San Francisco enabled him to set sail for
Japan where he remained till August 1957, studying and meditating
in a Zen temple. After an 8 months voyage, "working on a tanker . . .
visiting Mediterranean & Pacific oil ports" (A,P,444), followed by an
extended stay in San Francisco, he in January 1959 returned to
Japan, and with the exception of a journey through India in the
company of Allen Ginsberg, spent the following 6 years in Kyoto,
studying under Oda Sessō Rōshi (1901-1966), Zen Master and Head
Abbot of Daitoku-Ji.

This self-education within a non-Western framework provided

Snyder with an æsthetics that matches the radicalism of his sociological convictions. There are few Westerners the poet could claim as
predecessors in this quest. Rousseau and Blake, Whitman and
Thoreau, Lawrence and Jeffers, Pound and Rexroth are the names
Snyder most frequently mentions in this context. Otherwise, he
finds it difficult to relate to past America or Europe "because it's
Christian. I find it easier to go to the Greek Anthology, the Romans,
the medieval Chinese" (S,IA,112). In this way, a new understanding
of poetry and art, like a new society, can only be reached by a radical
break with our past. "It is a mistake to think," Snyder wrote in 1969,
"that we are searching, now, for 'new forms.' What is needed is a
totally new approach to the very idea of form . . . The future can't be
seen on the basis of the present; and I believe mankind is headed
someplace else" (B-M,P,358). A whole-hearted Primitivist at first,
Snyder came to recognize through his Far Eastern studies that
"traditional Hinduism and Buddhism have added a great deal onto
basic Shamanistic and primitive ritualistic, ceremonial practises and
life styles" (S,IR,59), and it is through a fusion of both that he
evolved this new approach to the idea of form.

Not unlike Olson, who demanded the "replacement of the
Classical-representational by the *primitive-abstract*" (O,W,28) and re-
defined form in terms of body-creativity (the poet's breath rhythm in
relation to the cosmic life rhythm), Snyder, by 1959, came to realize
that "the rhythms of my poems follow the rhythm of the physical
work I'm doing and life I'm leading at any given time" (A,P,420).
More recent statements come even closer to Olson's (and Far Eastern) breath-rhythm theory. According to one school of Mahāyāna
Buddhism, as Snyder points out, the whole universe is often thought
of as "a vast breathing body," while poetry is "the vehicle of the
mystery of voice" (S,E,118), a notion which is close to what is meant
by *Fushi,* the Japanese word for song, which literally signifies a knot,
or whorl in the grain of wood (S,T,114). "The bass tone of the
universe," Snyder explains, "stops for a few moments and does some
complex things, and then it goes on again" (S,IQ,49).

Unlike Olson, however, Snyder tends to equate this concept of
form with the void:

> form—leaving things out at the right spot
> ellipse, is emptiness.
>
> (S,E,5)

What at first may appear to be in contradiction with the breath-
rhythm theory turns out to be its natural counterpart when considered in the light of Eastern philosophy from which it is derived. As

an analogue of cosmic creation which emanates from the void and in endless cycles returns to it, the work of art must necessarily partake of the ultimate emptiness or *śūnyatā*. For as the Chinese philosopher Chang Tsai (1020-1077) puts it, the "Great Vacuity" is nothing but "material-force." "Things of necessity disintegrate and return to the Great Vacuity," which is omnipresent in all creation, both cosmic and artistic: in its "integration and disintegration, appearance and disappearance, form and absence of form" (Ba,C,460-1). Thus Chinese painters, for instance, follow the principle of *hsü shih*, or vacant space versus solid. For in the composition of a picture, as Hsun Tsu-yung writes in his *Ferry Boat for Painting* "there must be spiritual breath coming and leaving without hindrance" (Ch,C,212). Or as the æsthetician Lu Chi exclaims in his *Essay on Literature*: "A composition . . . is (like the act of Tao) the embodiment of endless change/ . . . it is Being, created by tasking the Great Void,/ And 'tis sound rung out of Profound Silence" (Bi,A,207,209).

Similarly, "true insight" to Snyder is "a love-making hovering between the void & the immense worlds of creation" (S,E,22), and poetry, as its subtlest medium of expression, walks "that edge between what can be said and that which cannot be said . . . [I]t's going out into emptiness and into the formless" while at the same time resting on "an absolute foundation of human experience and insight" (S,IR,64,67-8). The "pure inspiration flow" bringing it forth is "not intellect and not—(as romantics and after have confusingly thought) fantasy-dream world or unconsciousness." On the contrary, true poetry "reflects all things and feeds all things but is of itself transparent" (S,E,56-7).

True to this theory, Snyder's poetry, like that of his Eastern peers, often radiates with an almost unearthly clarity and precision, whereby the sensual concreteness of every detail seems as if suffused with this transparence or awareness of the void. What seems so deceptively simple, is, in fact, a unique, by now widely imitated, yet probably inimitable achievement within Western poetry. Little gaps of silence frequently seem to separate one utterance from the next, and, like the brush strokes of calligraphic paintings, each phrase or remark, like the phenomenon or event it embodies, seems to rest within the energy of its own tension, autonomous, and yet related to all others in the hidden field of force, creating its "complexity far beneath the surface texture" (A,P,421).

> What my hand follows on your body
> Is the line. A stream of love
>     of heat, of light,        what my

eye      lascivious
       licks
over, watching
far snow-dappled Uintah mountains
Is that stream.
Of power.       what my
   hand curves over, following the line.
   "hip" and "groin"
Where "I"
   follow by hand and eye
   the swimming limit of your body.

              ("Beneath My Hand and Eye the Distant Hills,
                           Your Body," S,C,108-9)

In the words of one of his earlier poems, there is a "leap of words to things and there it stops" (S,R,22), and, reminiscent of Olson's principle of "FIELD COMPOSITION," the poem, as the reduplication or reenactment of a natural process, seems to follow its own dynamics. In this way, the end of the poem often states the end of an activity ("we sleep in the sand/ and our salt"), the beginning of something new ("& got back in our wagon,/ drove away"), an activity that finds its only purpose in itself ("and made love on the sand") or, by way of a cyclical repetition, restates the beginning ("Three a.m.—a far bell/ coming closer") enhancing and deepening its effect ("A far bell coming closer," S,C,59-63,112). The lyrical "I" or speaker, as the inverted commas in "Beneath My Hand and Eye . . ." suggest, is generally represented as just another of the objects or events enacted and, in Olson's words, "can go by no track other than the one the poem under hand declares, for itself" (O,W,16).

A 1972 "British Assessment" tries to associate Snyder with the decadent Nineties poets in England, "who dissipated their technical expertise on an extraordinarily narrow range of emotion and experience."[2] Yet, despite *prima facie* resemblances, nothing could be more alien to Snyder's aims and achievements than the subjective impressionism of a poet like Arthur Symons, for instance, who in 1897 declared the "moods of men" to be the primary aim of his verse:

> There I find my subject . . . and whatever has once been a mood of mine, though it has been no more than a ripple on the sea, and had no longer than that ripple's duration, I claim the right to render, if I can, in verse.

                       ("Preface" to *London Nights*)

In fact, it is exactly this "ego interference," as Snyder once
commented, which "keeps someone else's poem from working" for
him (S,IT,22). Like Olson, Snyder is deeply aware of "that peculiar
presumption by which western man has interposed himself between
what he is as a creature of nature . . . and those other creations of
nature which we . . . call objects." And probably nowhere in contemporary American poetry has this dichotomy been overcome more
convincingly than in Snyder's. Many of his poems seem like
paradigmatic embodiments of Olson's notion that a poem ought to
be a "field of force" in which man, including the speaker, becomes
"himself an object" (O,W,24). As in "Beneath My Hand and Eye
. . .," there is a general tendency, not to present nature in terms of
man but to present man in terms of nature, both that of his body and
his surroundings. For according to Snyder we enter this world,
trailing not "clouds of glory," as we come from "God, who is our
home,"[3] but

> slippery clouds of guts
> incense of our flowery flesh
> blossoms;    crusht;    re-turning
> knots of rose meat open out to—over—
> five-hued clouds—
> the empty diamond of all space.

> (S,C,93)

In an insightful interpretation of "Sixth-Month Song in the
Foothills," Charles Altieri has shown how the poet, when speaking of
himself, usually "refuses to supply explicit referents to the partici-
ples modifying his own actions, so that they appear as if freed from
the limits of subjectivity." The effect of this, however, is not a "blend
of subject and object,"[4] as in Romantic nature poetry, but a total
elimination of that dichotomy:

> In the cold shed sharpening saws.
>        a swallow's nest hangs by the door
> setting rakers in sunlight
> falling from meadow through doorframe
>        swallows flit under the eaves.
>
> Grinding the falling axe
> sharp for the summer
>        a swallow shooting out over.
> over the river, snow on low hills
> sharpening wedges for splitting.

Beyond the low hills, white mountains
and now snow is melting.   sharpening tools;
            pack horses grazing new grass
bright axes—and swallows
            fly in to my shed.

                                                      (S,C,17)

The speaker or "subject" seems to be omnipresent in the poem. Yet,
except for the last line he only refers to himself as an anonymous
event amongst others, such as grazing horses or melting snow.
Similarly, Snyder avoids the direct or indirect article to single out a
phenomenon or event as an independent object, while presenting all
phenomena, including himself, in terms of interrelated actions and
movements. This is further enhanced by the frequent use of the
gerund (e.g., "sharpen*ing*") which gives the descriptions a presentational urgency that draws the reader into the poem to make him
become part of the "jewelled net" of nature's interconnectedness
(S,E,129) embodied in the language. Nowhere, however, does the
gerund create that momentary emotional intensity typical of the
traditional post-Romantic lyric. Instead, as in other of Snyder's
poems, it suddenly and for no specific reason, tends to switch into
the present tense, as if to suggest that what is presented in all the
immediacy of its here and now does—like

        the plank shutter
                set

    Half-open       on eternity

                                                      (S,W,28)

—partake of the eternal round of being, of what has always been and
always will be:

        —and swallows
        fly in to my shed.

    Given the scope of this essay, I have mainly focussed on what
seems to me Snyder's most outstanding contribution to Western
poetry. Yet, just as the Eastern poets he translated cover a wide range
of modes and tones, from the mystical luminosity of Chinese Han-
shan to the mythopoeic deep imagery or colloquial satire of Japanese
Miyazawa Kenji, so the poet's own work is by no means limited to the
lyric mode of his "Flowers for the Void" (S,E,134) "going out into
emptiness and into the formless which is the nature of pure joy"
(S,IR,64). Snyder often speaks with a funny, self-ironical, satirical or

outspokenly didactic voice, while a work like *Myths &Texts* (1960), hailed by Robert Bly as "one of the two or three finest books of poetry" of its decade (B,S,6,29), presents us with a subtly orchestrated structure, centered around specific symbols and myths that were inspired by "the happy collections Sapir, Boas, Swanton, and others made of American Indian folktales early in this century" (A,P,421). Julian Gitzen, in an extensive interpretation of the poem, has compared *Myths & Texts* with *The Waste Land*, though one may add that the "fragmental texture"[5] which in Eliot's poem expresses anguished spiritual chaos in the face of nothingness ("These fragments I have shored against my ruins") serves Snyder as a positive means for apprehending reality in its pre-conceptual suchness (*tathatā*) and as a medium for his poetic "re-enactment of [the] timeless dance: here and now, co-creating forever, for no end but now" (S,E,134).

> Intricate layers of emptiness
> This only world, juggling forms
>             a hand, a breast, two clasped
> Human tenderness scuttles
> Down dry endless cycles
> Forms within forms falling
>                         clinging
> Loosely, what's gone away?
>                         —love.
>
>                                   (S,M,34-5)

Another major poetic mode, that of his long poem in progress entitled *Mountains and Rivers without End*, at first seems to invite comparison with the American epic tradition from *Leaves of Grass* to the *Maximus Poems*. Yet as Snyder explained in 1959, it in fact emulates further models of Eastern literature and art. Its "dramatic structure follows a certain type of Nŏ play," while its overall structure (which "threatens to be like its title") was conceived "after a Chinese sidewise scroll painting" (A,P,421). In an even earlier statement to Kerouac recorded in *The Dharma Bums*, the poet jokingly anticipates that, just like the author of *On the Road*, he will be writing

> on and on on a scroll and unfold on and on with new surprises
> and always what went before forgotten . . . I'll spend three
> thousand years writing it, it'll be packed full of information on
> soil conservation, the Tennessee Valley Authority, astronomy,
> geology, Hsuan Tsung's travels, Chinese painting theory, re-
> forestation, Oceanic ecology and food chains.  (Ke,B,156)

It would be tantamount to splitting hairs to try to trace these various modes in terms of their successive evolution in the poet's life. Even in his beginnings, Snyder, unlike Robert Lowell or other poets of the "confessional" genre, for instance, displays none of the tormented, self-questioning, and often suicidal spiritual tendencies, so typical of post-Romantic poetry in the West. Instead, he seems to have evolved these several modes almost simultaneously and as from a common basis, and to have deepened, refined and elaborated them ever since. As Snyder points out himself, *Mountains and Rivers without End* (of which the first *Six Sections* were published in 1965) was begun as early as 1956, *Myths & Texts* (1960) "grew" between 1952 and 1956 (A,P,421), while the poems of the more "lyric order" as he calls them (S,IR,65), already dominate his first published collection of 1959 *(Riprap)*. Even earlier, in his diary of the years 1952-3, Snyder had begun to formulate the basic premises of his philosophy and poetics: his experience of *"no identity"* and "the void," his epistemological "love-making hovering between the void & the immense worlds of creation," his concept of form as "ellipse, is emptiness," the subsequent experience of linguistic disintegration ("my language fades. Images of erosion") and the attempt to reconstitute language after the model of Chinese poetry cross-bred with the primordial potential of the Anglo-Saxon heritage.[6] It was equally early in his career that Snyder assumed his clean-slate stance in favor of Primitive and Eastern mentality ("Let's be animals or buddhas," S,E,5,10,22,36) and against the Judæo-Christian world view:

> What use, Milton, a silly story
> Of our lost general parents,
>       eaters of fruit?
>
> .   .   .   .   .   .   .   .   .
>
>     In ten thousand years the Sierras
> Will be dry and dead, home of the scorpion.
> Ice-scratched slabs and bent trees.
> No paradise, no fall,
> Only the weathering land
> The wheeling sky,
> Man, with his Satan
> Scouring the chaos of the mind.
> Oh Hell!
>
>                     (August 1955, S,R,7-8)

By 1955, Snyder had also entered his now well over 20 year old discipline of regular meditational exercises or *za-zen* and "like a

blade which sharpens to nothing" (S,E,34), had started to gain insights which must have struck some of his early readers as being of
an almost frighteningly staunch and inhuman rigor:

> Sky over endless mountains.
> All the junk that goes with being human
> Drops away, hard rock wavers
> Even the heavy present seems to fail
> This bubble of a heart.
> Words and books
> Like a small creek off a high ledge
> Gone in the dry air.
>
> A clear, attentive mind
> Has no meaning but that
> Which sees is truly seen.
> No one loves rock, yet we are here.
>
> (S,R,6)

To be sure, Snyder's early work shows traces of the confessional
("Bitter memory like vomit/Choked my throat") or romantically
subjective mode, at times almost reminiscent of a poet like Matthew
Arnold, stoically resigned to the cruelty of life, yet at the same time
yearning for human compassion:

> In this burning, muddy, lying,
> blood-drenched world
> that quiet meeting in the mountains
> cool and gentle as the muzzles of
> three elk, helps keep me sane.

But far more forceful and ubiquitous is the impulse to negate all the
"pointless wars of the heart" (S,C,34,46) and to come to terms with
human suffering generally. Questioned about his attitude towards
the confessional school of poets, Snyder replied: "I'm a Buddhist,
which is to say you take suffering and impermanence for granted, as
a base fact of the universe, and then proceed on from there"
(S,IQ,50). Again, such an attitude is by no means new to Snyder and
was in fact assumed even before the confessional poets made their
first appearance in Anglo-American literature. As early as 1956,
Snyder, age 26, concluded that there comes

> a time when the poet must choose: either to step deep in the
> stream of his people, history, tradition, folding and folding
> himself in wealth of persons and pasts; philosophy, humanity,

to become richly foundationed and great and sane and or-
dered. Or, to step beyond the bound onto the way out, into
horrors and angels, possible madness or silly Faustian doom,
possible utter transcendence, possible enlightened return,
possible ignominious wormish perishing (S,E,39).

By his subsequent creativity, personal development and indefatiga-
ble involvement in ecological, social, cultural and purely human
concerns, Snyder has left no doubt as to which of these two paths he
has chosen as his own.

[1] This, of course, may be an at least partly inauthentic statement. See Snyder interview p. 105.

[2] P. E. Lewis, "Robert Creeley and Gary Snyder: A British Assessment," *Stand* 13,4 (1972), pp. 42-7, 46.

[3] Wordsworth, "Immortality Ode," lines 65-6.

[4] "Gary Snyder's Lyric Poetry: Dialectic as Ecology," *The Far Point* 4,1 (Spring/Summer 1970), pp. 55-65, 61.

[5] "Gary Snyder and the Poetry of Compassion," *Critical Quarterly* 15,4 (Winter 1973), pp. 341-57, 347.

[6] See S,IQ,47: "Then, in terms of poetic craft, one must not only have an ear for daily speech, but the particularly poetic sense of refining, purifying, and compressing daily speech into the kind of compact utterance that a poem becomes. So first of all, in my poetry my craft has a sense of compression, a sense of ellipsis, of leaving out the unnecessary, of sharpening the utterance down to a point where a very precise, very swift message is generated, an energy is transmitted. In doing that, I have paid particular attention to the Anglo-Saxon or Germanic derived aspects of the English language, and have made much use of mono-syllabic words, of compactness and directness of the Anglo-Saxon heritage in the English language, which I have cross-bred with my understanding and ear for Chinese poetry."

# Gary Snyder

*Faas*: The first thing I should like to discuss is your attitude towards Olson. You once called him "an apologist for Western culture" and his "trip from Sumeria to Gloucester a sort of justification for White-America."

Charles Olson

SNYDER: No, I never said "White-America," and altogether I don't think that's fair for me to say, really, because frankly I haven't looked at Olson that closely for a number of years; and when I first read Olson, I was feeling extremely partisan towards Eastern culture and my response to Olson was probably based on that excessive partisanship. So that all I can say in honesty is that I haven't studied Olson as deeply as I might have or should perhaps. And what I have read seemed to reflect a predominantly Atlantic and ultimately Occidental focus, which wasn't where my specific interests lay. My thinking comes together with Olson's direction when we come into prehistory and the Pleistocene.

*Faas*: You saw Olson's piece on Pleistocene Man?

SNYDER: Yes. And at this point I'm doing a lot more investigation of the Pleistocene horizon around the world than ever. Now, Pleistocene is before Eastern culture and Western culture diverge; your evidence would be from the artifacts that are essentially identical throughout the Eurasian landmass. And a number of other evidences coming right down to the upper Paleolithic give us in a sense a kind of international prehistoric culture. Olson's insights in this were interesting, but only point the way to some amazing possibilities that should be investigated further: prehistory.

Pleistocene Man

*Faas*: But then there also seem to be general points of affinity between Olson's poetic theories and your own.

SNYDER: Indeed! In intrinsic poetic theory: projective verse—I quote that right like everybody else as a starting point for thinking about the line's breath and the poem as a musical phrase or a *thala* (a rhythmic model). You know what a *thala* is? Well, you know the term *raga*.

*Faas*: Yes.

SNYDER:  A melodic mode for an Indian piece. Every Indian piece is
to a certain *raga* and also to a certain *thala*. And a *thala* is the rhythmic
mode that goes with a certain melodic mode. [Chanting]:
tatatatatatatata*ta* tetetete tatatata*ta*; the set-up for a *thala* should be
reproduced on the drum. And so from Olson's notion and from
other people's ways of seeing things, my sense of the form of poetry
is analogous to the form of a *thala* which is a long thing sometimes,
you know, completes itself and sets the tone, sets the rhythm and the
style for a whole underlying poetic development.

*Faas*:  It was interesting for me to find that a specific kind of Zen flute
music is based on breath rhythm.

SNYDER:  Shakuhachi.

*Faas*:  Yes, I think that's it.

SNYDER:  [Starts chanting]: and so forth. That's a Zen chant. Well,
what I was doing last night [refering to a reading at the New York
YMHA, early in 1974] in some of those poems, was based on *Nō*-
drama chant which is also breath rhythm. My source of inspiration
there is having attended many *Nō*-plays.

*Faas*:  But are there any specific points where you differ from
Olson?

SNYDER:  I wish you'd told me you were going to ask these questions
and I would have studied that. [Laughing]

*Faas*:  On the whole, I think, there is much more affinity than difference.

SNYDER:  There is actually a great deal of affinity and I'm fascinated
by the way Olson's mind works. I think, as I said before, my direct
teacher in these matters was Pound. I read Pound exten-

East and West   sively. I did not read Olson extensively because I had
Coast gurus    already absorbed so much of that from Pound. I came to
               Olson a little later, somehow I didn't feel the need. I felt
that Pound was my teacher already and that Olson had learned it
from Pound. For that and for other reasons which are curious and
which have to do with East and West coast differences. Like we did
not read Olson very much on the West coast in the fifties. There was
a remoteness there, and indeed it was Robert Duncan who was the
West coast guru as Olson was the East coast guru. Duncan sort of
shared West coast guru rites with Rexroth, and Rexroth never liked
Olson at all. Actually, he put him down terribly.

*Faas*:  I didn't know that.

SNYDER:  He said he was a second-rate Pound, and as a human being
he thought that Olson was too difficult. Of course, Rexroth was a
difficult man in his own right. So, you know, I'm trying to think now
what the actual facts were of those relationships between poets and

influences. In other words, thinking of Charles, I'm fascinated by the way his mind works, and he has a marvellous sense of phrasing and timing and a way of juxtaposing ideas which is, you know, absolutely brilliant. On balance, however, I find him too much of a head poet, over-intellectual, over-abstract, over-theoretical, his poems verging off too much and too often in the directions of reading lists to disciples and notebook jottings. I think he was rather indulgent of himself in that respect.

*Olson too much of a head poet*

*Faas*: Since we have started to talk about your contemporaries: How do you view the work of Robert Bly and his plea that American poetry will have to go through what he calls the "dark psychic woods of the unconscious," that is to say, through a period of Surrealism, before it will be able to become a really great modern poetry?

*Bly and Surrealism*

SNYDER: As I understand what Robert is saying, this is not necessarily a plea for Surrealism. I don't know if he would say that. What he has translated and praised in the way of, say, South American, American, Spanish and European poetry has not been really Surrealist poetry.

*Faas*: You mean not like early French Surrealism.

SNYDER: Well, it's been poetry of image. But Surrealism is another issue which I have questions about. It may not be fair, but I have a feeling that Surrealism skims off the top, it doesn't go deep enough into the unconscious, that it plays more with the subjective flow level of imagery which can be manipulated rather than . . .

*Faas*: Like automatic writing?

SNYDER: Yes, well, automatic writing or what we used to call stream-of-consciousness. And there's a deeper level that Bly is interested in, which is more . . . quiet, and which I'm interested in. Yes, I think we do have to go through that. I feel that American poetry probably will or should move further away from its rhetorical and rationalistic Anglo background, you know, Romantic Anglo background, and swing deeper into the mind. I would hope that my own poetry would do that.

*Faas*: You would hope?

SNYDER: Yes.

*Faas*: I always had the feeling that in a way you had bypassed that stage. Or, rather, what I mean is that with the advantage of a Buddhist education and years of meditational practice you did not have to pass through the Surrealist stage in order to get to the spiritual realms beyond that.

SNYDER: Oh yes, I don't mean I would wish to write like a Surrealist.

But I would like to work at deep sea levels, a little bit up from that absolute bottom transparency of the Chinese type poetry, a little more mythic, a little more archetypal. Well, I did that in *Myths & Texts*. That's the key poem in which I worked that kind of thing in. Actually, *Mountains and Rivers without End* is also where I'm writing that kind of poetry. Like that poem I read last night about the flowing, about the river mouth which finally just comes to a stop like that. I like that kind of work best right now.

*Faas*: À propos Surrealism, there is an interesting study by the German scholar Christian Kellerer entitled *Objet trouvé und Surrealismus* which tries to show that Surrealism is our Western access to a Zen Buddhist approach to life and art.

Surrealism and Zen

SNYDER: But there is one difference, there is a key difference, and the key difference is that the Surrealist conceived of that deep knowledge of himself as somehow still the ego.

*Faas*: Exactly. But then amongst the late followers of Surrealism you get artists like Jackson Pollock who are able to break through that ego barrier.

SNYDER: How does Existentialism fit in with that? Because Existentialism seems to me to have been working in the same direction.

Existentialism

*Faas*: I think the answer to that lies with a man like Robbe-Grillet whose essays *Pour un nouveau roman* in many ways read almost like a Zen Buddhist theory of the novel, although he doesn't seem to have been influenced by Eastern thought. One of Robbe-Grillet's starting points is the Existentialist notion of the absurd which to him is just the last form or rather inversion of our Western teleological concept of life and history—trying to find a meaning and a purpose in everything. To Robbe-Grillet, by contrast, reality is neither meaningful nor absurd: it is simply there.

SNYDER: It makes sense.

*Faas*: I find the same kind of "literal" understanding of reality in Creeley. He reports in an interview how he passed the same neon sign for weeks on end, read it every day and became so fixed on its literal *signifiant*—the words, the letters, the visual configuration—that it never occurred to him it contained an actual pun.

SNYDER: That happened to me yesterday in *Newsweek* magazine. There was an article about wildcat drillers in Texas. It quoted one of these wildcat drillers who had just begun to employ some young geologist, and this geologist came up to him as he was getting off his truck and the geologist said: "We have just gone through the Miocene." And then he came back a little later and said: "We are now going through the Eocene." And the driller said: "Well, young fellow, when you hit the kerosene let me know." [Both laughing]

*Faas*: Despite some obvious differences, you and other American poets seem to share the basic notions of a general open form poetics. Are we here dealing with a distinctly American phe-nomenon?

SNYDER:  It seems to be. I don't know of anything like it in modern Japanese poetry, and certainly not in India. I'm telling you of places I know about.

American open form poetics

*Faas*:  And yet there is at least one Japanese poet, I forget his name now, who began under the influence of European Dadaism . . .

SNYDER:  Takahashi.

*Faas*:  Right, and who now writes some kind of Zen Buddhist poetry.

SNYDER:  That's because Zen Buddhism seems like the better tag to sell it by.

*Faas*:  Speaking of world poetry generally, surely there are tenden-cies toward an open form poetics everywhere: Höllerer in Germany, Gustafsson in Sweden, but more at isolated points, whereas in the U.S. it seems to have caught on everywhere. Even with Lowell who, in his *Notebook*, went, I think, through an experience comparable to that of Williams when he found that he couldn't finish *Paterson*.

SNYDER:  Lowell's *Notebooks* really were a change, a tremendous breakthrough, and a good one, mind opening.

*Faas*:  Robert Duncan, during our recent conversations, jokingly said that you were a Marxist in disguise, and personally I find that there is a very strong sense of purposefulness and future-oriented pragmatism in you. Do you feel that Western teleological thought is compatible with Eastern philosophy?

SNYDER:  Well, Buddhism does have a teleology, has a whole es-chatology which is placed in a kind of mythic far future—a kind of Teilhard de Chardin vision of everything in the universe becoming finally enlightened together. Except for what do you do then? I suppose you start another universe, you will do it all over again. [Laughing] The Buddhist cosmic time span eschatology—you see the Bodhisattvas and the Buddhas all make vows not to achieve enlightenment until all sentient beings are saved. So all the Bodhisattvas and all the universes are working lifetime after lifetime for the salvation of all sentient

Buddhist teleology

beings. If Buddhism is doing its job, why then eventually all sentient beings would be saved. And then everything would be a Buddha. Zen mysticism says: well, wait it's already all a Buddha right now, if you can just see it, so that's ahistorical. It's the eternal moment. I think in those terms, but I also think in terms of organic evolution, and from that standpoint we have a critical time now in which decisions are being made which will have long reaching effects on the survival of many forms of life. All the time we are reducing biological diversity at a great rate with modern civilization. From that standpoint I don't know if I'm exactly a Marxist, but I'm committted to a biological Buddhist mystic defense of the diversity of life which I think is the work of poets as ancient shaman-poets and ancient servants of the Muse and the lady of wild things and non-human or extra-human realms. And I value the Marxist critique of Capitalism as throwing precise light on the economic reasons for the destructiveness of modern civilization.

*Faas*: But you have stood up for social progress as well, political progress.

SNYDER:  Not if social progress was so narrowly construed as to move at the expense of other beings, that kind of simple-minded progress.

*Faas*: You once took a stand against the political apathy and conformism of institutionalized Buddhism.

SNYDER: Well, I don't think we can afford political apathy any more, I don't think it's impossible, and I think it's required that poets, Buddhists and everybody else be functioning beings aware of history, aware of economics, aware of ecology. And the understanding of these systems and how they work is another extension simply of the Buddhist understanding of interdependence which is poetical in the extreme if seen right. And it's the embracing of this kind of knowledge which I think is valuable right now.

political engagement

*Faas*: I find that your concept of man leans heavily towards an almost Rousseauistic belief that "man's natural being," as you put it yourself, "is to be trusted and followed . . . and that in following the grain, one is being truly 'moral.'" On the other hand, you grant that "it is necessary to look exhaustively into the negative and demonic potentials of the Unconscious, and by recognizing these powers" symbolically act them out. Do you feel that your own poetry is doing that?

poetry and the demonic

SNYDER: In a few poems I have tried to do that.

*Faas*: In fact, there is one poem which reminded me of Ted Hughes, I just can't remember its title, about the skinned . . .

SNYDER: . . . the skinned wolf.

*Faas*: Could you mention some of the others?

SNYDER: Yes, there is a poem called "Down," there's a couple of poems in *Myths & Texts,* in the third section called *Burning,* especially the one that has the line *"Maudgalyâyana* knew hell," and the poems in *The Back Country*, in the group called *Kālī,* a number of poems that deal with the goddess of death and destruction.

*Faas*: And yet you mentioned earlier that there were certain aspects of your life which you had excluded from your poetry, certain explosive potentials that you had never acted out in it—like the relationship with your mother which you said was very much like Allen Ginsberg's—and that perhaps you might even write your own *Kaddish* one day.

SNYDER: Well, I am still working some of these potentials out.

*Faas*: There is also your curious paraphrase or rather interpretation of a famous passage of the *Bhagavad Gita* which seems to bespeak an almost St. Francis-like mentality of love and compassion—quite in contrast to the *Gita's* life-affirming, yet fatalistic acceptance of eternal suffering and destruction.

SNYDER: Now, I don't know what you're referring to, actually. The most useful place where I quote the *Bhagavad Gita* is where I refer to "all created things rushing into Krishna's devouring mouth," and that's a total vision of the negative possibilities of the whole universe.

*Faas*: Let me see, I have got it jotted down somewhere. Here we are: "After the mind-breaking Void, the emptiness of a million universes appearing and disappearing, all created things rushing into Krishna's devouring mouth; beyond the enlightenment that can say 'these things are dead already; go ahead and kill them, Arjuna' is a loving, simple awareness of the absolute beauty and preciousness of mice and weeds." Now, I felt that the emphasis here was on the "loving, simple awareness of the absolute beauty and preciousness of mice and weeds." *beyond emptiness*

SNYDER: That is the final step, yes, the final step beyond the complete comprehension of the "emptiness" of the universe.

*Faas*: But in your interpretation that would point towards an almost Christian understanding of the universe.

SNYDER: No, I don't see it as particularly Christian. Today we take for granted via the atheistic scientific conception of the universe, its drift toward entropy, the emptiness of it, the meaninglessness of it.

*Faas*: I am thinking of how differently Hughes, for instance, might interpret this passage, probably emphasizing the suffering and the horrific whereas you emphasize the need for compassion and love resulting from such insight.

SNYDER: That is because the compassion is not what you would expect. You would not expect that the perception of the meaninglessness and emptiness of the whole universe would result in compassion for mice. That's one more step.

*Faas*: Do you feel that this is what's actually taught by the *Bhagavad Gita*?

SNYDER: It is not taught by the *Bhagavad Gita*. It is taught in other spheres. The way I phrased it there I was taking a step beyond the *Bhagavad Gita*.

*Faas*: At one point in the sixties, I have to quote you here, you expressed hope that a new society might within approximately three generations be formed "within the shell of the old," so to speak, and that "automation plus psychedelics plus a whole catalytic, spiritual change or bend of mind that seems to be taking place in the west" would produce a "vast leisure society." Yet, more recently,

the future of mankind

in 1970, I think, you drew a somewhat gloomier picture saying that at the moment a breakdown would be better and that probably there will be a transitional period with predatory tribes "living off the remnants of civilization." What are your feelings about all this right now?

SNYDER: Well, I can say very simply what the changes were which my thinking underwent between those two statements. The first about automation and a vast leisure society is what I call technological utopianism.

*Faas*: Like Fuller's.

SNYDER: Yes. There was an enthusiasm for that at the time—that was about 1965—that I got swept along with, without perhaps thinking very clearly. I should have known better, actually, because I had thought out these things once before. The problem with technological utopianism is shortage of resources, of energy. Where do you get the energy from to run such a technology? I turned away

technological utopianism

entirely from that as I studied resource availability. I read things like D. H. Meadows' *The Limits to Growth,* Jay Forrester's computer-based study of various potential curves for our society in the next century, which has received a lot of criticism but which is nonetheless, I think, pretty thorough. I read Gofman & Tamplin's book *Poisoned Power* on energy which sketches out energy resource supplies and contradictions in any future energy use. On the basis of that study I came to feel that there was not going to be a vast leisure society. On the contrary, there was going to be a vast peasant class if we are lucky, and that technological utopianism won't hold up. My second statement which is rather gloomy, is probably a more accurate prognostication, although you have to allow that modern culture is extremely ingenious, sometimes takes amazing bypaths, and pulls itself out of problems at the last minute.

*Faas*: So there is hope that it might fall on its feet.

SNYDER: Yes, there is some hope that it might fall on its feet. We'll see how Americans and this economy as a whole take this winter's [i.e. 1974/5] energy crisis. I mean if people take it in good spirit and are ingenious and adaptable, that would be a good sign. If it sparks off a lot of frustration, anxiety and anger and selfishness, then that would be another sign. [Laughing]

*Faas*: You once said that everywhere you go, you meet so many people who live in neo-tribal communities.

SNYDER: Less of them around now. It seems like most of those communes probably were never very stable, although people always talked about their own commune as though it were built on solid rock. But they have all evaporated, very few people are doing it. Like they had problems of men and women, and nobody agreed to wash the dishes. I guess I'm in kind of a depressed mood about the American national character right now, which seems to be so intensely individualistic and selfish whether it's hip or straight, you know, long haired or not long haired, there is a streak of selfish individualism that the Chinese, for example, see as America's downfall. They look at the American character and they say: the Americans can't keep it together and they may be right.

*Faas*: A lot of the people living in neo-tribal communities seem to be in your area, Nevada County, California.

SNYDER: Well, it's everywhere, but the people that went out into the country five years ago from the city and started communes and things, went with very little idea of what they were doing. The first phase was sheer romanticism and sheer anarchy, and not in the good sense of the word. And that kind of thing failed, those people are all gone now. The survivors of that were the ones who became practical, so to speak, realized their limits and realized that they would have to do a lot of hard work and realized that they would have to get along with their neighbors. Those who did that are still there, and that element has become an extremely interesting new phase in American rural life. Formerly, urban and often college educated people establishing deep relationships and commitments in a rural area transformed themselves and in some sense their neighbors in the process. That is taking place in my area. My area is pretty well disciplined, actually, is really on top of it, and has no tolerance for this . . . One thing that we find very useful and shared with each other as much as Buddhism, has been reports on Chinese communities from People's China, as a model for what has to be done.

*Faas*: Mao's China.

SNYDER: Yes, the reports from a Chinese village, and other things like that which have given us a clue as to how to be cooperative and to work together without necessarily calling ourselves a community or a commune and banding together and so forth, and trying to hit a balance between American individualism and the need for coopera-tion. That's an interesting process. But I see how traditional run of the mill American individualism in this increasingly overpopulated, resource depleted world is a liability. It may have been a plus in frontier times, you know, because there was always some place to go to; the individual with no sense of cooperation would just go off by himself and do something else. That's not possible now, not even in the wildest countryside. So we have become like Europe and like China. We are now at the end of our resource and space freedom and we have to learn to live within the terms of what we've got. It will be interesting to see if we can do it.

*Faas*: From where do you get these reports?

SNYDER:  I buy them at the Chinese Communist Bookstore, down in Berkeley.

*Faas*: And that works, what they're doing?

SNYDER:  It really does work.

*Faas*: And do they keep up any of the old traditions?

SNYDER:  Sure they do.

*Faas*: In an unofficial way, I suppose.

SNYDER:  Well, some things are official, some things are unofficial. Some poets and thinkers are officially good, a few are officially bad, it's hard to get their works.

*Faas*: One biographical or rather semi-biographical question: What exactly did you do in Japan? I gather that you lived there from '56 to '57 and then again from '59 to '65, staying in a monastery.

Snyder    SNYDER:  No, for the first time I was in Japan I was in a
in Japan   temple right through, and the second stay I was in Japan I
           was part of the time living in a monastery, doing *Sesshins* (intensive periods), part of the time out, doing research work, trans-lating, work connected with Zen study, academic work in a Buddhist research library within the temple.

*Faas*: With other Americans and Europeans?

SNYDER:  A couple of other Americans, one I'm going to see this afternoon, who is professor of Japanese at Columbia now, a Bud-dhist scholar, Zen Scholar, Philip Yampolsky. He translated the *Sixth Patriarch Sutra* and the writings of Hakuin. So I was leading essen-tially a layman's life, a Koji's life in Japanese terms, a lay disciple, keeping a close contact with my teacher, seeing him almost daily, and at the same time, out of necessity, earning a little money for my support, and doing research and scholarship, and a little gardening, a little vegetable gardening. My teacher then died, and I stayed on in

Japan for another couple of years, finishing up studies and re-
searches that I wanted to pursue. Just before my teacher died I met
Masa, and shortly after he died we got married.

*Faas*: And you practised regular meditation all those years?

SNYDER: Oh yes, of course. All through that time and I still do. We
still get up in the morning and meditate.

*Faas*: Every morning?

SNYDER: Yes, and some of the people who live near us     meditation
join us. When you were at Kitkitdizze we were meditating, weren't we?

*Faas*: No, not really, we had a kind of discussion.

SNYDER: Oh right, that was weekend. Saturday, Sunday we take off.

*Faas*: And you meditate in that little grove above your blockhouse.

SNYDER: Where we went up for the discussion, that was our morning meditation ground.

*Faas*: So you have been meditating for quite a while now?

SNYDER: I started when I was 22. Over twenty years.

*Faas*: I think I mentioned to you that in my own meditating I usually
start to hallucinate after a while, I mean hallucinate in the sense of
what Claudio Naranjo calls "vivid dreamlike sequences con-
templated while awake with closed eyes."

SNYDER: You know, that's why we have sticks in the Zendo—

*Faas*: How do you notice that somebody is hallucinating? [Both
laughing]

SNYDER: Oh, you know, they start giggling or fluttering their eyes,
so you go whack!

*Faas*: I once told a Zen master about these experiences which to me
are really the point at which I enter some sort of quietude, and he
said: That has nothing to do with Zen meditation. You must be on the
wrong track.

SNYDER: Yes. [Laughing] Well, if you don't get hung up on it, on
hallucinating, it's all right. Don't make a career out of it. [Increased
laughter] *Za-zen* has been an intimate part of my life since I first
started in my early twenties, when I was a student at Berkeley. And
sometimes I do more, and sometimes I do less. It's a practise which I
find creative and stabilizing both.

*Faas*: How does it affect your creativity?

SNYDER: It moves me out of my daily-track mind, daily single-track
mind, puts you in a large universe, and takes you away, gives you a
perspective on the concerns and the work of the day and puts the
work of the day in its own place and makes it a pleasure. It reminds
you that the day's work is also your meditation and that the infinite

Buddha nature penetrates all things equally in multiple marvellous ways. And you live your life with more detachment and at the same time with more savor, which in a sense is what the whole Buddhist life is about: the detachment and selflessness which makes your life more rather than less.

*Faas*: Let me switch to your general interests. Do you read literary criticism?

SNYDER: Hardly ever. In fact, I probably haven't read criticism for 15 years. It isn't that I even look down on it, it's that I don't have time for it. That is to say if I make a choice of priorities of what I'm going to read, I'll read biology first, history second, anthropology third, poetry fourth and criticism somewhere at the end.

general interests

*Faas*: I seem to share some of your priorities.

SNYDER: Yes, I see you as a man of the history of ideas, and the history of ideas I'm very interested in, I respect highly. I just don't know what to do with it because there are too many ideas [laughter] and they keep getting out of hand. But it's not my business to try and figure out what we're going to do except as to simply make things work. Now, to put it in Buddhist terms, you study your own nature deeply, you come to some understanding of your own nature, but your understanding of your own nature is not done in purely individualistic Romantic terms. The Romantic split between tradition and individual talent is no problem for the Buddhist. It's understood that you go to the tradition and study the lore handed down by men who have gone through the same process of meditation and study as yourself, and you respect and appreciate the accumulation of wisdom that they have brought forward. You tune that back into your study of yourself, you turn the soil over, and you actually work back and forth between absolutely naked self-examination and reference to a tradition that you respect.

tradition and the individual

*Faas*: Do we have any of that soil in our Western heritage?

SNYDER: Oh sure we do. It's called poetry. It's called the poetic tradition, that's the soil that we go back to.

*Faas*: I thought you were referring more to some definite framework of ideas in which the Chinese sages were able to live.

SNYDER: Ah, but the framework is the poetry, and the ideas come secondary to that. Maybe that's the way it should be. I would argue that experience, the experiential always precedes the ideology. And the experiential predecessor to Plato is Shamanism, mind expansion, the experiential predecessor to science is alchemy which is also mind expansion, and the experiential predecessors to other schools of thought are the instincts, emotions and experiences that we find most clearly manifested in the poetic tradition. Like it's after Provençal poets that we have what in the history of ideas is Romanticism. And it's in that sense that I look to poetry for the history of ideas. Poetry and magic, poetry and Shamanism, poetry and whatever it is generally, I think, manifest these things prior to their appearance in the world of formal ideas.

*Faas:* Unless you get poetry with a distinctly didactic or even propagandist bias like some of Eliot's, for instance.

SNYDER: People do that. You can subsume that under the heading of a special kind of experiential use of ideas, like taking ideas as experience and then recounting them in poetry. Yet, fundamentally it's the biological and physical life itself that provides the benefit of it.

*Faas:* But do you feel that in this way the *Cantos,* for instance, can be read for the same kind of benefit as, say the *Divina Commedia?*

SNYDER: I remember I was reading the *Divina Commedia* about the same time I was reading the *Cantos.* I had read it once through before because I was told to in College. And then I read it a second time through much more closely because I was told to by another poet. That second time was while I was working on a job in the mountains, it was after I had put in a full day's work: every night I sat by a candle and read it till I finished it. And then I went through Milton after that. Now reading both Dante and Milton was more an exercise in cultural history, reading the *Cantos* was not. Maybe it is now, but it wasn't at that time. And so this much misused or overused word "relevance," you know, comes in. We do live in our own times, and mayflies though we may be, we make the field around us that we can make, and so it's that sense of immediate usefulness, immediate manifestation that makes the difference. Like, I can read any number of things from the past and enjoy them and appreciate them and see them in their historical context, but there are few things that are still useful. Blake is still useful, Coleridge is not, although Coleridge's ideas are perhaps as good or better than Blake's. Now I don't know critically how to say that, except to think of it, you know, in terms of tools. I haven't really thought that out clearly. I find certain Chinese poets still useful, their thinking is alive to us, to me. What underlies my use of the word usefulness is an implied and assumed value which, I guess, is evolutionary in some sense. I feel that there is a line of development of the potentialities of human consciousness that we keep working at, and that some works, some poetry, is useful for a while, some poetry is useful for a longer time and keeps coming back to us.

the usefulness of poetry

*Faas*: This is what Duncan would presumably call your Marxist understanding of literary history.

SNYDER:  Well, Duncan is very cute in calling it Marxist. I think of it as bio-classicism, because I really am curious about some basic paradoxes of evolution that are obviously still going on. McClure put me on to one of the most interesting things, a book by a South African anthropologist, Phillip Tobias, entitled *The Brain in Hominid Evolution,* an historical and evolutionary study of brain size. What it all comes down to is that the average brain size of the human race was larger forty thousand years ago than it is now, and that the increase of brain size over the prior million years to that was the most striking feature of evolution—that the legs, the hands, the knees, the elbows all evolved more or less at their own rate, but that there was nothing physically that striking about it. The one single notable thing is the rapid increase of brain size. Now according to everything we think about evolution so far, if any one factor or feature of the body shows remarkable and swift change, it does so for an adaptive function. The shrinkage of the brain then must have also meant that that function was no longer necessary or was superseded by something else. What superseded the brain was society, social organization. Social organization, the computer—it is no longer necessary for everybody to be so sharp. So the organism was at its sharpest in terms of the individual members of the species about forty thousand years ago, and we are now witnessing a kind of decline. It does not have the appearance of a decline because society has its own life which enables it to maintain and transmit vast bodies of information, and so the information and the skills and survival techniques belong to society at large but they do not belong to us as individuals.

*Faas*: Do you find the theory convincing?

SNYDER:  The argument seems to me plausible, and as such it should become part of our revolutionary, super-reactionary poetics, namely that we look back at that ground base of humanity forty thousand years ago again, refer ourselves back to that and ask the question again: Where were we going, where might we go?

*Faas*: At various points you have drawn attention to Rousseau, Blake, Whitman, Thoreau, Lawrence, Jeffers, Pound and Rexroth as the major Western influences on you.

SNYDER:  Matthew Prior . . . everybody. [Laughing]

*Faas*: Yet in a programmatic statement for *Naked Poetry* you wrote that the "future can't be seen on the basis of the present."

SNYDER:  Can't be *seen*, that's the emphasis.

*Faas*:  How do you see the role of D. H. Lawrence in the evolution of modern Anglo-American art and æsthetics?

SNYDER:  Oh, I have a great respect for Lawrence, great respect, and he was certainly one of my greatest teachers. He was my first modern poetry teacher. It was in my early years of high school when my focus was essentially mountains and nature, when somebody was passing around a copy of *Lady Chatterly's Lover*—wow—so I read that, and I thought: I would like to read some more of this fellow. So I went to the Public Library and I found *Birds, Beasts and Flowers* listed in the catalogue. And I wondered: Is this a novel or what? I took it out of the library and it was poems. You D. H. Lawrence see, I grew up in a very poor, relatively uneducated rural background in Washington State, but I knew about the mountains and the trees. And so I read this book and I said: This man knows what he is talking about, and I was converted to the poetry right there, and to modern poetry.

*Faas*:  Did you also read his essays?

SNYDER:  Much later. When I say much later, I mean when I was nineteen. I was reading the rest of Lawrence by the time that I was nineteen but I was reading Lawrence's poetry when I was fourteen.

*Faas*:  He really had it all together, and single-handed.

SNYDER:  Really single-handed.

*Faas*:  In Europe, a great many poets have been deeply affected by the language crisis to a degree you rarely find amongst American poets. Poets such as von Hofmannsthal or Ingeborg Bachmann virtually stopped writing poetry on account of the in-sights commonly associated with the name of Wittgen-   the language stein. You, by contrast, told me that reading Wittgenstein   crisis had turned you on to poetry.

SNYDER:  Of course, because Wittgenstein himself was saying: This isn't philosophy, this is poetry. So it's not philosophy, then let's write poetry. [Laughing] I mean, maybe some of these European poets who quit writing, secretly wanted to be philosophers. So Wittgenstein disappointed them.

*Faas*:  Concerning this whole issue, there is a curious point on which I can't understand Robert Duncan. He seems to have this belief in a Platonic, essentialist potential of language which appears to me almost like an escape from what has been happening in this whole area.

SNYDER:  It's not like scientific theory for Robert. It's part of his feeling for poetry, that's all. Like, it's a poetic view of language, I think, a totally poetic view of language.

*Faas*:  Did you actually read Wittgenstein?

SNYDER: I read the *Tractatus.*

Faas: Not the *Investigations?*

SNYDER: Yes, I read *Philosophical Investigations,* and then I read some papers about him by his disciples. This was years ago, shortly before
I went to Japan. I had a friend in those days, Paul Wien-
Wittgenstein    paul, who was a professor of philosophy at Santa Bar-
and Zen         bara, and Paul was working with Wittgenstein and
Wittgenstein switched him to Zen actually. And he came over to Japan and did Zen study for a while.

Faas: That's fascinating.

SNYDER: And then went back to Santa Barbara where he continued teaching and working in philosophy. He has written a couple of books about this, about the limits of language and moving into actual *practise,* one called *The Matter of Zen* and then another book since then about Zen.

Faas: Do you find them interesting?

SNYDER: They are very simple and very direct, yes. Quite interesting.

Faas: Have you read Whitehead as well?

SNYDER: I really have no knowledge of Whitehead. You see my intellectual theories and visions are not drawn from philosophers but inductively derived from reading history and anthropology and
linguistics. I formulate my theories that way rather than
formulating    by reading theoreticians, and that's what my reading has
his poetics    been over the years. So my poetics are in a sense a kind of
linguistic and anthropological poetics based on what human beings have done and extracting from that what the essence of poetry seems to be. So I use the shamanistic terminology of the magic of words and what that is, the mantric efficacy of sound, and the genres of poetry as derived from a Tribal concept: essentially work songs, power vision songs, love songs, courting songs, death songs, war songs, healing songs. That kind of terminology is what I feel comfortable with because that is how I see it.

Faas: There is some awareness of a language crisis in Williams and Pound with their experiments in fragmentation and the ideogrammic method. It has always been slightly puzzling to me
Whitman's    how after all that poets of your generation could go
rhetoric      straight back to Whitman and all his rhetoric.

SNYDER: We all wobble, I was going to say . . . we all swing back and forth, I guess, between that sense of needing to do the job with language itself, and occasionally thinking that the job can be done with emotions and ideas. Whitman is a great temptation, like it's the rhetorical temptation of just expressing yourself in big terms as against the work of doing it structurally. Convincing people with ideas is one system, the other is to change the structural basis. The structural basis is much less rewarding and much more time consuming, although if it works, it does the job. You see what I mean? But it doesn't have immediate results. So audiences don't respond well to poems which are structurally revolutionary, but they do respond well to poems which have a big rhetoric. This may be one of the dangers and temptations of the poetry reading circuit.

*Faas*: Also the dangers of a poem like *Howl*?

SNYDER: Well, *Howl* was also a structural innovation. Or not really an innovation, but nobody had done it well for a long time. Consequently that added something to the situation. It was people who imitated *Howl* afterwards that fell back into the old rhetoric. *Howl* itself for its time and place—I speak as one who saw and heard it read many times—was immediately appropriate and satisfying on many levels.

Ginsberg's
*Howl*

*Faas*: Duncan told me about the impact the poem had on him so that he tried to write his own *Howl* the day the poem arrived.

SNYDER: Well that was actually something which you couldn't copy, although people tried.

*Faas*: Yet even a poet as different from Ginsberg as Galway Kinnell admits to the important influence *Howl* had on his poetry.

SNYDER: Oh yes, it had a lot of influence on people who at the time didn't admit it and didn't speak of it till years later. Yes, it undoubtedly is the most influential poem of the mid-century in America.

*Faas*: You'd really go as far as saying that?

SNYDER: Undoubtedly. And, perhaps, the only other single poem that has had that kind of impact is *The Waste Land,* in this century so far.

*Faas*: That implies a tremendous respect for somebody whom you once, I guess jokingly, referred to as a "transitional figure."

SNYDER: It's obvious. And we are all transitional figures. Ginsberg is not just a poet, he is a social force, and *Howl* is not just a poem, it's a social force. But the poem is intensely moving, intensely moving in the context of its own time. It made people weep who had never wept before. Quite an achievement.

*Faas*: I'd like to come back to modern philosophers and the influence they had on you. Were there any others besides Wittgenstein?

SNYDER: I really can't think of any others.

*Faas*: Or anthropologists? I noticed that Lévi-Strauss, for instance, assumes a more and more prominent place in your critical writing. And who were your main teachers when you did your B.A. thesis on *The Dimensions of Myth?*

SNYDER: On the whole, I feel, I was more influenced by cultural historians, such diverse figures as Frazer, Frobenius, the Americanist Franz Boas, people like that were shaping my thinking, and to some extent Jung.

*Faas*: Benjamin Lee Whorf?

SNYDER: Oh yes, very much so. But we haven't mentioned Jung before, and Jung was important for all of us, I'm sure.

*Faas*: So Duncan would probably call you a Jungian like Olson.

SNYDER: I called *him* a Jungian.

*Faas*: While he calls himself a Freudian, which is rather strange considering his concept of imagery and poetic creativity.

SNYDER: I guess one of the reasons why I say that Duncan is my favorite poet is because I can't figure him out. So I'm always fascinated by what he does and I'm always puzzled by his poetry and I come back to it. Whereas with a lot of other poets, I think I understand what they're doing, so I don't come back to them. So it's the fascination with difficulty and puzzle. And also it's a funny personal feeling I have about him. I even dream about him once every six months or so. I have sort of funny dreams about Duncan. Shall I tell you one of the dreams I had about Duncan?

dream about
Duncan

*Faas*: Please do.

SNYDER: I've never been to Germany, but I dreamt that I was walking somewhere in Germany and I came down a steep grassy embankment, and there was Duncan standing there and he beckoned to me and said: Come right in, this way. And so we went into what was like a cave or an underground room, and we were under the ground and there was an earthen or stone wall that was entirely covered with breasts, and Duncan said: Drink from the one you like. And so I went up and like actually nursed on one of these breasts that were coming out of the wall. And Duncan was my guide.

*Faas*: Do you feel that there are any points of affinity between your work as a poet and recent developments in painting and music?

SNYDER: I'm really out of touch with that right now.

*Faas*: John Cage?

SNYDER: Cage's position I know, and I find that interesting.

*Faas*: And Pollock?

SNYDER: That also more like belongs to the early sixties as I understand it.

*Faas*: Oh sure, I didn't mean the last few years only.

SNYDER: Certainly, there was a period when quite a bit was coming together from Western avant-garde aesthetics and, what shall we call it, Zennist æsthetics. But that seems to have evaporated somewhat.

Like the whole field now is again wide open. Look at what's happening in every area: the population is exploding, economies are going up and down, more books are being published than ever before, and that kind of thing. So really everything seems out of hand, information overload. [Pause] It just occurs to me that I started talking about my kinds of reading and my inductive way of arriving at theories because I realized that I was being presented with questions about philosophers like Whitehead and Wittgenstein who are really not my intellectual direction. This is not to say that I can't comprehend them, but I don't find reading them as creative or productive as going to historical or anthropological facts or to direct experience. Now maybe that's a very modern thing.

*the seventies*

*Faas*: In fact, that in a way parallels my own change of interests in recent years.

SNYDER: It's a very interesting change of the mind. In my reading of Buddhist philosophy—here is a very interesting book concerning Gampopa I am studying right now—I switch back and forth between mythological poetic imagery statements and hard rational logical philosophical statements. Buddhism weaves in and out between those two areas in a very fascinating way. Plato does it a little bit when he invokes metaphors and mythical images like in *Phaedrus* or in the *Symposium*. Other philosophers generally don't. They don't use metaphors like the myth of the cave to talk about philosophical matters, they steer away completely from myth. But myth as a mode of intellectual dialogue is very interesting to me, because in a way it is able to deal with psychological complexities. And again the boundary line between psychology and philosophy is to me more interesting.

*philosophy and myth*

*Faas*: I mainly asked you those questions because I have dealt with the philosophers we mentioned in the context of a book I wrote on open form aesthetics, not because I expected you to have a very specific interest in them. Of course, I *am* interested in philosophy, and that is one of the things I found out about myself by coming to the U.S.

SNYDER: Just as when I went to Japan I found out who *I* really was. I found out that I was an American pragmatist. [Laughter]

*Faas*: In *Naked Poetry* you stated that we are not now looking for new forms and that what's needed is a totally new approach to the idea of form. Could you expatiate on this statement?

SNYDER: In stating that I was simply trying to break this thing of always saying: We are looking for a new form. And the question is:

Do we need any form at all, or, is there anything that is

everything not form anyway? It is more or less obvious that every-

has form thing has form, everything that we call a thing has form.

There is no formlessness in the world as we know it.

*Faas*: In the sense of Gestalt psychology.

SNYDER: Mm . . . like I discovered by practise that a lot of my poems were each unique and represent each a different form of strategy. Which is one way of looking at it. That the same form is never done twice.

*Faas*: So that would be the totally new approach to form?

SNYDER: That would be one totally new approach to form which is to see every poem as a different solution to a different problem.

*Faas*: When I read that statement I thought you meant a totally new consciousness.

SNYDER: That would be on the way to a totally new consciousness. A new consciousness is also very much part of our potentiality, one of our future potentialities, hopefully. But so often we find ourselves looking at the past, since we really haven't any ways of thinking about the future that well. Now since I said that, Jerome Rothenberg has brought out his books *Technicians of the Sacred* and *Shaking the Pumpkin* in which all of this fascinating Primitive, pre-literate American Indian, Oceanic, African, Polynesian whatever, all this poetry has been presented to us. And there are probably, you know, like sixty different new forms that are possible, that have been brought back to our consciousness by Rothenberg, forms that belong to our own archaic past.

*Faas*: And you think that the kind of feeling needed in order to really make these forms our own can be revitalized?

SNYDER: Sure, like we haven't used proverbs very well for several centuries.

*Faas*: Also in *Naked Poetry* you say that each poem should grow from an "energy-mind-field-dance" and that it has its own inner grain.

the      That, of course, reminds me of Olson, but also of the

Romantics concept of organic form as expounded by

Romantics Schlegel or Coleridge, for instance. Would you acknow-

ledge the Romantics as predecessors along these lines?

SNYDER: I have nothing against it, although I don't feel the influence on myself directly. Like I can't read Coleridge.

*Faas*: Not even the *Biographia Literaria*?

SNYDER: No, I can't even read Wordsworth, I really can't read him. I find it tiresome. It's just tiresome.

*Faas*: And yet it seems to me that Coleridge's definition of the imagination as "a repetition in the finite mind of the eternal act of creation in the infinite I AM" was a first major step towards open form æsthetics, a definition he partly derived from Schlegel.

SNYDER: And where did he get it from?

*Faas*: As far as I can tell it was Herder who first modified Aristotle's mimesis theory in the direction of open form æsthetics by saying that the artist does not mirror nature, *natura naturata*, but imitates creation or *natura naturans*. And then Schlegel goes one step further by saying that the poet does not *imitate* cosmic creation, but repeats it, reenacts it.

SNYDER: That's beautiful.

*Faas*: And it's from there that Coleridge picks it up, I guess.

SNYDER: I think of form in terms of biological forms, like in the work of people such as Adolf Portmann, the biologist. Those people's work offers to me the most interesting information about what form is and how form changes. Form is always moving and adaptive and always has a function.

*biological concept of form*

*Faas*: How about the influence of Buddhism on your concept of form?

SNYDER: It's not very far from the biological sense of form.

*Faas*: Turning to your poetry, I noticed that you often tend to avoid articles or personal pronouns. For instance, instead of "*the* tree" you would just say "tree."

SNYDER: Really?

*Faas*: Not so much in the longer as in the shorter poems.

SNYDER: Well, I hope I haven't done it in any way that makes the poems obscure, because that's not my intention. My intention is just throwing off extra weight or what seems to be extra weight, and maybe in that I am influenced by my liking for Chinese poetry which has that stripped down feeling.

*Faas*: I also found that both your longer and shorter poems occasionally have an outwardly closed form. For example, you would repeat the first line of the poem at its end, or you conclude the poem with a kind of summary, or as in "It was when" (from *Regarding Wave)* would structure an entire poem around one long sentence. Do you feel that the open form impulse, as these examples seem to suggest, can include closed form devices?

*closed form poetry*

SNYDER: I don't see any objections to such devices and I have no antipathy as such to closed form. Like, anything that works, I'll use. I'm impressed by the fact that almost all the poems that I can remember by heart are poems with regular meters that rhyme and that it is very difficult to memorize poems that don't have these regular meters and rhymes. Right there, you see, there is an obvious function for that kind of form, that it's mnemonic, that it sticks in your mind.

*Faas*: That sounds like Ginsberg picking up on the old song traditions.

SNYDER: Exactly!

*Faas*: And taking poetry back to where it came from.

SNYDER: Right.

*Faas*: Yet that would be a slightly new use of rhyme and metrical devices.

SNYDER: But using ballad meter and using any of a number of easily available forms surely has its value, just as it's very difficult to sing songs that don't have these forms. You end up singing art songs, and art songs are the worst of all.

*Faas*: What do you mean by art songs?

SNYDER: Ah . . . I don't know how to describe art songs. Like if you set free verse to music it sounds like art songs. There is an area of the power of poetry that cannot be denied, which is the area of rhythm and structure, the area of drama.

*Faas*: Drama in what sense?

SNYDER: The drama of ballads, for example.

*Faas*: One of your critics claims that a main characteristic of your poetry is its lack of tension, its lack of drama. Is that because drama, along with tragedy, would be a specifically Western mode of literature to you?

poetry
and drama   SNYDER: It's not really Western. Chinese poetry has the upper class literary style but then it has that huge body of folksong and ballad that belongs to the people, that's full of drama. And, of course, the poetry of India is all drama, all rhetoric. I don't use that strategy very often, but I respect it. And I would use it, you know. Whenever the time comes, I'll use it.

*Faas*: Isn't the Eastern concept of drama different from ours?

SNYDER: Well, I'm using it in the broadest sense of getting your interest aroused, keeping your interest up, and then fulfilling your interest. And also surprising it, and the surprises are the most interesting thing. It's like getting people going on something and then surprising them, that's the oldest literary trick of all. And it still works. And form is useful for that, just as *mantras*, the singing of *mantras* harmonizes with the rhythms of the breath rate of the body. The body is a closed form.

*Faas*: But then that particular body rhythm might open up into the rhythm of the whole universe.

SNYDER: The universe is a closed form.

*Faas*: Not a form of expanding boundaries?

SNYDER: But that's closed too, yes, expanding boundaries are closed, you're still talking about boundaries.

*Faas*: But they are open to the outside, to what surrounds them. Just like in Gestalt psychology you have one pattern or form, but it's expanding into, if not to say, constituted by all the surrounding patterns, and there is no end to it.

SNYDER: It's still form.

*Faas*: Oh yes, it's definitely form.

SNYDER: So all form is closed.

*Faas*: It's rather funny that I should be manœuvred into the role of an apologist of open form while you are defending closed form. [Laughter]

SNYDER: I'm not defending closed form. I'm just saying it's another strategy. And if you want to talk about emptiness, the universe is not empty, the universe is full. And any conception of the universe is still a conception that involves the nature of form.

*Faas*: And this is where poetry moves.

SNYDER: Poetry moves off the edge of that, that's where it is exciting.

*Faas*: And meditation would go beyond that.

SNYDER: Well, in and out of it. In Buddhist terms, the body is form, the mind has the potentiality of formlessness, and speech or language mediates between the two. It seems very accurate. But the mind is usually caught up in form because it is generally playing with linguistic tricks or replaying impressions that it has taken in. But the mind also has the possibility, like a mirror, of not necessarily reflecting anything, and that is the ground nature, the fundamental nature of consciousness. We tend to think of it as being full of forms because that's how we see it. Just as every time you look into a mirror you see something in the mirror. But a mirror need not necessarily have anything in it. It would still be a mirror.

*Faas*: At one point you speak of poetry as riding the razor's edge between the expressible and the inexpressible, and you criticize those poets who move too far into the realm of the inexpressible. Wouldn't you say that your own poems sometimes cross that borderline as well, moving into the realm of *mantra, koan*, etc., of those sacred magic genres which have usually evolved through generations and generations and derived their form from there?

SNYDER: Well, the borderline is probably something like this: When you are in a territory where there are no special expectations of your listener, you can still make a song, you're in poetry. If you have a request, ask a special practise from your listener, if you have to say:You must meditate two weeks before you listen to this poem and maybe observe some special diet, then you are in the specific realms of shamanistic or religious training. Now, messages are transmitted and things are taught and songs are sung within the shamanistic special realms of practise, but that's a very special world, it's a professional world almost. We bring poetry back from our special practises, so to speak, to the open realm of human dialogue where we can address it to anyone. That's the known international definition of poetry, after the fact. Otherwise it becomes like an esoteric tradition. There are poems that move in, so to speak, esoteric traditions.

*Faas*:  In contemporary American poetry?

SNYDER:  In some senses, yes. Poems that require special inside knowledge, special knowledge of the theories and so forth. That is not so interesting to me as public clarity.

*Faas*:  Could you give an example?

SNYDER:  Some kind of Surrealism perhaps. And even maybe the poems surrounding Olson and his group, in some ways, are a little bit esoteric. They require a certain amount of initiation. And, of course, this has been a charge which has been levelled at modern poetry generally, that it required special initiation. But that's in a much broader sense. Talking about the uses of language, there are ways we use language which are open to everyone, which *koan* and are public dialogue. There are private and esoteric ways *mantra* of using language which belong generally to religious traditions. There are other specializations today like the sciences which are again another question. But you see what I'm driving at. Like a *koan* functions in a very special realm that requires thousands of hours of meditation per minutes of utterance, whereas in the realm of poetry the proportion is less. [Laughing] And something like a *mantra* is a special use of language which requires repetition. There is a whole territory in which language gets its power by repetition. "Hail Mary, full of grace," and so forth. Poetry in "civilized" times does not use repetition as a device for gaining power, but it also is a method of gaining power.

*Faas*:  Ginsberg talks about his use of *mantra*-like strategies.

SNYDER:  He approaches that, yes, he fuses them with his poetry. And I involve similar things in a way in my poetry. What we're doing, I suppose, on that level, is that we're bringing back some territories of language use that belong to traditional and archaic cultures and *archaic uses* that have been neglected in contemporary times quite a *of language* bit. The "poetry reading" is what makes this possible. The fact that we do poetry readings means that we are led to using techniques which are extra-Western and in some ways archaic because we're using the voice, and we can sing, can chant *mantras,* create some special things around us, so that my poetics start with the voice, pure sound, and voice line melody, voice line rhythm possibilities, then explores mantric, that is, meaningless sound possibilities which I see in *mantras* and in various kinds of chants and in nonsense songs of children, and then move into rhythmic rhyme poetry of children.

*Faas:* Like yesterday at the YMHA.

SNYDER: Yes, I did some of that. That catches the minds of people and catches the minds of children, and then goes out into the trickier melodies that you get associated with open poetry, where you are steering between rather complex feelings and ideas on the one hand and ways of pushing language up against what it can say. It's a very paradoxical thing, poetry is in one way the finest use of language, but at that point it comes up to the very limits of language. In some ways it's the densest, the most concentrated use of language outside the technical scientific language. I mean by content analysis standards. But then it comes up against an end which is that razor edge boundary line. That's when I try to do some things with those silent poems, those quieter poems, because hopefully they do echo some non-linguistic, pre-linguistic, pre-verbally visualized or deeply felt areas. Like in that little bit of *haiku* æsthetics which says: The words stop but the meaning keeps going. That's another angle which is at work in Chinese poetry very much, in those little Chinese quatrains or double quatrains where the poem is very intense and very short.

*Faas:* Talking about the actual structure or texture of your poetry . . .

SNYDER: I like what Duncan says: that we are all writing the same poem.

*Faas:* Like weaving a big endless tapestry.

SNYDER: And in that sense no beginning or ending, just contributions.                                                        poetic closure

*Faas:* But then there always is a beginning and an end the way the poem appears on the page typographically.

SNYDER: No, but the end goes on, it goes on in your mind. Like the end of the poem is just the beginning of whatever causal or karmic function it might have in the world, like what effect it has on people, like how it echoes.

*Faas:* William Stafford, talking about Olson's æsthetics, once said in an interview that he usually ends a poem when his powers to homogenize an experience come to an end.

SNYDER: I stop a poem when I feel it has been well enough begun that the reader can carry it from there. That the rest of it is for his mind.

*Faas*: You have rarely commented on your actual practises as a poet. Do you find that the order in which the poem appears on the page usually reflects the sequence in which its words and sentences occurred to you while you were writing it.

SNYDER: In short poems, yes. Short poems I write very quickly, very swiftly.

*Faas*: And you don't revise them?

revision    SNYDER: Not too much, because I don't write them down before I've got them more or less ready. I resist the impulse to write a poem down until I feel that it's fully matured. I keep poems in my mind for months.

*Faas*: Duncan showed me some of his manuscripts a couple of days ago. He says that he treats each of his revisions as separate poems.

SNYDER: I have thought about that. It's kind of charming. [Laughing] Except it takes more paper. The longer poems of *Mountains and Rivers* are real field compositions in which things do not belong according to chronology but according to place.

*Faas*: And that means rearranging, shuffling things around.

SNYDER: Yes. I've been doing twenty-five sections simultaneously over the last ten years, working a little on this poem, a little on this poem, a little on this poem, and, hopefully, like all the field    sheep will be driven into the corral at the same time, and composition    then the poem will be done. I don't know anybody who is writing a poem like that, who's writing the whole thing at once clear out here, and trying to herd them all into the same gate at once finally.

*Faas*: Does one know anything about the writing practises of Zen Buddhist poets, like Basho, for instance?

Zen poetics    SNYDER: Pretty quick. You get that impression from reading Bashō and the literature about Bashō as a great *haiku* writer. Also, Bashō was quite a critic, he had created a circle of disciples, and he was very quick in describing what were the shortcomings of various people. In fact, that's one of the most interesting things about the evolution of *haiku* with Bashō and his circle: the importance that criticism played in it and how they made their living as *haiku* teachers. And as teachers their function was to be critics. They didn't make their living by giving poetry readings or by publishing poems. The money came from criticizing the people who studied under them.

*Faas*: Do you feel that a poem, if it doesn't have closed form, should at least have texture and coherence?

texture    SNYDER: I'm not convinced of that necessarily. But from my own poetry I noticed a tendency towards texture and coherence. But I can enjoy incoherent poems if there is something else to it. I don't want to overstress coherence. Too much texture and too much coherence leads back to that old trap of formal perfectionism which cuts off the possibility of the idea and meaning going on in the mind of the reader afterwards. So the kind of coherence that I will strive for would be a communicative coherence ✓ that liberates the reader to go on with it. You see what I mean? Coherence in the sense of usefulness and relevance, and stimulation and excitement and imagination, not coherence in the sense of: I have shown you what I can do, I have now closed it up and now it's done. I am a striver, not a finisher. [Laughing]

*Faas*: As opposed to a man like Yeats who felt that a poem was finished when you could hear the clicking of the lid closing in on the box.

SNYDER: Well, but I can't deny that some of Yeats's poems really do that, beautifully, and yet they keep on going on in your mind.

*Faas*: Because Yeats being a great poet ever so often transcended his own poetics.

SNYDER: Exactly. [Laughing]

*Faas*: In a previous interview you stated that your poetry tries to explore the full landscape or architecture of consciousness from contentless ground through the unconscious and conscious and on through sense perception and immediate emotion to the realms of abstract scientific theorizing and pure mathematics. Yet it seems obvious that your poetry inhabits some of these areas much more than others.

*the scope of his poetry*

SNYDER: Obviously, my poetry does not occupy all of these niches, and I don't even try to. The niches that I occupy, or that I hope to occupy, are the warm humane mammal family niche, the archetypal and mythic niche, and the transparent intuitive direct perception niche.

*Faas*: Transparent, I guess, in the sense of form as emptiness, as ellipse, leaving things out at the right spot, as you once put it.

SNYDER: At some points. The "form as emptiness" is not quite the same as you understand it, I think. The quotation "form equals emptiness" is from the *Prajñā Pāramitā Sūtra,* and it's a key term of Buddhist metaphysics, *the* key term of Buddhist metaphysics, and it has a whole history of ideas and traditions that fits around it for Buddhists.

*Faas*: I'd now like to turn to your long poems. In which ways do the strategies of fragmentation which you use in *Mountains and Rivers* compare with Pound's? In fact, I see some even more striking similarities with Hart Crane's *The Bridge.*

*ideogrammic method and fragmentation*

SNYDER: I haven't read that poem for a long time.

*Faas*: That peculiar kind of American fragmentation,

the juxtaposition of rhetorically unrelated bits of narrative, dialogue, dramatic monologue.

SNYDER: Yes, I really don't know. [Laughing] I haven't been thinking in those terms.

*Faas*: How then do you relate to Pound's ideogrammic method?

SNYDER: Well, the ideogrammic method was useful for us when we were young. Later, I went to study Chinese and I realized how little Pound or even Fenollosa understood about how Chinese works. I feel that as far as Pound goes, it's clear to me that I have more of a sense of clarity; I don't introduce things that are particularly obscure unless I can't help it.

*Faas*: Some of your poems in *Mountains and Rivers* seem to me extremely difficult.

SNYDER: You think so? I don't think so. [Laughing]

*Faas*: Especially "The Blue Sky" with all those names.

SNYDER: There's a lot of names, that's true. But hopefully when the whole thing is put together there will be enough reverberations and echoes from the various sections so that it will be self-informing. What I find is that every poem I do in *Mountains and Rivers* takes a different form and has a different strategy, and I have to let the strategy work itself out. When I get enough distance from it at some point I'll be able to understand more clearly what I've done. But like every poem has a very different strategy and they come in various ways from various quarries, many-faceted.

*Faas*: Is there any comparable technique of fragmentation in Chinese poetry?

SNYDER: No.

two kinds of consciousness

*Faas*: That's why I'm puzzled that you should go back to that kind of technique.

SNYDER: Doing what?

*Faas*: Fragmentation.

SNYDER: Well, that's because of this kind of poem. I'm writing two kinds of poetry.

*Faas*: But isn't a poetic mode always the expression of a specific kind of consciousness?

SNYDER: I have two kinds of consciousness. [Laughing] I don't know, I do *Mountains and Rivers* and then I do these other shorter poems.

*Faas*: So that would be your Western consciousness. [Laughter]

SNYDER: Perhaps. It's a mythic consciousness, myth fragments.

*Faas*: Have you seen the *Norton Anthology of Modern Poetry*?

SNYDER: Yes, I have.

*Faas*: In the introduction to your section, the editor speaks of your

relaxed, often cheerful acceptance of a world composed of fragments in contrast to Eliot's "These fragments I have
shored against my ruins" at the end of *The Waste Land*.     *Myths & Texts*
And that unlike Eliot "who juxtaposes cultures to point     and *The Waste Land*
up a disaster, [you see] in a pluralistic world of fragments
our salvation."

SNYDER:  It's going in the right direction. But the next step would be
to understand that nothing is not related, that everything is interrelated. And that there really are no fragments.

*Faas:*   The *shih shih wu ai* or what you called the "jewelled net of
interconnectedness."

SNYDER:  Yes. It's different ways of connecting your network. The
Buddha says: "Bhikshu, you see this rice stalk. If you understand
this rice stalk, you understand the law of interdependent origination. If you understand the law of interdependent origination you
understand the *dharma,* if you understand the *dharma,* you know the
Buddha." A fundamental Buddhist position.

*Faas*:  And how does Chinese poetry express that interconnectedness?

SNYDER:  It expresses it in images, small images. "A high tower on a
white plane. If you climb up one floor, you'll see a thousand miles
more." [Laughing] That's why Zen as a training uses Chinese poetry
extensively, because they understand the uses of those images as
expressions of interpenetration.

*Faas*:  And how do the images link up?

SNYDER:  You just juxtapose two images.

*Faas*:  With a gap of silence in between.

SNYDER:  Sometimes. Well, what we're talking about now is very
interesting, but it's something I haven't really got clear enough
myself. If you want you can look up this book on the Buddhist
philosophy of interdependence by a man called Chang, entitled *The
Buddhist Philosophy of Totality;* it's a marvellous book, published by
Pennsylvania State University. It has many images that are used in
discussing interpenetration on many levels and how Chinese poetry
is doing that.

*Faas*:  Do you want to discuss this issue of interdependence and
fragmentation any further?

SNYDER:  Okay. There are two things. One is, say, a fragmented text
which appears fragmented and which is fragmented and which
leads nowhere. Another is ideogrammic method, a fragmented text
which appears fragmented but actually leads you somewhere because the relationships that are established between the fragments
express a deeper level of connectedness, which becomes clear to the

reader's mind if he is able to follow it. We have phony obscurity and we have obscurity which serves to communicate. Two differences. The ideogrammic method is intended as a method of communication in the sense of juxtaposing apparently unrelated things that show the connections automatically. That, of course, is what I'd have in mind in my work. Not that I want to make fragmented form but that I want to make a whole form.

*Faas*: But didn't you plan *Mountains and Rivers without End* as an open ended endless poem?

SNYDER: Endless? No, not really.

a poem "without end"?

*Faas*: Do you remember what you told Kerouac, or at least what he claims you told him in *The Dharma Bums?*

SNYDER: I said that as a joke. Yes, I was saying that facetiously. That wasn't really what my sense of it was. I was talking about *Mountains and Rivers without End* and I was tripping over the word "without End." But, obviously, what you do with "without End" is that you feed it back into itself and make a circle of it.

*Faas*: But you mentioned previously that your conception of the poem changed.

SNYDER: It has changed some, sure.

*Faas*: What were those changes? Say by comparison with open form poems like *Paterson* or the *Cantos*.

SNYDER: I would not like to get caught in between open and closed. If the universe is circular, which it is, does that not mean it is a closing world? We don't know. Actually something like the Möbius strip moves in and out of two dimensions; it is closed but it is also open. I'm not really worried about that. I would like to have the poem close in on itself but on some other level keep going.

*Faas*: What would be the other level? In the reader's mind?

SNYDER: Yes.

*Faas*: Or structurally, too?

SNYDER: Well, structurally in that each of the sections of the poem implies a direction that you can complete yourself. I don't do it, you know, once I have done it, I leave it, and people can play with that more if they want, do more with that if they want on their own.

*Faas*: But for you there would be a definite point where you leave off and think it's done.

SNYDER: Yes.

*Faas*: Do you have any idea right now when that's going to be?

SNYDER: Mm . . . a few years from now. I'm working on another book right now, about Japan, which is taking me away from writing poetry.

*Faas*: You told me that each of the 25 sections would center around a *ku* or key phrase.

"key phrases" in *Mountains and Rivers without End*

SNYDER: An image, a focal image.

*Faas*: Could you point one out, in "Bubbs Creek Haircut," for instance.

SNYDER: Well, the key in that is the third line in from the last, "double mirror waver." That shows you what the whole structure of it is.

*Faas*: I thought it would be "Goodwill."

SNYDER: That's another one. That runs through other poems, too. But "Goodwill" is more a content point. "Double mirror waver" is a structure point. Mutually reflected mirrors. Like, you see yourself many times reflected in a barber's shop. You look and you see yourself going that way and you see yourself going that way. It's a key image in *Avatamsaka* philosophy, Buddhist interdependence philosophy. Multiple reflections in multiple mirrors, that's what the universe is like.

*Faas*: So each poem would have that kind of central image or key phrase.

Buddhist interdependence philosophy

SNYDER: Yes, there is a key phrase in a sense. I'm not playing on it, but there is a place where I have the picture of what I'm doing somewhere in the poems. I was not always that conscious of it.

*Faas*: What exactly does *ku* mean?

SNYDER: A *ku* just means a little phrase. On page 20* in "Night Highway Ninety-nine" it's "—Abandon really means it/—the network womb stretched loose all/ things slip/ through," and then: "Dreaming on a bench under newspapers/ I woke covered over with Rhododendron blooms/ Alone in a State Park in Oregon." That again is the center of the structural principle in "Highway Ninety-nine" which is "slipping through." The "network womb" where all things slip through is a Buddhist image, the image of the *graha,* the great womb of time and space which intersects itself. And being sort of continually through that network. And then I put it again in the image of "Dreaming on a bench under newspapers" which is like waking up in another place, covered with blossoms. That's what I'm trying to show in "Highway Ninety-nine" as it moves across different space and time—paradigms again.

*Faas*: Do you come across these images in the process of writing?

SNYDER: Yes.

*Six Sections from Mountains and Rivers without End Plus One.* Writing 9. San Francisco: Four Seasons Foundation, 1970.

*Faas*: It's not that you have an image and organize a poem around it?

SNYDER: No, well, when I hit the image then I know what the poem is going to be.

*Faas*: It's not like James Dickey who once said that he always has any number of subjects ready in his head about which he could write poems.

SNYDER: Well now those, that's what you make the body, the meat of the poem. But this is the bones of the poem.

*subject matter versus structure*

*Faas*: But you don't have the latter as preconceived notions.

SNYDER: Well, when I see it, I know what I've got. I know what I'm doing, when I finally hit something like that. Until I hit that, I don't know what the poem is, so I haven't really begun to write the poem. I've just been doing some work with some images.

*Faas*: Would all that still be at the stage of thinking about the poem, of writing it in the mind as you say?

SNYDER: It's on the level of visualizing and re-visualizing and re-experiencing and projecting the images and then writing some of the images down and keeping a lot of it in mind.

*Faas*: Not like writing and rewriting the poem in your mind and then finally writing it down almost without corrections as in the case of your shorter poems?

*the writing process*

SNYDER: Well, *Mountains and Rivers* takes a little bit more replay than that. You have to do it because it's complicated. I have to go back, I have to re-look at it, I have to re-tune it, re-adjust it sometimes quite a bit, not too much but . . . You want to see some more of that?

*Faas*: Yes, please.

SNYDER: In "Hymn to the Goddess San Francisco in Paradise" on page 24, in the very first section there, starting with "—amazed to see under their clothes they are/ naked/ this makes them sacred/ & more than they are in their own shape/ free." I take that to be the center of what's being developed there. Going back to very ancient ideas of women and of goddesses which saw nakedness as a sacred state at the time of the pre-mycenaean mother goddess temples, when the priestesses only appeared occasionally but then they appeared naked. The nakedness was a sacred epiphany of itself. And the funny thing about nakedness is that it is the closest thing we have about ourselves, and yet it has this curious magic and always has had as far as we can tell. It evokes all in some curious way, and yet it's the plainest simplest thing on earth while having that awesome quality. That's what I was trying to evoke with the "Hymn to the Goddess." And the city is being contradictory in that way. [Pause] "The Blue Sky" which is all about healing and my ideas of language is a very complicated poem and I'm not sure that it hangs together exactly like that. But the most useful lines in it are (on page 41) "'Where'd you get the buttermilk?'/ I'd been looking all over for buttermilk. He said,/ 'At the O K Dairy, right where you leave town.'" That's the healing word in that. [Laughing]

*Faas*: That's more like "Goodwill."

SNYDER: Yes, that's like "Goodwill," it's a lot like "Goodwill." The other thing that's important in "The Blue Sky" is on page 42, that little comment on "[*comrade*: under the same sky/ tent/ curve]/ Kamara, Avestan, a girdle kam, a bent curved bow." I tried to imagine the poem arching like the bow of the sky, I didn't really do it very well, but I tried to think of the poem as going from one horizon over to the other horizon. It starts eastward from here, looking east, sunrise, and ends "Thinking on Amitatha in the setting sun" towards the center "where the Eagle/ that Flies out of Sight/ *flies*." So the blue sky is the sky itself, the arch of the sky, the kam, the camber, it is the structure of the poem, starting from one end to the other and then going back to the center, and ties into the idea of bow and comrade. Let's see, we didn't do "The Market," eh? [Pause] It's weird poems, isn't it? [Laughing] Page 32. The pivotal point there is "when the market is closed/ the cleanup comes/ equals." Again, this is a poem about interconnections and exchanges, interchanges, and again I'm trying to lead to that with the last phrase about buying "bananas by the ganges." That's what happens when you break your customary set of equivalences, then where do you go? Which I hope will be taken up in another poem which will answer that. [Laughing] This poem essentially poses a question which is not yet answered in the body of the poems that are done. Just as "The Blue Sky" raises a question which is the Eagle, so I'll have to do another section which will clarify that.

*Faas*: So one important structural device in the framework of the whole work would be to raise questions in one poem and then, in a way, to answer them in another.

SNYDER: Yes, on many levels I hope to be doing that.

*Faas*: How do you see your poetry in relation to the reader or listener?

SNYDER: Well, poetry starts with breath, breath of life, spirit, voice, voiced, you know, breath voiced becomes voice, and then voice as a vehicle of signaling, which becomes language, lingua—lang—

tongue, all that physiological fundamental of it is very
interesting to me. And then it moves out from there into
poetry as expression of inward states of being, fundamentally, but inward states of being which are more than
private, that invoke similar states of being in the hearer, that trigger
the same response, the same inward state, and in that triggering
establish a bond, a communication.

the reader's
role

*Faas*: Eliciting some kind of creative participation?

SNYDER: Right. And the bond is established on a deeper level than
the intellectual front brain consciousness level of bonding. I'm talking biologically now, because this is really where I draw from, especially lately. Signaling and bonding is essential to a particular social
species like ourselves and the more complex and elaborate and deep
inward states of being are expressible, the higher level of
consciousness and higher level of evolutionary organization you find in the organism. There is a book by Adolf
Portmann, the Swiss zoologist, entitled *Animal Forms and
Patterns,* which contains a very interesting theory about animals.
Now this is philosophy for me, this is my kind of philosophy. What
Portmann says is this: Catfish, squirrels etc., have no faces, they have
no facial expressions that signal to another animal. They signal with
their whole body. Their hair stands up, for instance. So moods or
states of feeling in animals are communicated by whole-body gestures, whole-body manifestations, also by sounds, the tone of the
sound. But as animals develop larger brains and higher biological
organization, the face and head become more important. Portmann
gives diagrams how the simple mammal forms have hair and fur
patterns that run right up and over their face and do not make any
formal distinction betwee the head and the body. With the higher
forms like tigers, the head gets a special patterning which accen-
tuates eyes and ears and which indicates that the head is the focus.
What that evolves into is the face. Now the face and its expressions
and the voice become the mode of expression of the inward state of
the animal. Wolves have a variety of expressions, as Konrad Lorenz
has pointed out. They communicate different states of feeling to
each other in that process, or rather by that means, and humanity
finally takes it another step, of course, to the capacity of communication. But the capacity of communication has many levels and the
most fundamental in a sense still remains the communication of
inward states of being.

poetic com-
munication as
"bonding"

*Faas*: So you establish communication by taking language back
from the purely conceptual, cerebral level to an animal body
physiological level.

SNYDER: Yes. And the more accurately the inward states of being can be expressed, the more remarkable it is. Like, sea urchins or sea slugs cannot see each other, they are completely locked in their own organisms. And in this sense there is a direction which is very beautiful, and that's the direction of the organism being less and less locked into itself, less and less locked into its own body structure and its relatively inadequate sense organs, towards a state where the organism can actually go out from itself and share itself with others. And poetry in language is of the greatest order of that sharing of the inner self with the outer, with the non-self. In a way, that's the whole value of poetry, in a way it's on the highest level of human bonding, that is to say that humans can share their real feelings with each other, which solves the need to be aggressive for one thing. That's the foundation of genuine communication and genuine love. Now, I'm no utopian. I see that working on some levels. So that's another angle which does not have to invoke magic.

*poetry the highest level of human bonding*

*Faas*: That reminds me of another question I wanted to ask you. Do you have any specific idea as to how you use myth in contrast to other poets?

SNYDER: I don't know how I use myth in contrast to other poets. I probably know as much about myth as anybody. Probably Duncan is the only other poet who has studied it as much as I have.

*Faas*: But his poetic use of myth is very different from yours.

SNYDER: I have a double sense of it: on the one hand myth in a way is our primary intellectual and poetic vocabulary, is the 50,000 year old international myth lore corpus, the world folklore motifs, world mythologies, world themes, world gods and goddesses, that whole thing is our fundamental vocabulary. Western literature uses its own myth vocabulary all the way through from Homer to James Joyce. India uses its own myth vocabulary all the way through in its literature and its thinking.

*poetic use of myth*

That is a fundamental kind of human lore which as an objective study is fascinating in the extreme and has amazing historical connections and cultural connections, and so forth. That's the one side. The other side is the more Jungian sense of the collective unconscious and the archetypal images. According to Jungian thought the myths are simply the surface manifestations of things which are deep in the unconscious. But I know enough about mythology and its complexities to realize that you can't simply explain mythology by a Jungian principle. Mythology is an inner thing that is almost biological and in a sense almost pre-cultural. Mythology also is man's most archaic lore and one which culture by culture incontrovertibly binds men together. It both liberates and binds. And you use those images as they come out of your own body. If you feel that a particular myth image or a particular god or goddess image is extremely attractive or interesting to you, then you have a relationship with it, and then you play that out from yourself against what is known about it in the world at large, in the external body of mythology. So that's what I do.

*Faas*:  There is a kind of erudite mythological eclecticism in Pound.

SNYDER:  I'm more interested in a poetical rather than a comparative mythological way, demonstrating what I think to be main strands in the world body of myth and how they relate to us today. I can only identify with what I consider to be main strands by a process of inner examination of those strands as well as by looking at them, you know, statistically. [Laughing] It's a dual process. "Bubbs Creek Haircut" is working all around that.

*Faas*:  Some of your poetry is full of esoteric allusions which seems to call for something like Eliot's "Notes on the Waste Land."

SNYDER:  But everybody knows about Shiva and Pārvatī, don't you think?

erudite
allusiveness

*Faas*:  I really doubt it. [Both laughing] I would guess that amongst your listeners of last night about 10% would really know who they are.

SNYDER:  Really? That's where I'm getting out of touch with my audience. [Laughing] Well, you know what I thought of, Ekbert? I thought, when I will have finished *Mountains and Rivers* to write a final poem section which would be footnotes and glossary all as one poem.

*Faas*:  Number 26.

SNYDER:  Or to break the page with a line here and write the footnotes as kind of another poem underneath. [Laughing] It would be fun to do something like that. It may be that that's necessary. As I say, I don't put any prime value on obscurity, it's not my intention to appear overly learned.

*Faas*:  And then, of course, who would really enjoy reading a poem which needs too much learned documentation?

SNYDER:  Sure, the reader reads it because it's interesting. That's why Pound fell down. That's why big sections of the *Cantos* aren't interesting. There are some very dry Cantos in the mid sections which don't hold up for that very reason. So, you know, like Pound dug a hole for himself there. I think I'm avoiding that, I think that the level of meaning, content, interest and music is going to be strong enough in *Mountains and Rivers* to sustain the reader through it. *Myths & Texts* has been very successful and *Myths & Texts* is a difficult poem, but it sells more copies per year now than it sold in 1959 when it was published. It has been in print steadily since 1959 and it sells a thousand copies a year—with no footnotes.

*Faas*: How do you respond to confessional poetry?

SNYDER: It's a work they have to do and probably it's work that has to be done. Also, certainly, there is an audience that benefits from it in some way. I read it, fine. I wouldn't consider that a main poetic stream.

confessional poetry

*Faas*: When I first met you in Kitkitdizze you said so nicely that nobody seems to take much notice of the number of establishment poets that are deeply neurotic, while on the other hand there were endless outcries against the supposed craziness of the Beat poets.

SNYDER: Yes, we have noticed that over the years. There was in many ways more tension and frustration and suffering and breakdown and alcoholism and so forth in the lives of the straight academic poets, at least as much and maybe more, than in the non-academic and supposedly crazier and freakier world. And the greatest model of sanity of all, of course, is that old madman Allen Ginsberg. [Laughter] Olson was a very sane man essentially, far stabler, say, than John Berryman or Anne Sexton. So it's very curious in a way, it's just that people don't notice it.

*Faas*: What do you think is the main reason for neurosis amongst establishment poets?

SNYDER: I suppose it's because when you're caught in the establishment, you are referring yourself to a set of expectations and trying to meet those expectations which are exterior to yourself. But when you step out of that you're only answering your own expectations and if you have high expectations for yourself, well, then you may get something interesting done. But you are not frustrated because you are not trying to please someone else. And whatever obscure demons there are in the white middle-class mind. I mean Berryman had some obscure demons since it's hard to locate why he should have had the difficulties he did really.

*Faas*: Duncan is reported by Bruce Cook to have said that your poetry is based on your "conception of the taste of the reasonable man."

SNYDER: I guess I must be a reasonable man because people keep telling me that. [Laughing] What I think I would be doing is trying to win the credibility of the reasonable man and then take him deeper. And I have to do that because I live in a very common-sense world. I always lived in a world where you had to be pretty straight because nobody would tolerate too much bullshit. I mean, who do you speak to? You speak to

the reasonable man

people who are fellow workers, and so you have to start off on some level of communication which they will listen to, then you take off from there. So in some senses maybe Duncan is right.

# Robert Creeley

Photo: Gerard Malanga

# ROBERT CREELEY (1926 -    )

"I've never felt that writing was fiction, that it was something made up about something. I've felt that it was direct evidence of the writer's engagement with his own feelings and with the possibilities that words offered him ... Wherever it is one stumbles (to get to wherever) at least some way will exist, so to speak, as and when a man takes this or that step—for which, god bless him. Insofar as these poems are such places, always they were ones stumbled into . . ."

One place Creeley, much against his natural inclination, has stumbled into all his life, is academia. He attended Harvard for a period before and after a year in the American Field Service in India and Burma during World War II (1944-45), but left the university just in time to avoid completing his B.A.—which was later awarded him by the rector of Black Mountain College. "Olson [in 1955] said, well, you taught the courses, therefore you should have credit for them—we'll give you a degree. It served." In 1960 he received his M.A. from the University of New Mexico and subsequently taught at various academic institutions before becoming a Professor of English at SUNY, Buffalo in 1966. Yet the unceasing restlessness of his diversified existence seems to belie this *curriculum vitæ*: while in Europe he became associate editor of the German Rainer Gerhardt's *Fragmente* and the Japanese Katue Kitasono's *Vou* and ran his own Divers Press in Mallorca; he edited the *Black Mountain Review* while teaching at the college, tutored the children of a coffee finca owner in Guatemala, or divided his life between Buffalo, New York and Bolinas, California. The major turning point in his life came through contact with Olson, with whom he conducted a four-year-long (soon to be published) correspondence before the two poets met in 1954. A poet *(Poems 1950-1965,* 1966; *Words,* 1967; *Pieces,* 1968; *The Finger: Poems 1966-69,* 1970; *A Day Book,* 1972; *Selected Poems,* 1976), novelist *(The Island,* 1963), playwright *(Listen,* 1972), short story writer (*The Gold Diggers*, 1954, 1965) as well as critic-æsthetician (*A Quick Graph*, 1970; *Contexts of Poetry: Interviews 1961-71*, 1973; *A Sense of Measure*, 1973), Creeley has also done important editorial work (*Mayan Letters* by Charles Olson, 1953, 1968; *New American Story*, 1965; *Selected Writings* by Charles Olson, 1966; *The New Writing in the U.S.A*, 1967, etc.).

# Robert Creeley

By way of introducing his seminal review of Robbe-Grillet's first novel *Les Gommes* (1953), Roland Barthes remarks: "Above the entrance of Montparnasse station . . . there presently . . . is a big neon sign 'Good Mileage' of which several letters are usually extinct." This, he suggests, would be an ideal subject for the French novelist who tends to strip things of their anthropomorphic significations and to describe them in their literal, non-referential suchness. "All the artist's craft aims at giving the object a 'being there' and to deprive it of 'being something'" (Bs,E,29,31).

For Barthes, *Les Gommes* was a startling confirmation of his theory, mapped out in *Le degré zéro de l'écriture* (1953), that modern writers, ever since Flaubert and Mallarmé, had increasingly tried to strip language of the socio-ideological connotations tacitly inherent in its normal usage. After the Surrealists, after Camus and Sartre, it was Robbe-Grillet who had finally reached that "perfection dans l'imitation du réel" which before him had only been realized in a non-Western culture like the Chinese (Bs,D,33).

The work of Robert Creeley, whose artistic and intellectual career resembles an ontogenetic repetition of this development, could have provided Barthes with a comparable—and even earlier—confirmation of his thesis. Explaining the extreme "particularism and literalness" of his writing, the poet relates an anecdote oddly reminiscent of the neon sign in Barthes' review:

> I'm by nature and circumstance a very literal man. There was a sign over a diner as one drove from Albuquerque to Santa Fe, and it said: "Ly'n Bragg." For years I drove past that café and it never occurred to me that it was a pun. Lie and Brag . . . As far as being literal, I can be extraordinarily dumb in that way. (Pa,C,213)

If Creeley remained unknown to Barthes, there was a critic of comparable genius to help him turn this "dumbness" into one of the most astounding and puzzling achievements of contemporary American letters. Olson first wrote Creeley on April 21, 1950, and the long correspondence and friendship that was to follow helped Creeley, who in 1950 was still writing in the mode of Wallace Stevens, fully to come into his own as a poet, short story writer and novelist. But if the older poet started out as Creeley's mentor, Olson, in turn, became the younger man's beneficiary. Olson acknowledged having learned from Creeley "more . . . than from any living man," and called him "a subtle & beautiful man, worth more than all the rest of us" (N,C,46-7). And indeed, out of their correspondence grew the second part of Olson's essay on "Projective Verse," while Creeley's short stories, "the push beyond Lawrence" (N,C,41), as Olson called them, provided the latter with a heretofore unprecedented parallel in prose to his concept of poetry as a reenactment of Nature's forces. As Olson hurried to announce in his introduction to Creeley's *Gold Diggers* (1954), there are two apparently self-contradictory narrative "methodologies" to achieve this aim: "that the narrator stays OUT, functions as pressure not as interpreting person," or, alternately, as Creeley illustrated,

> the NARRATOR IN, the total IN to the above total OUT . . . the narrator . . . taking up the push of his own single intelligence to make it, to be—by his conjectures—so powerful inside the story that he makes the story swing on him, his eye the eye of nature INSIDE (as is the same eye, outside) a lightmaker. (O,U,127)

Creeley found in Olson—just as Robbe-Grillet did in Barthes—a critical intelligence to match his creative achievement, and he gladly yielded to Olson's advice. According to his bibliographer Mary Novik, he, for instance, revised "3 Fate Tales," so that the "narrator was allowed to intervene in all the ambivalence of his stance at the beginning of the first and second tale," and on further insistence by Olson, also "revised the ending of the first tale, putting the equivocal narrator fully IN," so that the tales, "previously separate exempla, are connected in the final draft by the qualifying presence of the narrator" (N,C,36). The result is a text which reads like *Dans le Labyrinthe* in miniature and can best be described in terms of *nouveau roman* theory or of the diverse statements, in which Creeley, following Olson, has paralleled, or even anticipated several of its major critical tenets.

Apparently unaware of post-Existentialist French fiction, Creeley found little in the modern novel besides D. H. Lawrence to presage the narrative mode he first developed in his short stories. The "divers techniques used to confront *time*" such as "[f]lashback, recall by certain of the characters, juxtaposition . . . of . . .'time' sequences" appear to him "ultimately makeshift" and of little use in his own attempt to portray a universe of "things shifting among themselves" (C,G,21-2), in which time and space have been reduced to their true nature of "qualifications" or what, using Whitehead's terms, Creeley might also have called "extensional and cogredient properties of events" (Wh,I,67). Equally inappropriate to him are the frequent digressions made use of by Joyce, Faulkner, Céline and others, because they only obscure or conceal the underlying symbolic pattern or "explanation" imposed on the material "anterior to the instance" of creation (C,G,43).

Creeley, like Olson, feels a "closeness of sympathies" with Existentialist writers like Sartre or Camus. For they, at least, were aware of the world in its simple "being there," underneath the anthropocentric projections of our thinking and language, aware of that "world *without appeal*" which Sartre's Roquentin discovers to his repugnance while looking at the roots of a chestnut tree. But Sartre's *La Nausée* or Camus' *L'Étranger* remain within the closed "universe of discourse" which their thinking repudiated. A scene such as Roquentin in front of the chestnut tree reads like an exemplum to prove the inadequacy of description, but staying in the descriptive mode itself, it becomes an ironic *reductio ad absurdum* of its message. In Olson's words it accomplishes nothing because it "does not come to grips with what really matters: that a thing, any thing, impinges on us by a more important fact, its self-existence" (O,W,56). In this way, Creeley felt that "the bulk of prose writing, 1930 to 50," including the Existentialist novel, and only excepting the work of D. H. Lawrence, was "of no consequence . . . in that it assumes, arbitrarily, a knowledge of event, of significance, which it does not make a means to in its own substance" (N,C,43).

Narratives like "3 Fate Tales" or Robbe-Grillet's novels, by contrast, are totally self-contained and non-referential to an exterior, "authentic" reality. As Robbe-Grillet puts it, "the work is not a substitute for an exterior reality, but is its own reality to itself" (R-G,R,166); or as Creeley declared,

> It's my own belief—any instance of the ASSUMPTIONAL knowledge of referents, which is to say, any case wherein the reader is referred to a *reality* not literally made a presence, given actuation, in the content, is a direct sapping of that writing's to-be-respected DEMAND on the reader's attention. (N,C,43)

This is most obvious in the use of ellipses or "holes" interrupting the narrative sequence. Robbe-Grillet, for instance, deliberately fails to tell the reader whether or not his voyeur Mathias has tortured and murdered the young girl that obsesses his imagination in *Le Voyeur*. As he comments himself, "Everything is told before the 'hole,' then again after the 'hole,' and there is an effort to bring together the two edges to eliminate this troublesome emptiness; but the opposite occurs, the 'hole' engulfs everything."[1]* Similarly, there is little to explain the fatal accident which forms the climax or rather anti-climax in Creeley's "First Fate Tale" (C,D,45-7):

> It is still quiet. But then out, it goes by me, and down. Stops. But I can't do anything, sit only for a moment, and then, jump, and look out, see there, down, the girl and the people already around her. Nothing of the woman until her head is just opposite mine, the mouth wide, scream, and someone I see the face of below, looks up and calls to her. It's all right. She isn't hurt. A miracle.

As the narrator emphasizes, the reason or motivation for all this "isn't known." If he is to "make . . . sense of it" it is exactly "that it isn't known, any of it. This woman or this girl or what has happened, and how I would have it, or my hand there." There is nothing even to set what happens into an analysable context of time and space. Everything seems to take place in an "eternal *now*" (R-G,R,134) in which time and space seem to annul each other: "I say time, to mean place," as Creeley's narrator puts it: "Any day of the week this could happen, to any, this girl, to others, me, you." And what may happen any day, may not have happened at all, not even to the narrator of the story. All he is able to affirm at the beginning of his narrative is that "[o]ne day, any day, there could be these people, or make them three people, this man and this woman and this little girl."

Unlike the traditional first person narrator reviewing the follies of the past from the armchair vista of maturity, Creeley's narrator, like Robbe-Grillet's, appears "*always* . . . engrossed in a passionate adventure of the most obsessive kind, to the point of frequently distorting his vision and of producing fantasies close to delirium." This is the "subjectivité totale" (R-G,R,148-9) of Robbe-Grillet's novels, or what Creeley, distancing himself from the Romantic "use of the *subjective* method as an excuse for emotional claptrap" calls "The subjective in a more basic character" (C,G,19), a concept which, after his controversy with Olson, came to amount to a total transcen-dance of the subject-object dichotomy.[2]

Even in his short stories, however, Creeley's subjectivity "in a

*Notes to this section on p. 164

more basic character" results in strategies of self-reduction similar to Robbe-Grillet's universe of disembodied abstractions, but alien to Olson's passionate ontological involvement with the world. The narrator of the "First Fate Tale" or *Dans le Labyrinthe* does not only invent his story in the very process of narrating it; in order to do so, he also has to invent himself—a "je néant" of guesses and specula- tions, circumscribed by the chimera of his own phantasizing. In other words, the story is not invented at all, but invents itself. What- ever happens, happens exclusively in the imagination of the reader, who through his creative participation becomes the story's real pro- tagonist: "it is in his head that the whole story takes place, a story which he in fact imagines himself" (R-G,R,166). In imitation of the serpent swallowing its own tail, the line of systematic self-reduction comes full circle, and the story's final words return the reader to the introductory "I put it this way. That I am, say, myself," in which the narrator made a tentative, hesitating and unsuccessful attempt to posit his own identity: "Any day of the week this could happen, to any, this girl, to others, me, you. I suppose it is something, even, done with. As it turned out. Past, and even complete. I am left with it, made different, because of it. Or, am I? We are back to that" (C,D,47).

But how did a text like the "First Fate Tale" originate in actual fact? Both in the introduction to his short stories and in similar comments on his poetry, Creeley describes this creative process as the open-ended self-realization of a linguistic event. "[W]hat emerges in the writing I most value," he declared at an international poetry conference in Berlin, "is a content which cannot be antici- pated, which 'tells you what you don't know'" (C,G,72). Even before he met Olson, Creeley had adopted this notion from modern jazz and abstract expressionism. In his interviews, reviews and prog- rammatic statements he has again and again referred to Charlie Parker's uses of silence and rhythmical improvisation, or has quoted Pollock's famous statement about being inside the canvas, or Franz Kline's "I paint what I don't know" as models for his own sense of creativity (C,IR,174).

The particular use Creeley made of these influences is suggested by his belief that the true following of abstract expres- sionism is to be found in the "antithetically disciplined formalism of Frank Stella, and those akin to him as Neil Williams and Larry Poons" (C,G,349). Like Piet Mondrian before them, these artists are pursuing what Werner Haftmann calls the "active creation of 'no- thingness,' "[3] trying to eliminate from their painting all reference, not only to exterior reality, but also to the very act of creativity.

According to Mondrian, this is achieved by opposing "the colour plane to the non-colour plane (white, grey, black), so that through this duality, the opposites can annihilate one another." "Line and colour must be composed *otherwise* than in nature,"[4] while (in Stella's terms) the painting becomes its own reality in which "only what can be seen there *is* there."[5] Or as Creeley himself put it, commenting on minimal art in general: "the painting is not a reference to another reality . . . but remains unequivocally its own occasion" (C,G,349). Stella himself has denied the reductionist approach to reality which critics have often imputed to him.[6] But it is clearly that "active creation of 'nothingness' " his paintings seem to reflect which explains the fascination they have for Creeley.

Creeley has often emphasized that there is "never a 'subject' *about* which one constructs an activity called 'poetry' "(C,G,72). Even T. S. Eliot's notion that the poet should embody emotions in "objective correlatives" seems to him a "disastrous mistake," since it proposes "that the thing for which there is an objective correlative is in some way a symbol of that object" (C,C,100), giving the poem the kind of referential meaning it should most try to avoid. If the work of art has any meaning at all, it must, as Olson says, "exist through itself" (C,G,54). What Olson's phrase suggests, of course, is a psycho-physiological "concrete," derived from a creative reenactment of nature which turns art into "the only twin life has" (O,W,61). Again, Creeley uses Olson's phrase in order to express a notion somewhat estranged from this original significance when he claims that art " 'means nothing,' [it] doesn't have a point." No wonder then that in this journey towards emptiness, the minimal artists gradually replaced Pollock and Olson as Creeley's main travelling companions, and that the "*zero* set" of an artist like Arakawa, "the real nitty gritty for any head-trip," as Creeley called it in a recent essay on "The Creative," has become a model for his poetic pursuits (C,Cr).

It is with a curious impatience that Creeley has inveighed against that "goddamn Zen" (C,B) which various friends keep drumming into his ears. Nonetheless, he admits to being "fascinated by Japanese writing, the haiku, and by people like Blyth in *Zen and English Literature*" (C,C,132-3), and he is as well aware as others that "the present attraction of the *Dhammapada*, or other Buddhist texts" is explained by the fact that they seem to offer a panacea for that hypertrophy of the ego, left to us as a burdensome legacy by Romanticism. As he seems to imply, this remedy has proved genuine for a poet like Gary Snyder, whose insights are the outcome of lifelong study and meditation in those fields. Yet if Creeley, as early as 1961, acknowledged Snyder's achievement as "a successful relation of hope" (C,G,209), there was little in his own work, written up to that time, to suggest that he might be headed towards a similar goal.

Like Snyder, Creeley was looking for ways to avoid the pitfalls of egocentricity, or what, after Lawrence, he calls "*sensationalism*, i.e., the repetition of a known sensation" (C,G,209). But the solutions worked out in their poetry up to 1961 were diametrically opposed. Unlike Snyder, who abandons his ego to the world of phenomena and action, Creeley tries to reduce it to zero. After its destructive raid on the universe, his "active creation of 'nothingness' " finally returns, like a boomerang, upon the creator—the poet, in Creeley's own words, working "towards a final obliteration of himself" (C,G,39): "[I] feel it [i.e., the poem] with the intensity of all the perception that I . . . that the ego bit can recognize, and then destroy the ego by its own insistence" (C,C,39).

If there is truth in C. Kellerer's claim that many Western artists have moved closer and closer to a Zen Buddhist approach to reality during recent decades, it seems equally convincing that this gradual change of consciousness is resulting in what A. Ehrenzweig terms "the definite schizoid tinge of modern art."[7] Whereas the action painters, for instance, outdid Far Eastern *Sumi-e* artists in their emphasis on *ch'i-yün shêng-tung* (or the "resonance or vibration of the vitalizing spirit and movement of life," Si,A,21-2), filling every nook of their canvases with the turbulent psychographs of the unconscious, the minimal artists or their precursors seem to present us with the schizophrenic counterpart: final emptiness, the ubiquitous background in Far Eastern painting, becomes an aim of analytical demonstration to men like Mondrian, Stella or Flavin. The "automatic effusions" of Kerouac (in Creeley's words "a simplification of that chaos, familiar to us now in Zen teaching," C,G,249) versus the work of Robbe-Grillet or Creeley himself present us with comparable polarities in the world of literature.

In a more recent poem Creeley summed up his general approach to reality:

> All I knew or know
> began with this—
> emptiness
> with its incessant movement.
>
> (C,F,95)

This has been taken as Creeley's own testimony for the "continual threat of the void" at the center of his experience, stemming, as Charles Altieri has argued, "from his sense of isolation, of being cut off from all roots or grounds—in concrete experience, in tradition,

and in his relationships with other people."[8] Yet instead of threatening him, the void seems to attract Creeley with the power of a
religious mystery. His "mind locked" while watching "The Mountains in the Desert" as the light fades—"such geography of self and
soul / brought to such limit of sight"—the poet is yearning for a state
of mind which transcends the limitations of his ego:

> Tonight let me go
> at last out of whatever
> mind I thought to have,
> and all the habits of it.

(C,P,166)

A similar abandonment to emptiness results from his insight into the
futility of trying to describe our existence in this world:

> I keep to myself such
> measures as I care for,
> daily the rocks
> accumulate position.
>
> There is nothing
> but what thinking makes
> it less tangible. The mind
> fast as it goes, loses
>
> pace, puts in place of it
> like rocks simple markers,
> for a way only to
> hopefully come back to
>
> where it cannot. All
> forgets. My mind sinks.
> I hold in both hands such weight
> it is my only description.

(C,P,190)

In the wooden sculptures of an unidentified artist Creeley found an
embodiment of the mindlessness and quiet he is approaching here.
The poem about these "Figures" reads like an indirect description of
his own poetic aims:

> Did the man
> who made them find
> a like quiet? In
> the act of making them

it must have been
so still he heard the wood
and felt it with his hands

moving into
the forms
he has given to them,

one by singular
one, so quiet,
so still.

(C,P,147)

Creeley is well aware that this artistic pursuit of the void must itself result in artifacts of nothingness, and that the "poem supreme, addressed to / emptiness" (C,P,29), as he called it, can be at best an allegory of silence. Such a poem is "Waiting," in which through certain stylistic devices, common to most of Creeley's earlier poetry, a discussion of these very issues is turned into a *monumentum ære perennius* to commemorate the self-annihilating act of creativity. This is achieved by an almost totally abstract vocabulary, a frequently ungrammatical or deliberately nonsensical syntax, the recurrence of certain phrases like the leitmotifs of a musical score, and above all by the use of key words which through repetition are slowly emptied of all the meaning they had in the context of their first occurrence and which finally—like lights in the mirror cabinet of the poem's total structure—fuse in a blinding glare of nothingness:

He pushes behind the words
which, awkward, catch
and turn him to a disturbed
and fumbling man.

What if it all stops.
Then silence
is as silence was
again.

What if the last time
he was moved to touch,
work out in his own mind,
such limits was the last—

and then a quiet, a dull
space of hanging actions, all
depending on some time
has come and gone.

God help him then
if such things can.
That risk
is all there is.

(C,P,167)

In the poem entitled "After Mallarmé," which deals with the
theme of quiet found in mindlessness (C,P,152), Creeley seems to
acknowledge that he is not the first and only poet who had the
courage necessary to take that risk. (See also C,P,29.) Despite many
formal dissimilarities of their verse, there are deep affinities between
the French and American poet. Of course, it was more than mere
courage that impelled Mallarmé to disclaim his allegiance to the
Christian God—"that creature of ancient and evil plumage"—and to
delve, before any other Western poet or artist, into the utter depths
of nothingness. The story of anguish and suffering, told in his
letters, describes how the first glimpse of the void, which Mallarmé
had while composing the *Hérodiade*, revealed an abyss that
threatened to engulf him in mental insanity. "My misfortune is," he
wrote to Henri Cazalis in March 1866,

> that, when I had polished my poetry down to this depth, I
> came upon twin abysses which drove me mad. The first was
> Nothingness, which I found without any prior knowledge of
> Buddhism.

This overwhelming vision of emptiness, both in himself and in the
world around him, soon became the conscious aim of all his artistic
endeavours. Henceforth his poems, those "Sumptuous Allegories of
Nothingness," as he called them, were created by an "*elimination*" of
all referential meaning and by methods of "self-destruction," rigorous to the point where Mallarmé had to look into the Venetian
mirror on his writing desk in order to preserve a sense of his identity.
"[I]f it were not in front of me here on the table," he confessed to
Cazalis,

> I would become Nothingness again. Which means that I am
> impersonal now: not the Stéphane you once knew, but one of
> the ways the Spiritual Universe has found to see Itself, unfold
> Itself through what used to be me.

Unlike Creeley, Mallarmé came to identify emptiness with a traditional concept of beauty, and adhered with painstaking assiduity to all the established rules of prosody. Yet, common to both poets is an autotelic, music score-like use of language, and Mallarmé's discussion of this characteristic culminates in a brilliant feat of critical synthesis that Creeley has often tried to formulate: "[O]ur principal aim," Mallarmé wrote on December 5, 1866, "should be to make the words of a poem self-mirroring (since they are sufficiently autonomous to begin with and need no outside impression) to such an extent that no one of them will seem to have a color of its own, and all of them will be merely the notes of a scale" (M,E,88,92-5). Here we have Creeley's frequently repeated plea for a non-referential use of language, to be achieved by techniques such as "feed-back" or "repetitive relocation of phrasing" (C,C,88). These will reduce the communicative meaning of words to the minimum or rather nonexistence of "existing through themselves" where "they [i.e., the words] speak rather than someone speaking with them," returning them "to an almost objective state of presence," and will thus engender a poetry or "complex of sounds and rhythms, which move in a parallel to music" (C,G,55).

Of course, Creeley has also remarked that he does not wish "to confuse poetry with music" and has repeatedly drawn attention to the emotion underlying and informing "the order and movement of *sound*" (C,G,53,131) determining the form of his poems. And naturally there are several poems, even amongst his earlier work, which do not reach, or even approach the etherealized purity of the "poem supreme, addressed to/emptiness." Yet until the early sixties nearly all of them seem to revolve, as if drawn by a mysterious force, in an ineluctable orbit around nothingness. Take a poem like "The Pool." In terms of description that can be visualized, and of narrative that can be summed up, it far exceeds the limits which usually keep the scope of such mimetic features down to a very minimum. But what actually do we see and hear?

> My embarrassment at his nakedness,
> at the pool's edge,
> and my wife, with his,
> standing, watching—
>
> this was a freedom
> not given me who am
> more naked,
> less contained

by my own white flesh
and the ability
to take quietly
what comes to me.

The sense of myself
separate, grew
a white mirror
in the quiet water

he breaks with his hands
and feet, kicking

There is the speaker and his wife with another man and probably the latter's wife. The speaker feels embarrassed, "less contained/ by [his] own white flesh," maybe jealous, contemplating his alienated self in the water, until the other man, by diving into the pool, breaks the reflection "with his hands/ and feet, kicking." Yet even a bare outline such as this tacitly fills in gaps in the narrative and provides us with circumstantial description or psychological motivation which the poem itself stubbornly withholds from the reader. It also evokes a scenic authenticity totally lacking in the labyrinthine world of isolated details and unrelated emotions created by the poem. Conversely, the outline fails to render the poem's real impact on the reader: the aura of total elusiveness conveyed by the fragmented geometry of surface description and the faltering staccato movement of utterance—that "graph of indeterminate / feelings" which "despairs of its own / statement, wants to/ turn away, endlessly / to turn away" (C,P,159,184). Mainly through repetition of certain key words, self-reflecting and mutually self-effacing, this vagueness finally condenses into an ideograph of nothingness, and the poem goes on to end in a thematic statement, expressing the speaker's yearning for a state of quiet, silence and emptiness, reached by "the risk" of his self-annihilating creativity:

pulls up to land
on the edge by the feet

of these women
who must know
that for each
man is a speech

> describes him, makes
> the day grow white
> and sure, a quietness of water
> in the mind,
>
> lets hang, descriptive
> at a risk, something
> for which he cannot find
> a means or time.
>
>                    (C,P,141)

In the "Boogie-Woogie" series, painted during the years shortly before his death in 1944, Mondrian started to fill the static configurations of his former style with bands of variegated color and to infuse them with the throbbing rhythms characteristic of his early work under the influence of Van Gogh and the Fauves. Sometime after 1960, a similar change seems to occur in the poetry of Robert Creeley. As early as 1962, the poet felt that he had begun "to relax," to feel "more settled, more at ease in [his] world" (Os,A,60). But the real change must have occurred at a level far deeper than that. Thus, most of his recent poetry seems to have been written by a man who, after emerging from the depths of mystic experience and still blinded by the glaring vision of emptiness, has come stumbling back into reality, groping for a hold in the bewildering chaos of a world, deconceptualized by his former quest for the void. After a ten-year-long effort to write the "poem supreme, addressed to / emptiness," we find him wondering around 1960: "then what / is emptiness / for." And his own answer: "To / fill, fill" (C,P,178) announces the earthbound drive of his new poetic idiom, and the direct thematic concern of several of his subsequent poems. There is the old fascination with "infinite emptiness," but now there is also a yearning for concrete reality and life, as expressed in the poem entitled "Joy":

> I could look at
> an empty hole for hours
> thinking it will
> get something in it,
>
> will collect
> things. There is
> an infinite emptiness
> placed there.

Even if the marmoreal stillness of the earlier work has turned into a "broken silence,/ filled with screaming," Creeley seems unperturbed in his new programmatic belief that "There is / a silence / to fill," because "It is possible, in words, to speak / of what has happened—a sense / of there and here, now / and then" (C,W,106,107,113,122).

An "absolute failure as a 'visual artist' " (Pa,C,210), Creeley had to relearn reality's alphabet and to return to his childhood's most primal cognitive gesture of simple enumeration in order to achieve this aim. "A Piece," Creeley's best known and most controversial poem since 1960, is the odd, but at the same time most direct expression of this effort.

> One and
> one, two,
> three.
>
> (C,W,115)

As he once pointed out in conversation, "the first way I could know that the world existed was in my ability to count it." Only from here could he proceed to register the "Small facts / of eyes, hair / blonde, face / looking like a / flat painted / board" or to tentatively posit his identity: "Here I / am. There / you are." This anxious questioning of himself in relation to others—"You are not / me, nor I you" (C,F,43-4,56,61)—finds an affirmative answer in the poet's discovery of the female principle. A creature of veritable flesh and blood, but also of mythic dimensions, comprising the polarities of light and darkness, she suddenly arises from the maze of lifeless abstractions that form the world of Creeley's earlier poetry:

> She was largely warm—
> flesh heavy—and smiled
> in some deepening knowledge.
>
> .   .   .   .   .   .   .   .   .
>
> She laughed and turned
> and the heavy folds of cloth
>
> parted. The nakedness
> burned. Her heavy breath,
> her ugliness, her lust—
> but her laughing, her low
>
> chuckling laugh, the way
> she moved her hand to the
> naked breast, then to
> her belly, her hand with its fingers.

A symbol of everlasting life, she embodies all that humans want or need to know,—"her eyes / the depth of all one had thought of, / again and again and again" (C,F,50-2). And the poet who follows her turns into the Yeatsian fool who has recognized the essential oneness of all being, yet also knows about the unending flux of creation, life and death:

> In secret
> the out's in—
>
> the wise
> surprised, all
>
> going coming,
> begun undone.
>
> Hence the fool dances
> in endless happiness.
>
> (C,F,55)

Thus none of his former vision has been lost, but the poet has learned to approach reality from a realm "beyond despair" (J.-P. Sartre), bringing to it the insights gained in his earlier quest for the void. It was obviously understating the case when Creeley declared only a few years ago that he had recently tried to develop a writing "that simply says: the road is going this way down the hill and there are trees here." No doubt it was new for him "to make a statement of what seems to be physically actual" in a specific place (Pa,C,210). But his poetry in no way limits itself to such phenomenological transcripts of reality. Like Rilke before him, he not only records, but celebrates existence: "I love water, I *love* water— / but I also love air, and fire" (C,B). And while formerly he had conceived of his poetry as an uncommunicative way of talking to himself (C,IR,173), he now feels a need to speak to others, even at the risk of having to be "descriptive":

> a *description,*–hey!
> see the dog
> walk—
>
> (C,B)

The most obvious outcome of this whole development is that Creeley, in abandoning the attempt to write the "poem supreme, addressed to / emptiness," tends to consider his more recent poems as one continuous testimony to his own life experience. In this sense his 1963 description of *The Cantos* or *A* as "a day book or journal," which "attempts to deal with reality over a man's life" (C,C,17) seems to anticipate the impulse behind his lyrical output since *Pieces* (1969). However inappropriate when related to Pound's and Zukofsky's poems, the statement also shows the poet's recent tendency to re-define his position within the tradition of American poetry. Asked if he considered *Pieces* as an open poem like the *Cantos, Maximus* and *Paterson,* Creeley described his work as

> a kind of open writing in the sense that it was composed in a journal as daily writing . . . I wanted a mode that could in-clude, say, what people understandably might feel are in-stances of trivia . . . in the same sense that Williams says—"the total province of the poem is the world"—something of that order in *Paterson* somewhere—the sense that poetry isn't a discretion, that it is ultimately the realization of an entire world. (C,C,192)

As his most important overall achievement, however, Creeley's recent poetic idiom can rise to a totally new vibrancy and transparent clarity evoking a world of concrete sensual detail while retaining the mystical luminosity of the "poem supreme, addressed to / emptiness." Such are the qualities to be found in a poem like "The Moon" which, without abandoning its Creeleyan tone and diction, is reminiscent of Chinese poetry, and equal to the best of Snyder's work in that mode:

> Earlier in the evening the moon
> was clear to the east,
> over the snow of the yard
> and fields—a lovely
>
> bright clarity and perfect
> roundness, isolate,
> riding as they say the
> black sky. Then we went
>
> about our businesses of the
> evening, eating supper, talking,
> watching television, then
> going to bed, making love,

and then to sleep. But before
we did I asked her to look
out the window at the moon
now straight up, so that

she bent her head and looked
sharply up, to see it.
Through the night it must
have shone on, in that

fact of things—another
moon, another night—a
full moon in the winter's
space, a white loneliness.

I came awake to the blue
white light in the darkness,
and felt as if someone
were there, waiting, alone.
.    .    .    .    .    .    .    .    .

(C,F,59-60)

[1] Quoted by B. Morrissette, *Alain Robbe-Grillet*. Columbia Essays on Modern Writers, No. 11 (New York: Columbia University Press, 1965), p. 19.

[2] See above, p. 25.

[3] *Painting in the Twentieth Century*, 2 vols. (London: Lund Humphries, 1965), I, 202.

[4] Quoted by H. L. C. Jaffé, *De Stijl* (New York: Harry N. Abrams, Inc., n.d.), pp. 120, 189.

[5] Quoted by G. Battcock, ed. *Minimal Art, A Critical Anthology* (New York: E.P. Dutton & Co., Inc., 1968), p. 158.

[6] Ibid., p. 159.

[7] See C. Kellerer, *Objet trouvé und Surrealismus* (Hamburg: Rowohlt Verlag, 1962), passim; A. Ehrenzweig, *The Hidden Order of Art* (Berkeley: University of California Press, 1971), p. 66.

[8] "The Unsure Egoist: Robert Creeley and the Theme of Nothingness," *Contemporary Literature* 13, 2 (Spring, 1972), pp. 162-85, 162.

# Robert Creeley

*Faas*: In the introduction to Olson's *Selected Writings* you say that Camus "may speak of a world *without appeal*, but the system of discourse he makes use of is still demonstrably a closed one." All he accomplishes is a *description* of reality, which in Olson's words "does not come to grips with what really matters." One finds a similar critique of Existentialism in Robbe-Grillet.

Robbe-Grillet

CREELEY: There is a lovely joke à propos Robbe-Grillet. We have some old friends in New Mexico, a young French architect and his wife, and apparently Robbe-Grillet came travelling through the country, and stopped there to give a lecture or something, and they introduced themselves, and asked him if he knew Robert Creeley. And he said: Robert Creeley, that's me. [Both laughing]

*Faas*: I find there are extraordinary affinities between his and your work, and I wondered if you are familiar with Robbe-Grillet.

CREELEY: I know him somewhat, but the insistent abstraction in his writing is really distracting to me. I mean by that the frame of the writing. *Last Year in Marienbad* is an obvious instance. When I saw the film, I was really depressed incredibly, but very impressed also.

*Faas*: Have you read *Pour un nouveau roman*?

CREELEY: No.

*Faas*: Do you know if he is acquainted with your work or Olson's?

CREELEY: I don't know if he is or isn't, because these friends said he really became so comically involved with the play on the names.

*Faas*: So probably it was just a pun. Did you ever meet him yourself?

CREELEY: No, I happened to be away at the time. I briefly met Michel Butor and I liked him very much as a man. But when he was talking about the opera he was then trying to design as a chance operation, it really turned out that the parts of the opera, the very segments of it, were highly defined. You know, it was sort of "three acts." He was only using chance factors for the way in which one act would follow another, and I felt that doesn't really do it.

meeting
Michel Butor

*Faas*: That's like early Stockhausen.

CREELEY: Yes, that's still too didactic.

*Faas*: Of course, Robbe-Grillet goes much further than that.

CREELEY: Yes, Michel Butor really seemed like the classic French-man, but a very pleasant man.

*Faas*: Did D. H. Lawrence in any way anticipate your own techniques as a short story writer?

CREELEY: I read Lawrence intensely when I was a younger man.

*Faas*: Of course, in general philosophical terms the resemblances seem obvious but when it comes . . .

CREELEY: . . . to the actual writing, there are two writers: Lawrence and Joyce. When I was a junior at high school about a year away from graduation, the *Dubliners* really hit me. That's perhaps the text of Joyce's that hit me most, that whole sense of the epiphany where there was a moment of incredibly inten-sive consciousness that flooded the whole context, that kind of focus, that really fascinated me, whereas I remember read-ing again and again and again *The Turn of the Screw*, and truly not getting anything out of it, I was very frustrated by it.

Joyce,
Lawrence and
Dostoyevsky

*Faas*: Also by James's theory of the novel?

CREELEY: Yes, I love James, I mean, but when it's used as a text for writing, it curiously leaves me cold. Whereas with Lawrence, it was the intense revelation, that highly charged situation of emotion created. What I most remember reading decisively of his work is *The Fox* and *The Captain's Doll*—the so-called novellas which I thought were extraordinary, and the short stories. I was also reading a lot of Dostoyevsky, the novels, the shorter novels and the short stories. All three of them, Dostoyevsky, Joyce and Lawrence, are, I think, writ-ers that use intensive emotion as revelation, moments of extraordi-nary intensity.

*Faas*: But your own style of writing is so different from theirs.

CREELEY: Oh yes, but then I read a lot of Williams' short stories, *Life along the Passaic River*.

*Faas*: Do you feel that he anticipated your actual prose style?

CREELEY: Well, in the forties, my stories were felt to be sketchy. Williams in turn would call my stories sketches, very interesting sketches. [Laughing]

stories without
a plot

*Faas*: So you must have taken it one point further than him.

CREELEY: Yes. I remember one time when one story was accepted for publication in the *Kenyon Review*, the editor John Crowe Ransom was really nonplussed by it. He said he didn't understand it, and he sent it to Robert Penn Warren. Anyhow, to make a long story short,

Robert Penn Warren's comment was that he found it without plot and he couldn't truly understand a story that didn't have a plot. He said that he was constitutionally in favor of plot, as he put it.

*Faas*: By hindsight all this seems so ludicrous, of course.

CREELEY: But then it was like being the awful kid at school who was doing something irrevocably wrong.

*Faas*: Even Cid Corman sometimes commented negatively on the short stories.

CREELEY: Although Cid without question was the person who found them good enough to publish. But he also was confused by them, I think.

*Faas*: You have commented negatively on the so-called Modernist treatment of time, on devices such as flashback, recall, juxtaposition, etc.

CREELEY: Yes, I think all that's very limited.

*Faas*: By contrast, you say that one should treat time and space as mere "qualifications" of the narrated events or, as you call it, "the things shifting among themselves." That term "qualifications" reminds me of Whitehead describing time and space as "cogredient or relative properties of events." Did you derive your own notion from him?

Whitehead and Heisenberg

CREELEY: I didn't get it from him. I finally bought a copy of *Process and Reality* about a week ago. [Both laughing] Yes, it seemed ridiculous not to, you know, have read it. But I had so much of that information from Olson and friends like Duncan. Personally, I never read texts of that kind decisively.

*Faas*: In "The Creative" you write that recently in Berlin you were delighted to discover that Heisenberg "has fallen upon the arts as though upon a blissful bed of flowers, *knowing*, in his age, as Gregory Corso would say, that the *conceptual* dilemma of the sciences leads them round and around the careful maze of their various *contexts*."

CREELEY: Yes, that's from Arakawa who was in residence at Höllerer's Literarisches Colloquium. Arakawa is a very interesting painter, a man using incredible situations of speech and linguistics, similar to the kind of things I'd like to say with images and words. He is fascinated by Heisenberg and said that Heisenberg, according to the men working with him, had come to believe that the assumptions in the sciences were disastrously romantic and that the formulations of the premises were so assumptive that the information derived from them was becoming more and more arbitrary.

*Faas*: In a way that has been his general trend of thought all the way.

CREELEY: Unhappily I never read him. The book of Arakawa's that I

really like is *Der Mechanismus der Meinung (The Mechanism of Opinion)*.
It's a very curious book, it's a continuous text and it doesn't have any
stated end in view.

*Faas*: I find the closest parallel to your short stories in Beckett.

CREELEY: I had the honor once of meeting Beckett and dug him
entirely. Thanks to John Calder who is a publisher in England, and
thanks really to Mrs. Bettina Calder. One day in London,
meeting Bettina said to me: later tonight John is going to see Sam
Beckett in Paris and they'll be talking a lot, so why don't you fly
over to Paris: he's going to meet him at the Café de Lille.
So bring a bottle of Irish whiskey and introduce yourself and I'm
sure things will go well. And so I went and we stayed talking from
about eleven at night till six in the morning. It was incredible!

*Faas*: Did he know your work?

CREELEY: Yes, he did, and he really liked it and I was enchanted. He
is an extraordinarily generous and humble man. The things he was
saying were so energized that I did what one does as a child when the
energy is so concentrated that all of a sudden you giggle or blurp,
sort of making aha. And he thought that I was, not mocking him, but
that I was laughing. And suddenly he said: you find that funny? And
I said: heavens no. But I was just so concentrated that I had to relieve
the tension. And he was describing or stating what he had as an
imagination of a word that would be entirely autonomous
the self- in its creation and existence. It was his dream to realize
created word one word that was absolutely self-created. And he said it's
about this big [indicating a height of about seven inches,
both laughing] and it has the situation of stone. And then later I was
reading in Jung or somebody about the phallic stone, and it was very
much the same. I don't know if Beckett was aware of Jung's image,
but it was very similar to it. Beckett literally said it was that high and
he wasn't being metaphoric. Somehow he had the imagination that
this word would physically take place.

*Faas*: Which of your works had he read?

CREELEY: My stories, I think, and possibly the novel. I know that
mainly through Bettina who's a close friend of his and I knew that *she*
had read them and talked to him about it.

*Faas*: What did you talk about with Beckett?

CREELEY: For a time John discussed the plays which had just been
put on in the Place de l'Odéon, which was mainly to make Beckett
relax enough so that he simply talked about senses of language and
the imagination of reality. He spoke in this very, not tentative way,
but at times there'd be pauses, he'd begin to say something and then
he'd sort of test it in his mind, then return to its continuance, say a

little more, check it out, you see. He spoke, not haltingly as though he were impeded in some physical way, but constantly checking what he was saying so that I had no idea what time it was. I mean I realized finally it was six in the morning, so the thing I most specifically remember is that extraordinary creation of a word that should have no other cause but itself.

*Faas*:  Did you know Beckett's work by the time you wrote your short stories?

CREELEY:  I first heard of him, I believe, through Alex Trocchi and a group of expatriates living in Paris in the early fifties, who ran this magazine called *Merlin*, which published Beckett's first French writing in English.

*Faas*:  That was in the early fifties. But you had already written some of your short stories by that time.

CREELEY:  Yes, I'd written a lot of them by 1954.      Beckett's

*Faas*:  I was just wondering if Beckett could have had any   influence direct influence on you.

CREELEY:  Not really. *Waiting for Godot* I reviewed in the *Black Mountain Review*. But by that time it was already sort of wide information. But I must have gotten a lot of equivalent information from the so-called Existentialists whom I certainly read. Now, I remember a story by Beckett that really blew my mind, called "The End." It's a story in which a man simply recedes, to where he is finally lying in a boat, in a boat-house. He has a whole contrivance of physical realities so that he manages to exist, and he defecates by shifting his body this way and that way a bit. He's a beggar and has this drop-board that permits the patron to give money without actually touching this awful person, so that he can beg but in no way offend the donor. It's kind of a classic Beckett trip. So I can't truly date when I first read his work but I remember that story vividly. And I wrote stories after that, but I'd already written quite a few before that.

*Faas*:  You had already written some before 1950.

CREELEY:  Right.

*Faas*:  When did you write the "3 Fate Tales"?

CREELEY:  I wrote those in New Hampshire, so that's previous to 1950.      "3 Fate Tales"

*Faas*:  They seem to me the most interesting and the most extreme, in a way.

CREELEY:  That comes out of a kind of wild blend of Dostoyevsky and Stendhal.

*Faas*:  Stendhal?

CREELEY:  I mean the way that Stendhal would substantiate some attitude in reality by giving you an instance of it.

*Faas*: While telling the story becomes its very subject.

CREELEY: Yes, exactly, which I really loved in his writing.

*Faas*: How about the influence of Existentialist writers?

CREELEY: My generation, the group of friends I had at college, grew up flooded with them. But I finally broke down trying to read Sartre's sequence of novels.

Existentialist writers

*Faas*: *Les chemins de la liberté.*

CREELEY: Yes, I got through one or maybe two, but I just got bored. Equally, *The Stranger* always irritated me. Years after I read it, Bert Almon, a student of mine who had done research on it, pointed out that the first draft of the novel was in the first person, was proposed as a personal narrative, and then Camus began to abstract and objectify it to the point where I felt that he kind of blew it. I mean I would have been very curious to have read it as a personal narrative. But then Ionesco was a great relief, I thought he was terrific.

*Faas*: Let me switch to Hart Crane. In 1954 you wrote: "We know, we know, we know, etc., that *The Bridge* was a 'failure'— though why, and how, we are not at all quite so sure of." This was obviously stated in reaction against the New Critics.

Hart Crane

CREELEY: And particularly the teachers of the forties that I had for instructors, who very smugly felt that the structure of *The Bridge* didn't arrive at any coherence. And demonstrably, I suppose, they are right: there isn't any great realization of a coherence finally in the poem. But I don't know. It's very hard for me to speak objectively about Crane, I was so moved by what he was trying to do. His incoherence to me is really attractive.

*Faas*: Crane once said that *The Bridge* might be published like *Leaves of Grass*, every new edition incorporating new additions. So at some point he did conceive of it as an open-ended poem.

CREELEY: I think that the people who were sympathetic to Whitman at that time were primarily sympathetic to him for "sociological or historical purview." They really weren't interested in the structure at all, and those who considered his structure were Williams and Pound. Williams thought it was too amorphous, and Pound, I think, intuited that it was really useful, this sense of an expanding center, and really recognized that Whitman was one of the basic keys to the possibilities of the long poem. Williams was funny, he shifted back and forth on the subject of Whitman. At one point he is calling him America's greatest poet, at another point he's saying that he is too blowzy. I

Whitman

think Williams tacitly is also responding to his homosexuality. Williams was very Puritanical, I mean, he was a very double man. I don't know if he is a Gemini, but he sure feels like one. He led this crazy diversity of lives.

*Faas*: Would you say that *The Bridge* fails mainly because Crane tried to fit it into some alien concept of unity?

CREELEY: Well, it doesn't fail. I had the experience of teaching it, like they say, last spring, sort of leading these tender students into this incredible chaos. What's—what does this mean? It's like walking through the sky or something. What are all these clouds doing here? [Laughing] And then we'd refer to Crane's sense of his purpose, you know, either his plan for Otto Kahn or some such text, and, you know, forget it. Yes, I think, had he let it move on impulse and trusted that impulse, he would have had an extraordinary thing, instead of trying to fit it into a pattern. In fact, Williams rather comes across in the same way, with his concept of the order of *Paterson* in four books.

*Faas*: But he finally broke through that, didn't he?

CREELEY: Yes, with *Paterson V*.

*Faas*: Which Crane never did. Of course, that was much later, so Williams had a much better chance, with the model of the *Cantos*.

CREELEY: No, Crane really had a bleak life.

*Faas*: At one point Robert Bly accused Olson and the Black Mountain School of a positivist Objectivism which tries to evade the human psyche.

CREELEY: I don't think he'd say that today. It's akin to Gregory Corso calling me an intellectual gangster. [Laughing] I suppose, that was probably because of Charles' kind of intensive razzle-dazzle vocabulary. It must have been intimidating if you a) don't understand what he is talking about and b) see what the authorities implicit were. Again Bob Bly's sense that a whole spectrum of European literature was being ignored was a little in error, simply that for various reasons a number of us had read that writing pretty widely. As a younger man I had, happily, Rainer Gerhardt as a friend and he made me aware of many European poets, in particular Trakl.

*Faas*: Do you like Trakl's work?

CREELEY: I was very moved by it, he is really haunting. There must be innumerable translations of "Grodek" but I never saw one that really got it.

*Faas*: The other poet whose criticism of Olson has always puzzled me is Gary Snyder.

CREELEY: I think Gary, being a Buddhist, has the usual Westerner's distrust of the Easterner, and he is also fearful of a situation which is continuous in the European tradition, or Western world in that sense. Gary is an extraordinary intellectual actually, but he has a lot of distrust of head-trips, and Charles is a fantastic head-tripper. I remember talking to Joanne Kyger about it, who had been married to Gary for a time, and she felt that Gary literally never understood Olson. So there was some of that resentment and confusion with the texts. I think he just hasn't really centered on it.

*Faas*: The same I think is true of Robert Bly.

CREELEY: Yes. I don't think it has been a key situation for their own interests.

*Faas*: But I think there is some truth to Bly's contention that Objectism to some degree evades the psyche.

CREELEY: What Olson is trying to do is break a condition which is possibly much more disastrous the closer you are to the European tradition, not sentimentally, but growing up, you know, on the East Coast. Neither Bly nor Snyder really have the onus of Eastern intellectual European thirties, forties kind of thinking. And what Olson is, I think, most involved in doing is trying to find an alternative to the heavy humanist tradition. I mean, it's all very well to speak of the human psyche and its value to human experience, but Olson was trying to work, not just towards an attitude, but towards an experience of humanness that would be as explicit, say, as any other physical event in the world. Going back to Whitehead, he is trying to "clear out the gunk," as Olson says, that gave the psyche that peculiar "soulful" state—the "center of the sinful earth," etc.

*Faas*: I recall that in 1951 you had a controversy with Olson about Objectism versus, what you termed, "the *subjective* in a more basic character."

CREELEY: Olson's Objectism, that's the way he puts it in the "Projective Verse" piece, means to be as clean, to be as specific, or to be as actual, as actualized, not as realized, but as actualized, to be as substantively the case, to be as "firm as fish is," as he says in one of the *Maximus Poems*: that the poem should be as firm as fish, like a physical event, as actual as that, not metaphorically but substantively it should be an issue of a physical condition—that true.

*Faas*: So in other words you gave in to his position?

CREELEY: Not entirely. I was really charmed, at the University of Connecticut last weekend, seeing Charles Olson's literary executor and George Butterick, who both told me variously that Charles was at times intimidated by me. I was so intimidated by him that it never occurred to me he was having anything of the like feeling. And they said that the letters would really reflect that.

*Faas*: But don't you feel that your creative impulse does essentially derive from the unconscious?

CREELEY: Sure, I mean, I couldn't think where else it should come from. As a writer I am possibly the one among my own friends and immediate companions, like it or not, who uses books least. I can't work from books, I paradoxically can't work from literature except through absorption in some very obvious and simple ways.

*creativity and the unconscious*

*Faas*: Yet you have few Surrealistic, dreamlike or hallucinatory images in your poetry.

CREELEY: What's interesting to me is the inability to rewrite. That has fascinated me all my life, that I basically can't rewrite so I'm stuck with what I first get. And that I don't really have much design or determination except that I attempt, when I'm writing, to let it be as accurate as possible. I mean I have very little predetermination as to what literally is going to get said. I used to feel kind of glib, saying, like, I wrote "off the top of my head" or on impulse. It sounds a little jazzy and presumptuous. But it has been so specifically the case over the years that now it just is the case. And writing a novel, for example, I had some sense of the area of experience and the factual events otherwise that I wanted to discuss, wanted to bring in as material, in some very vague sense of, not plot, but sequence of events, that I found I might involve. But other than that what I used as a context was the number of chapters. *That's* the plot. And I do the same thing in a text that's to be published by Scribner: a collaboration between myself and the sculptor Marisol, a number of images of her work, reproductions of her sculptures interweaving with a sequence of prose pieces. And that at moments becomes markedly surreal. Duncan, thank God, is very impressed by the Marisol text, because I really use him as a close reader. I think he is the closest reader I have.

*Faas*: In a letter, published in *Origin* (1953-4), Duncan makes a statement concerning his "entirely differentness" from Charles Olson, defining poetry as "a revelation of language not personality." Similarly you have often stated that you are "frankly and selfishly interested in words," that writing to you is "primarily the experience of language" and that you believe in poetry "determined by the language of which it is made." Yet there seems to be a crucial difference between Duncan's concept of language and your own. When Duncan says "I follow the word," "the word takes over" or "the word for me is the living flesh"

*concept of language*

he really speaks of language in a deeply neo-Platonic and Orphic sense.

CREELEY: Yes.

*Faas*: Or he calls poetry the ground on which we participate in the "cosmic language." Do you share any of these notions?

CREELEY: I don't feel as comfortable with them. I feel awkward with that terminology. I would feel closer to Wittgenstein's "words are all acts," that the structure of words that one composes, that one comes to compose, constitute reification rather than revelation, and reification of some specific situation of the human. I mean they bring news of that order. That's why I said, selfishly: my writing constitutes a revelation of myself to myself in ways that I find otherwise very awkward to attain.

*Faas*: And yet all that is at the center of Duncan's poetics.

CREELEY: Yes, he's got this incredible "cosmic consciousness." Probably it was the West, those very vast sunsets and so on. I mean Duncan can move in the largesse of that Romantic temper.

Duncan's largesse

*Faas*: Yes, it's deeply Romantic.

CREELEY: He is like Victor Hugo in that respect. I remember Olson saying towards the end of his life that Duncan has become, not the Man of Letters, but the Master, that he had really become possessed of that power, and that it was extraordinary. I've always felt that Duncan's ability to realize an incredible compass of reality was frankly more expansive than Charles'. I don't know, it's hard for me to judge. Charles' insights, in their depth of perception, are to me extraordinary. Robert's are really more like exfoliating this extraordinary *extending* world, like Whitman's.

*Faas*: So when *you* talk of language as something which reveals itself or unfolds in the process of creation you mean it in a sense closer to Wittgenstein.

CREELEY: Yes. You know that extraordinary piece of Wittgenstein's, I've got it here, it's a recollection of a lecture on ethics and religion, and at the end of it he makes a statement that's just dazzling, which I believe so deeply, he says:

> Now I am tempted to say that the right expression in language
> for the miracle of the existence of the world, though it is not
> any proposition *in* language, is the existence of language itself.
> But what then does it mean to be aware of this miracle at some
> times and not at other times? For all I have said by shifting the
> expression of the miraculous from an expression *by means of*
> language to the expression *by the existence* of language, all I

have said is again that we cannot express what we want to express and that *all we say* about the absolute miraculous remains nonsense. Now the answer to all this will seem perfectly clear to many of you . . .

And then at the end he says:

that is to say: I see now that these nonsensical expressions were not nonsensical because I have not yet found the correct expressions, but that their nonsensicality was their very essence. For all I wanted to do with them was just *to go beyond* the world and that is to say *beyond* significant language. My whole tendency and I believe the tendency of all men who ever tried to write or talk Ethics or Religion was to run against the boundaries of language. This running against the walls of our cage is perfectly, absolutely hopeless.

[Laughing]

*Faas*: And it is so nice to see that Wittgenstein was kind of a mystic.

CREELEY: Right. I remember the first time I read that, I had taken some acid, and I read that thing hour after hour and it just glowed.

*Faas*: Have you known Wittgenstein's works for a long time?

CREELEY: The person who turned me on to him was Zukofsky: "a point in space is a place for an argument."

*Faas*: When was that?

CREELEY: Fairly early, in the fifties. I don't read Wittgenstein in any heavy didactic sense, though.

*Faas*: You mean, you read him for pleasure.

CREELEY: Yes. [Fetching a book] That's the most recent I read, *Zettel*. Look at this one!

*Faas:*    Looks like a *maṇḍala*.

CREELEY: Yes, it's very much like Jasper Johns. You see this pattern over here. [Pointing to a grouping of numbers on a piece of paper stuck on the kitchen wall] These are figures that come of numbers being written on top of one another. I really like that. I am fascinated by the experience one has of words saying things. I realize as I get older that one's experience of that activity is increasingly subjective. Especially in the relation with Bobbie, for example. We have lived so long together that the assumption as to what the other means becomes so didactic. It's almost impossible for us not to hear what we hear in our own heads if the other says something.

*Faas*: Being aware of the language as language.

CREELEY: Yes.

*Faas*: Rather than as meaning.

CREELEY: Yes, right, [laughing] we leap entirely to the quote, to the words.

Faas: Ted Hughes makes an interesting statement to that effect saying that conversations between people to a large extent are like the twittering of birds, and the liking one develops for another person's talk usually depends on certain rhythmic and melodic structures rather than on the content and meaning of what is being said.

CREELEY: Yes, again the evening with Beckett was so delightful because of listening to him *physically* talking. It was only a few, you know, very intensive things said otherwise that I really remembered.

Faas: Let's move on to a related question. At one point you say "I feel poetry as a complex of sounds and rhythms, which move in a parallel to music." What exactly is your position on that?

poetry
and music

CREELEY: I suppose it's something like Schwitters', where there was a strong intent to have poetry be a pure structure of sounds and rhythms. Like he really got bugged when some Czech told him that he'd used the Czech word for bread, he really hated that somebody should say, you have a word there or sound that means something apart from its physical event. But then it's linked up with the whole question of semantic meaning. It can't be gainsaid, I mean, that music does not have that situation to pay attention to. I hate programmatic music, music that sounds like something.

Faas: Late nineteenth century music.

CREELEY: Yes, and the kind of blowzy trip of the 1950's, Prokofiev and so forth. That just bored me out of my head, or that kind of interpretation music, you know, some kind of groaning voice telling you you hear the wind through the forest.

Faas: So, analogously you want pure language?

CREELEY: Yes, not even "pure" language, but language that never forgets that it is language.

Faas: Is there any modern music which you feel moves in directions you follow in your poetry?

serial order
in psychology

CREELEY: Well, sure, Cage is fascinating to me, for example. I've been fascinated by re-qualifications of senses of "serial order." I was reading a text called *The Psychology of Communication*, by George A. Miller. For example, the human situation has difficulty regaining the context if there is something interpolated, like; "That man, whom you saw yesterday, is my father." "That man is my father" is the basic statement—"whom you saw yesterday," is the element that's being inserted. This is also applicable to computer structure. If you keep putting in statements into the basic statement, after about three or four such insertions, the hearer or witness gets very, very confused. The human attention apparently is not recursive and tends to be always where it is, so the more there is interpolated in that fashion the more difficult it is for the human to regain locus. And Miller points out that we can usually pick up where we left off in a simply physical context. Painting a fence, for instance, we know where we stopped because there is the new paint, physically it is. Poetry obviously is a way to regain a situation in the recursive that is to remind us where we are constantly by a structure. Now I am    Cage fascinated by what happens when we aren't so reminded, when we break and move into different patterns to locate the experience of being somewhere, and that's what I find extraordinary with Cage: the attempt to requalify the experience of serial order, which to me is really crucial.

*Faas*: Could you give me an example of something analogous in poetry?

CREELEY:  Say, you write a poem about "a day at the beach" or a poem in a certain meter, or a poem having rhymes of this or that order. All of these elements could be variously used to locate the reader, to give him a reassurance that he knows where he is. If he can't understand what's happening in the third verse, then the very structure of the fourth verse relocates him and lets him continue. Williams towards the end of his life was fascinated by what he called measure, because the nature of experience apparently began to alter, senses of location in life began to yield, began to give up the sense of overall purpose, became increasingly secular. What does it all mean? That's the kind of crisis that occurred in the forties with the Existentialists, just one long individual intelligence trying to find a place in a world that seemingly has no recognition and no response. I am fascinated by how one thing can follow another, and how diverse that pattern can be. Bill Eastlake is a very pleasant friend and novelist and in one of his books this Navaho lady is saying that she knows the TV story is over when she sees the lady hand another the box of soap. That's the end of the story. It's like: *and so they all went home* or something.

*Faas*: Or your four pages.

CREELEY:  Yes, exactly. I am fascinated by what can be used as a mode of coherence in that way.    coherence

*Faas*: But it is coherence after all.

CREELEY:  Yes, because without that coherence it's like Williams' contention that it all simply spills on the page without a particular condition.

*Faas*: But it's a totally arbitrary containment.

CREELEY: Yes, but it still is a containment. And Cage to me was its most clear exponent.

*Faas*: At the moment he seems to move in a kind of weird paradise of mathematical abstractions, a profoundly happy man; I met him in New York the other day, such an impressively gentle man in the best sense.

CREELEY: Isn't he? That's a picture of him over there. [Showing Cage picking mushrooms]

*Faas*: Yes, that's exactly like him.

CREELEY: I really dig him. He's an extremely sweet man.

*Faas*: There is one statement of yours which has always puzzled me, namely that the follow-up of abstract expressionism is to be found in the "antithetically disciplined formalism of Frank Stella and those akin to him, as Neil Williams and Larry Poons."

CREELEY: That probably comes of my friendship with Neil Williams and to some extent with Larry Poons. I suppose what I was saying was that those artists who most saw the experience of abstract expressionism, its completions or its successes, minimal art tended therefore to move towards alternatives, instead of continuing its situation, instead of making it a tradition, moved on from its containments to areas that hadn't actually been used. Neil, for example, pointed out to me that Frank Stella had really moved away from Robert Motherwell, in particular from the kind of anthropomorphic shapes that Motherwell had used. I don't really know anything about Neil's own really early paintings.

*Faas*: Werner Haftmann talks of an "active creation of 'nothing-ness' " in artists like Mondrian, and I think the same would apply to painters like Stella.

CREELEY: I don't think that's quite true.

*Faas*: Frank Stella, of course, doesn't agree with it either. But you have said yourself that a painting of Stella "is not a reference to another reality . . . but remains unequivocally its own occasion." So you would grant that he tries to obliterate referential reality.

CREELEY: That's for sure. The thing in Stella I was fascinated by was the paintings of the middle sixties which would influence reality with extraordinary impact. He worked with these shaped canvases just using line grids and it changed scale entirely around it, so that people walking by would be getting constantly smaller and larger.

*Faas*: And then his non-referential use of paint.

CREELEY: Yes, wanting it to be the thing in itself.

*Faas*: Like you with language.

CREELEY: Or like Williams, for example. The heteroclite and the diverse and the specifically common. That's particularly interesting to me, especially in Chamberlain.

*Faas*: I'm not too familiar with Arakawa's work and I wondered what you meant by "*zero* set," "the real nitty gritty for any head-trip," in talking about him.

CREELEY:  Let me get that book I talked about previously. [Fetches book] *The Psychology of Communication* by George A. Miller. He's speaking about grammar situations [reads]: "Our college students seemed unable to reinvent the concept of zero . . . In [the] linguistic context, it simply did not occur to most people to use the perfectly familiar concept of zero in order to simplify their classification scheme . . . In a numerical context they thought of zero, but in a linguistic context they did not." That was the point that really got to me. "*Zero* set" is really a fascinating place to be. [Both laughing] It's like the ultimate imagination. I don't know what "*zero* set" is obviously, but as I understand it, it would be the concept of something that neither is nor is not. It wouldn't be less than and obviously it wouldn't be either more or less. It would be nothing. Zero.

*Faas*:  Not unlike Sanskrit *śūnyatā*, I guess, "the void of inexhaustible contents," as D. T. Suzuki paraphrased it.

CREELEY:  Yes, how you could state that which by being is not, you know, that which by being is not is not by being. A curious paradox. And Arakawa was talking to me about "*zero* set."

*Faas*:  What particular work of his are you referring to?

CREELEY:  I'm referring to this book *Mechanismus der Meinung*. I wish the hell I had it here.

*Faas*:  But all that is exactly what, using Haftmann's terms, I mean by "active creation of 'nothingness.' "

CREELEY:  Yes, trying to realize something that doesn't have, that isn't more or less, or isn't something added or something subtracted. The invention of zero was the greatest step forward in the history of mathematics. Zero is a fantastic concept.

*Faas*:  All throughout your earlier poetry I find a yearning for destruction not only of outward reality but also of yourself, a striving for

> some time beyond place, or
> place beyond time, no
> mind left to

*Marginal notes:* Arakawa's "*zero* set" · *śūnyatā*

say anything at all,
that face gone, now.

At some point you say that in your creative efforts you are working
"towards a final obliteration" of yourself. I feel the poem,
self-         you write, "with the intensity of all the perception that I
reduction    . . . that the ego bit can recognize, and then destroy the
ego by its own insistence." Is that kind of experience a
pleasurable or an anguished one?

CREELEY: I have some insistent pattern in my own nature that makes
me extremely restless and, not so much bored, but just that the
moment something becomes familiar to me, known to me and relax-
ing to me, I simply tend to reject it, I don't know why. It just really is
insistently the case. Presently I almost feel a delight in that way. For
example, I was in New York last weekend in the company of a friend
I have there, a girl I really enjoy and like to be with, and we were at a
club, I mean a place that frankly isn't literally my kind of interest nor
is it suitable to my age, so to speak, to be there. But there I was
nonetheless and at one point I realized that she was splitting with this
other fellow and I thought, wow, that's really heavy. So she says, I'll
call you tomorrow or something. [Both laughing] In the meantime
I'm stoned out of my head in this mad place, the Club 800 which is an
old time apparently transvestite bar that's now a rock and roll scene.
It's about 5 o'clock in the morning and the vibes are up to 80,000
whatever, two, three hundred people dancing like mad in this place.
And I don't know where the hell I've got to. But again on some kind
of weird persistent intuition I find my coat, I hit the street and it's
raining, a kind of nice gentle spring rain and I feel like wow, isn't the
world sweet, and I think: What in the name of heaven makes me so
pleased? It's as though I'm stepping out onto the earth again, not
sentimentally but it's all beginning again. And somehow the kinds of
                    anticipation, the responsibility, not responsibility, but the
That's all          kinds of assumption and argument, and the plot, let's say,
fallen apart,       it's broken again, thank God. I love the excitement of
what's next?        something like: here it is, that's all fallen apart, what's
next?

Faas: It seems similar to the kind of experience I have had in the
past of somehow getting drunk, until you finally don't quite realize
any more where you are going and where you are, and then wake up
next morning: and here are walls, furniture, curtains, a window you
have never seen before, and it makes you laugh.

CREELEY: I love it.

Faas: And of course one goes around deliberately looking for these
experiences.

CREELEY: Once as a kid in New York I was like in some boredom and loneliness. I saw these five guys get into a car and just got in line with them and got into the car with them, and thankfully they didn't turn out to be offended. I mean that would be characteristic.

*Faas:* But in those quotes I read to you, you were saying something very specific about the act of poetic creativity as being an obliterating of your ego.

CREELEY: Yes, like turn the ego into material. So again with a bad relationship like last weekend, the ego was instantly offended like: how dare you leave me? But then the situation became so immediately more interesting to me, and now I was a far more real person to myself than I had been even moments before, you know. It's like I was back in business, whereas even moments before I knew all too well where I was: I was an older man with a younger woman, in that kind of old time familiar place.

*Faas:* So the act of creativity would be breaking away from the old familiar ego.

CREELEY: Yes, so that all the condition of the material has to reveal itself, has to pertain, because there can't be any assumption. Finally, that evening, I was very stoned and I couldn't find my way to where I stayed, so finally I asked a bum who walked me all across the city, and it was terrific. [Laughing] I mean I felt that this was a weird and unexpected blessing that other kinds of containment would sadly never be able to stop for. I don't mean to be sentimental about it but I mean the world breaks open in a beautiful way when there can't any longer be assumptions about it.

*Faas:* And writing a poem somehow helps you experience the same thing.

CREELEY: Yes, somehow.

*Faas:* So it's really a kind of self-transcendence.

CREELEY: Well, whatever, self-revelation more than self-transcendence.

*Faas:* You describe that experience in "Figures." Who was the artist in that poem?

CREELEY: A really moving New Mexican, sadly but lovely drunken sculptor named Patrocinio Barela, and he lived in Taos and used to peddle these little santos figures. He'd peddle them mainly for drink, and he finally burnt to death. There are pictures of his work in the *Black Mountain Review*.

*Faas:* The sense I got from that poem is that these figures gave you the same feeling of self-obliteration and quiet.

CREELEY: Right.                                              Mallarmé

*Faas:* There is a poem of yours entitled "After Mallarmé."

CREELEY:  It turns out it's Jouve. [Both laughing] Somebody told me he couldn't find that poem in Mallarmé, and it's actually a poem by Jouve, and it was quoted to me by Philip Guston.

*Faas*:  Really! Nonetheless, there are striking resemblances between you and Mallarmé.

CREELEY:  I have read Mallarmé, but only in a very kind of scattered way.

*Faas*:  Have you read his letters?

CREELEY:  No.

*Faas*:  It's just a few I am referring to, from around 1866, describing his mystical insights into nothingness.

CREELEY:  Rexroth once referred to me as the corn-fed Mallarmé. [Both laughing] It's kind of sneering but still.

*Faas*:  Charles Altieri has argued that "at the center of [your] experience is the continual threat of the void" stemming from your "sense of isolation, of being cut off from all roots or grounds—in concrete experience, in tradition, and in [your] relationships with other people."

CREELEY:  I think he is unwittingly a little sentimental, I think he is overstating it.

the void

*Faas*:  And interpreting you too much in humanistic terms.

CREELEY:  Yes, the void can be at moments like the whole of creation or something in an almost punning sense, you know. When younger I felt probably fearful that everyone was going to go away through the fact of being a kid whose father died young, and various other realities thus, losing an eye and whatnot, having very few people as family to relate to and feeling awkward in the social milieu.

*Faas*:  When did you lose your eye?

CREELEY:  When I was two, and my father died when I was four, and then our social habits changed because of losing him. But I don't find myself presently particularly threatened by the void. A poem like "The Hole" is curiously positive.

*Faas:*  You also talk of "The poem supreme, addressed to/ emptiness."

CREELEY:  Yes, I don't think it was an awful word.

*Faas*:  I have the impression, perhaps equally overstated, that the void, instead of constituting a threat, represents some kind of *fascinosum* to you, something compellingly attractive almost, in an Eastern or mystical sense.

CREELEY:  I was really struck when I read that sequence of poems called *Numbers* in Texas a few years ago and there was an

*Numbers*

Indian novelist that New Directions publishes, I think his

last name is Lal, and he came round afterwards and told and Buddhist
me charmingly that that sequence of poems— theosophy
particularly "Nothing," the zero poem—were fantastic, realizations
of Indian, you know, Buddhist theosophy, I guess he'd call it. And
really dug it. The delight in zero.
*Faas*: Why then did you inveigh against that "goddamn Zen"?
CREELEY: That's the Zennies. You know, I'm teaching
here, and I've just got a large cluster of papers, and one or the "goddamn
rather several of the students are really and understand- Zen"
ably washed away with contemporary, generalized
Buddhist thought, and they are very boring. It has nothing to do
with friends like Gary who have made it a very distinct part of their
own condition.
*Faas*: Gary to me has this almost frightening kind of sanity and
balance which doesn't seem to leave much loophole for the ordinary
neurotic.
CREELEY: Oh he's not that sane, really, he's very healthy, so things
that would occur in a patterning of the neurotic for others of us or
me, for example, would occur in Gary in a completely uninvolved
straightforward condition of health. When he was here, I suddenly
realized that I've lived here for six years, and one of the students
comes back and I sleep with her. And then I get all these neurotic
echoes of it in my own head: like what have I betrayed—X, Y or Z
[both laughing], what's happening? Gary has really worked to rid
himself of all that.
*Faas*: I must admit that I tend to feel more like you, too.
CREELEY: Of course, I am at times obviously hooked on the tensions
and energies I get from irreconciliations, so to speak, and
I am obviously much more attached to the tensions than Snyder
he is, he doesn't like them at all.
*Faas*: Have you known him for a long time?
CREELEY: I've known him since '56.
*Faas*: Has he always been like that?
CREELEY: When I first met him he was a markedly shy fellow.
*Faas*: The way Kerouac describes him in the *Dharma Bums*.
CREELEY: Never pompous, never careful particularly, but serious.
He was more tender and more serious than others were, in a very
deliberate sense. Then I didn't see him for a long time, when he was
in Japan and when he and Joanne were married. And then the next
time I saw him at all was when Don Allen and he came up to stay with
us in New Mexico, when he and Joanne had just broken up, and that
was a heavy time in his life, that really hurt him and confused him,
1965. He didn't really know what happened. It was like a sadly

incongruous marriage, although both of them were extraordinary. But Joanne has a level of nervous energy which just frustrates Gary. And Masa, his present wife, has a crazy wry particular humor. We had a lovely conversation with her, where she is describing to Bobbie all of Gary's twelve pairs of shoes which he has for every condition of weather and terrain [both laughing] and she is like kind of wryly describing all these shoes with Gary sitting next to her. At first it was almost flattering, but then it got obviously pretty ironic.

*Faas:* What most impressed me when he came to New York was the complete ease with which he conducted himself in front of a huge audience.

CREELEY: He feels very at peace in the world. His reading here was of the same order, and the one impression which everybody seems to have literally taken away was this sense of an extraordinary peacefulness. It wasn't that he told them to be that, but they really felt completely relaxed and well used.

*Faas:* Duncan seems to share some of your impatience with Westernized Zen. When I talked to him in 1973 he called

Duncan and
Snyder

Snyder some kind of Prussian officer—said in a joking way, of course, but still . . .

CREELEY: And it's Duncan that Gary is paying homage to. [Laughing] Robert loves all the double-edged, the double-faceted, the double-faced, he sees as I see "the underside turning" and the double nature of reality, due to the condition of his eyes etc., etc. And there is something about the will to purity that really bores him. Robert's life has been incredibly intensive and diverse and I think both of us in various ways at first had difficulty, I know I did, hearing the rhythmic structure of Gary's writing. He has moved very much from Rexroth, and I missed the sensual texture, I missed an experiential kind of intensity, I felt that its physical skill was very interesting but . . .

*Faas:* What do you mean by experiential intensity?

CREELEY: In contrast, say, to Allen. To me Allen was terrific, just that he moves so directly to the personal center of his own reality whereas Gary would tend to always be at some distance, I wouldn't really know who Gary was at all. But then his later poems would have some beautiful sensual texture, like "Wash in the Sun."

*Faas:* Or "The Bath."

CREELEY: But it's still a curious objectifying of the body state.

*Faas:* I sometimes feel its simplicity may be just beyond my understanding.

CREELEY: His health seems to speak for him at this point. It would really need some weirdly perverted or distorted sense that would want to question where he is at.

*Faas*: I told Snyder: I find it very difficult to write about you because there are no problems.

CREELEY: Right. Yet it seems that his early life was anything but easy. Something seems to have really freaked him as a younger man, possibly the relationship with his mother.

*Faas*: So your insight into emptiness or what the Indian novelist called your "realizations of Buddhist theosophy" are a direct outgrowth of your own individual development?

CREELEY: Yes.

*Faas*: No direct influence of Buddhism itself?

no direct
Buddhist
influence

CREELEY: No, not really. Like Lawrence Ferlinghetti really spent so much of his life on the West Coast, and last summer we were down at his place in Big Sur and he was saying that despite his long friendships with many people who are decisively involved with Buddhism—Gary, for instance—his own sort of American East Coast upbringing made him, not wary of it, but it wasn't where the center of his own experience seemed to find its place. In a like sense I would just feel that I am very interested in it, much like Thoreau or someone like that, but the reification of that experience would occur to me in a very different vocabulary, that's all.

*Faas*: In 1961 you said that Gary Snyder's work presented "a successful relation of hope."

CREELEY: Gary has an incredibly strong will, resourceful, extremely, yes, not serious in a heavy sense, when younger it did seem so, he just eschewed the whole anxiety head trip which was so familiar in the East. This part of the country uses it so much, you know, as an energy turn on.

*Faas*: And you think he eschewed all that.

CREELEY: Or he worked through it. That long long time in Buddhism must have had a lot to do with it. At least my understanding is that Zen is a formal practise to break that kind of consciousness among other things.

*Faas*: Let's turn to your more recent development. I got the impression that sometime in the '60's your work and your sense of yourself underwent a profound change.

CREELEY: Yes.

*Faas*: I'll briefly mention some of the things I noticed. A couple of years ago you said that all you had recently tried to achieve was a kind of writing "that simply says: the road is going this way down the hill and there are trees here," and that you were now simply trying to make a statement

development
since the
sixties

"of what seems to be physically actual" in a specific place, which obviously is the opposite of your earlier poetry where you are trying to say . . .

CREELEY: . . . what I feel . . .

*Faas*: . . . and also trying to write "the poem supreme, addressed to / emptiness."

CREELEY: Right.

*Faas*: I wonder how this change occurred.

CREELEY: We'd moved here in the middle sixties. Almost always my changes have to do with relationships or with people, and mainly with Bobbie. Also, in a book like *Words* I began trying to think of ways in which I could break habits of writing and composition. Using long hand instead of typing, even something as simple as that, had a profound effect. And then I think the key book is *Pieces*, that really is where the decisive change occurs, where the concept of poems as set instances of articulate statement yields to a sense of continuity. I was fascinated by my friends' ability to continue, and I realized that I didn't have a thematic proposal for that situation. I'd written a novel but that seemed to me something else and I'd seen Duncan work with *Passages* and Allen with various texts of his, or Olson's *Maximus Poems* or Zukofsky's *A* or whatnot, and I wondered what kind of modality would really give me something that could also in a sense continue as a situation of writing, that wouldn't each time contain itself in a singular statement, so I'd really just write it as a common audit of days.

*Pieces the decisive step*

*Faas*: But doesn't this new concern with reality and things contradict what you said about your autotelic use of language?

CREELEY: Yes, it's like easing oneself down into the physical world.

*Faas*: To me it almost seems like the poetry written by a man who has been blinded by a glaring vision of nothingness and now comes stumbling back into reality.

CREELEY: Yes, and starts to see that there are real things here. In the sixties there also was that extraordinary experience of acid for the first time, and that had a large impact on ego-structures. I mean that doesn't *solve* the question, for the previous habit structures are very, very tenacious and recur soon afterwards. But in any case it stays as true information. So I was trying to think of ways in which the statement could include the diversity and variousness of experience rather than always choosing these moments of intensive crisis which tend to be singularizing and thus contained.

*taking acid*

*Faas*: So there is a whole new sense of the real which seems to go hand in hand with a new sense of language.

CREELEY: Yes.

*Faas*:  Ginsberg recently told me that your poem "Oh No" provided him with an illustration of his new concept of space which he developed under the influence of Chögyam Trungpa. You know the poem I mean:

> If you wander far enough                    "Oh No"
> you will come to it
> and when you get there
> they will give you a place to sit·
>
> for yourself only, in a nice chair,
> and all your friends will be there
> with smiles on their faces
> and they will likewise all have places.

CREELEY:  Oh no! That's kind of ironic, the poem itself is meant as a kind of awful irony.

*Faas*:  Isn't it! [Both laughing]

CREELEY:  It's like Wittgenstein's "A point in space is a place for an argument." How one can transform it into beatitude, terrific! It's like the pie in the sky, forget it. That's funny. [Laughing]

*Faas*:  Was it at the time of the Vancouver poetry conference in 1963 that these changes in your development came to a fulfillment?

CREELEY:  It was rather the beginning of it. In fact, it was Allen who said to me one night: You don't really have to     Ginsberg's
worry about writing a good poem any more, you can write     advice
what you want to. We talked of modes of composition and
how constricted I felt by how I had developed as a writer, and we
really went into that, that's the text of "Contexts of Poetry." I had
recognized increasingly how modalities of saying things had become
ends in themselves, and their use otherwise was getting more and
more impeded. So I was trying to think of ways to break out, and
partly it was thinking of other modes of transcription which would
change the experience literally. And then shifts in senses of what the
occasion, I suppose, of the writing really was. Like I
respect Galway Kinnell and like him as a person, and yet     Galway
feel some distance from his writing, not criticism in some     Kinnell
awful sense, but I really don't turn on to the way he writes,
and I keep on wondering why. And perhaps what happens is that in
his writing there is such an intensive signal of its occasion, there is
such an insistent program, that I'm really bored.

*Faas*:  Yes, he so loads his poetry with all kinds of poetic, symbolic or allusive imagery, that in the final analysis it all seems a little tenuous, paradoxically.

CREELEY:  Yes, he overworks it in a funny way. And so whatever could be called the impulse is curiously smothered, and the program of the purpose overrides the actual writing. So he is like a very skilled workman, like putting all this stuff on.

Faas:  So your own development involved a getting away from this notion of poetic creativity as a conscious craft.

CREELEY:  Yes. The real breakthrough begins just about the end of *Words*, and then it really is manifest with *Pieces*. That's the key book for me. In some ways I tried to continue the information of that into *A Day Book*. But I tend increasingly to believe like Duncan that the formal situation of *A Day Book* is possibly too arbitrary and that the conjoinment of prose and poems in that book doesn't really mesh in the way that I'd hoped it might. It really is too hard, and the congruence of one to the other is not particularly informative. So I really ought to do what Duncan reminds me I should do anyhow: put together three prose situations of thirty pages each as a cluster, a new version of the three tales, like Flaubert's, which has been weightily in mind for years. I have been fascinated by that sense of three tales like "3 Fate Tales." That sense of the three is really insistent.

Faas:  Personally, I can't quite understand your fascination with numbers.

fascination with numbers

CREELEY:  I can't really tell you why that's the case, it's not in some symbolic sense. When I was a kid preparing to go to college my rating in some mathematical skills was way above everything else. I love patternings that can be situated in numbers. I don't have any sophisticated information in numbers but I'm fascinated by conditions in which numbers can be used either to demonstrate or to describe.

Faas:  Your more recent poetry also shows a marked impatience with imagery and in particular with "the damn function of simile, always a displacement of what *is* happening." By contrast there are a lot of similes in your earlier poetry which almost reads like John Donne's very often.

imagery

CREELEY:  Yes? He was a heavy influence, of course, at one point.

Faas:  Of course, Donne's conceits and similes, although they are cryptic, always contain a solution, whereas your early poetry offers the same kind of riddles, but without solutions.

CREELEY:  Yes. Contemporary. [Both laughing]

Faas:  So Donne was a direct influence?

CREELEY:  He and the whole cluster of poets of his period. Wyatt, Herrick, although they are much different, no not so much Marvell, but Vaughan, and, oh God, Crashaw, I was trying to remember the edition of metaphysical poets, edited by Saintsbury?

*Faas*: Grierson?

CREELEY: Yes, Grierson. That was really a heavy book for me.

*Faas*: There is a final point concerning your more recent development. Up to some time ago you conceived of your poetry as of an
uncommunicative way of "telling something to yourself."

CREELEY: Yes. Now I just write it because I enjoy writing it. I don't
think I have any greater sense of purpose, except in those instances
where there is a kind of very shy or minimal commission or sense of
occasion, like for a birthday, yes. Right now I'm working on prose.

*Faas*: *Mabel*?

CREELEY: Yes. I'm off poetry for a bit, not in the sense that I don't
like it or something, but at the moment I'm just too
emotionally hung up. I mean I'm not Gary and I'm just       I'm off
too questioning of my own life at the moment to find the    poetry for
kind of, yes, it's funny, it's a blend of relaxation and     a bit.
intensity, I don't know. The last time I felt myself really writing
poetry in the way that I love it, was at the very end of *Pieces*, that
whole section "Mazatlan: Sea." That to me is the last poetry that I
have written in a body state, I want to say, or at least in a conscious
state of experience that was to me absolutely delicious. Subsequently
poetry has been like stabs and seizures and fits and irritations and
explanations and bullshit. I mean I liked it, wrote a whole book of it,
so to speak, but I felt too little in it, and too much practise. The most
moving poem to my own imagination would be the poem for my
mother's death which is a kind of attempt to realize what had happened and to honor her, you know; and one or two things of that
order that I have done. Those weren't poems of any human ease,
they were deeply compulsive and painful. And I haven't felt at home
in poetry for about four years, I guess, which is an awkward and
difficult thing to say, but it doesn't particularly worry me because I've
gone through periods of that nature before. I mean it worries me
like hell, but . . .

*Faas*: Are you aware of any reason for all that?

CREELEY: Duncan again has been very useful: like body changes,
emotional changes one goes through in one's late forties. Senses of
boredom with previous conduct, ah, senses of questions about going
on, doing it. Just to do it seems a kind of random way. Really being
tempted to move off entirely, but questioning as to what that means.
Thinking of Gary, who is a good friend, I don't see that constantly
changing the place and subject is really going to do anything at all. I
don't really feel depressed but it's like: is this poem necessary? I'd

really like to write prose in this way because it lets me move out . . .

*Faas*: Anyway I find your short stories really fantastic.

CREELEY: I'd better write some more, yes.

*Faas*: I like them much better than the novel.

CREELEY: Yes, I do too. I think the short stories are singular, whereas the novel, I wrote it just to have written a novel. But it didn't really get to anywhere.

*Faas*: Let me just read a couple of lines from a more recent poem, "The Finger":

"The Finger"        She was largely warm—
                    flesh heavy—and smiled
                    in some deepening knowledge.

                    .   .   .   .   .   .   .   .   .

                        Her heavy breath,
                    her ugliness, her lust—
                    but her laughing . . .

and so forth. What was the actual circumstance that prompted these lines?

CREELEY: This was in this house we were staying at in Gloucester and Bobbie was sitting by the fireplace; we had taken the acid quite late, about two o'clock in the morning, and we'd started a fire. Bobbie shifted to some lighter clothing so she had on this lovely kind of orange velvet wrapper, just lounging in front of the fire, like this incredibly beautiful woman, this firelight and this velvet and this chuckling woman, it was just incredible.

*Faas*: Of course, in the poem she also has these demonic, threatening aspects.

CREELEY: Right, you don't fool around with that, no no, she is not at all to be tickled, as Olson would say. [Both laughing] What's fascinating to me is how these states of experience, however they are gathered, may be obviously simple recollections unwittingly of a whole context of information that's been got, but has been forgotten.

mystical
experience

I remember at one time talking to my eldest son—he's a classic New England fellow, he's at Harvard, a graduate student in art history, and has been brought up largely by his mother from whom I've separated. We do get on without question, but he finds it very awkward to propose anything that has any "magical" situation in his life. So Bobbie and I were talking to him once about thinking, and he obviously loves to think. And I asked him if he had ever found while he was thinking any kind of transformation occurring in it, physically or otherwise. So he said, once he'd been working late at night in the stacks and concentrating upon some text when suddenly, unexpected by himself entirely, he experienced that the light around him seemed to alter. There, all of a sudden, was kind of a magnesium blue permeation of light all around him, and a humming, a distinct sense of humming, not like birds' wings but like a vibrating, a very curious vibrating sound that he could hear distinctly as a hum, and that the light wasn't just like a light-source but that it seemingly permeated the air, this intense whitish blue light. And this went on for a few seconds and then dissolved, and he felt very confused and thought he'd possibly fallen asleep and dreamed it. But he said he felt very high—of course, he doesn't use words like that—but curiously untired. And I said: Well you know, friend, you've described one of the classic trips. [Laughing] I mean, we don't have the books in the house, but you could go and check them out yourself. Now whether it's obviously a physiological state or whether it's some mystic state is up to you to determine, but I mean that's it. So he was pleased to know that.                 "The Moon"

*Faas*: Do you feel that there is a comparable new mystical dimension to your recent work? I'm thinking of poems like "The Moon."

CREELEY: I feel that my danger in such situations is that I become coy about them. Like last night I was lying in bed, still affected by this flu and I'd been watching TV and reading variously, and suddenly I was aware of this intense light from the window. And when I looked out of the window I thought: full moon. But I couldn't see the moon actually. So I went out and saw it sure enough and then I checked the calendar and it was full moon. And I was really feeling depressed the last week and the full moon really excites me and pleases me and reassures me. And so I thought: well, that's just what I needed, that moonlight. And to suddenly get it so specifically through the window. It was really good news to know that moon hadn't forgotten me somehow. [Both laughing] But you see I can't get off and be easy about it and say: isn't it sweet and it has such affection for me. It's like a Jewish puritanism, sort of.

*Faas*: Your recent attempts to write a long poem have been compared with *The Cantos*, *Paterson* etc.

CREELEY: I came upon a quote of Thoreau's talking         the long
about what he calls a "day book" in which he collects the     poem
events of the day and so on, and then he translates them
into some information and judgment of his own. I'm interested in the phrase "a day book" where he uses it for notations of what happened. But the point is that I don't transfer or translate, but let it stand. It's interesting as a form but I don't have any impulse to continue it, no. *Pieces* was really the success of that sequence.

*Faas*:  Yet I don't really see any kind of resemblance to *The Cantos* or *Paterson*. Maybe Zukofsky's *A*?

CREELEY:  But then *A* is a different pattern also. *A* has a very diverse and specific sense of structure. I mean Louis has a very formal composition among other things, with a number of things in mind to accomplish. So he would have pieces of it ahead and backwards and he has a very strict sense of formal composition that he is working to realize whereas I was fascinated to know what happened if you accumulated rather than designed and determined, that is, if you made the accumulation the crux of the situation rather than the moment to moment determination, let that collect rather than say: this is a good poem, this is a bad poem.

coherence    *Faas*:  And which would be the element of coherence?

CREELEY:  That it was written. I mean that could be coherence.

*Faas*:  Ginsberg says that the coherence is dependent on the concentration with which you observe the movement of the mind while writing, in other words that the coherence would dissolve as soon as the concentration slackens. So the poem would reflect some kind of inner coherence of mind experience. Again when he talks about the beginning, middle and end of a poem he uses these terms in a totally non-Aristotelian sense, so the beginning, middle and end of a poem would be determined by the beginning, middle and end of a thought process and the poem would leave off when the thought process . . .

CREELEY:  . . . reaches a stasis . . .

*Faas*:  . . . or a decisive turning point. Does that make sense to you in terms of your own work?

CREELEY:  It does make sense to me in terms of his but not too much of mine. You see, Zukofsky speaks of writing as a way of getting to or realizing or arriving at that which gives the hardened piece, and I could certainly believe in that, or do believe in that; to write in order to realize what brings you to rest, you know.

I don't          I don't certainly try any longer to do something that
write to     will be simply extraordinary or brilliant or whatever, as I
resolve      don't write to win prizes any longer. Again Allen's sense
the world.   from a few years ago: You don't have to write good poems
any more. In any case, I don't see any point of stasis in any human situation that to me would be more than temporary, I don't mean this pessimistically, but I don't see how the experience of being human can be in any point a stasis, I just don't see how it can be. It can arrive at a containment but I don't see how that containment can be more than a momentary situation even though that moment may last for twenty years. So that I write now primarily to recognize and

thus to register states of consciousness, of feeling that are in various ways constantly changing and constantly in flux. I write to see what stays the case and what changes, that's all. I don't write for peace, I mean I write for peace in the sense that writing these things gives me peace, but I don't write to resolve the world. What we were saying earlier: using art to reify all the states of human consciousness that do occur in all the states of human experience, to give, not simply a record but a reification of all those diversities. It sounds pessimistic, I assume, to say that each one of us dies so that that resolution in itself seems ample and sufficient. You know, I was extremely moved by Williams' late poems, simply that they continued an information that was to me extraordinarily valuable. And the one or two times that I had a chance to talk to him, he said: You hear a lot about old age being a time of fruition, that you feel you have accomplished X, Y and Z and that you can relax and enjoy the world and realize that you have done things in it, etc., etc. But actually it's an awful drag, you know. There is no rest in that way ever apparently, and what works to accomplish it, is always defeated by the very physical experience we have as people. So I think of myself much more like Burroughs' lone telegraph operator. I am simply a re- cording instrument. That's what I really love in Bur- roughs, where he says: I'm merely a recording instru- ment and I'm not here, you know, to make plots or . . . I would far more feel that I'm here simply to write it down, don't mind me if the news is good, bad or otherwise. [Both laughing] I'm not here to bring enlightenment or a resolving of human ills, I am here to tell you what happens as best I can. Not at all to insist on myself but just to give manifest of that one consciousness among myriad others, and the information can be as desultory or insignificant as proves the case. So the only act that's valuable is that which is used to articulate these states, you know. I think that's probably where Duncan and myself would sheer off from Gary who wants the poems to realize a state of beatitude and to work to that purpose possibly. To me that's an indifferent object. I mean it isn't that I don't care about human suffering or the human dilemma, but I don't particularly care about it as an artist.

the lone telegraph operator

I personally find extremely valuable those poems which make manifest human states of consciousness, physical states and various experiential states at all points of age and condition. And the resolu- tion is fine, but the resolution, as Jess Collins would say, curiously throws out the baby with the bath water. I mean, I want the full condition of the experience not so much so that I can make a judgment but so that I can compare. I know, for example, that in

points of my own despair or even delight it's been extremely useful
to me to be able to read Williams' poems written when he was in his
forties. I find them valuable simply because they give me information about where I'm at. They don't teach me but they give me
companionship. Perhaps I'm simply tired of endless plans to tidy up
the world. Phil Whalen tells me charmingly that there are a lot of
young kids crashing on the Zen Center, some of whom have to be
relegated to the steps because they are rather obstructive in the
Center itself, and I mean Zen just ain't gonna save them.

*Faas*: Many people just aren't aware of the fact that Zen involves
very rigorous discipline.

CREELEY: It's the ability to yield your ego and your will to an author-
ity. You see, to an American that's almost unthinkable, you spend all
your life getting out of it and here you have to give yourself back to
your father.

*Faas*: Does the term "open form" make sense to you?

open and
closed form

CREELEY: It's confusing to me. What is it, *Naked Poetry*,
that whole stupid thing. You know, this country has had
such a bleak battle between "free verse" and so-called classically,
conceptually formal verse or previous senses of metrical pattern. I
keep wishing there was a word that was more accurate. I mean,
projective verse is one sense, but that too is a kind of final cliché, it
doesn't really locate very much. Closed and open I guess. I don't
know. Open form? Yes. What's your sense of it?

*Faas*: Generally speaking there seems to be a tendency now to
incorporate closed forms into open form æsthetics. In various ways
you find that in Duncan, Snyder and Ginsberg, for instance.

CREELEY: I certainly use closed forms with very decisive patterns
that are very familiar.

*Faas*: And you don't feel that closed form relates to one type of
experience, and open form relates to another?

CREELEY: The thing that really made more sense to me was, years
ago, Pound trying to inform me by letter about ways in which a
magazine might be edited—trying to make me back off my heavy-
handed seriousness in various respects. He said, first of all, get three
or four people you really dig, and depend on them and publish
them, let them publish anything they want and that will be your core,
your constant, so to speak. On the other hand, he said, let about a
quarter or a half of the magazine run hog wild so that any idiot

the constant
and the
variant

thinks he can get in. And he said, verse consists of the
constant and the variant. Any element that stays decisive
in the context can be used as the variant, any element that
stays decisive in the context can be used as the constant.

It's like Duncan's sense of enclosing the closed in the open. Pound's ✓ presumption was that in order for the situation to have a coherence there must be an element that stays sufficiently stable to offer meas- ure for the remainder of the activity. For example, if you have a strong rhythmic situation, use that as the constant and keep it factu- ally persistent. Or Kenneth Koch, well, he simply uses a very steady heroic couplet, and into that he can literally pour anything, throw in all this lovely garbage. He uses a contained, reasonably stated line of bullshit and you can read on and on and on despite the fact that it's obviously going nowhere.

*Faas*: So you think there is an absolute necessity for *some* kind of coherence, rhythmical or otherwise?

CREELEY: I tend to, yes.

*Faas*: In 1953 you spoke of the poem as a whole defined by a "relevant and actual tension between diverse parts." That almost sounds like Cleanth Brooks.

CREELEY: Yes, Brooks and Warren was a text I used as a kid.

*Faas*: Would you consider that statement as dated now?

CREELEY: I would still regard it as interesting. I mean, I would now tend to read it as the situation of words energizing one another. I mean Kenneth's writing, for instance, gets too flaccid for me. He's a funny guy, I saw him like last weekend.

Kenneth Koch

*Faas*: What did somebody call it? Transcendental high camp, yes.

CREELEY: It *is* high camp. Restoration wit carrying a handkerchief in his sleeve or something. It can be very charming and very funny, and one poem of his that hits me very much is "Sleeping with Women" where there is a crazy curious sound pattern.

*Faas*: But then that kind of funniness often conceals so much ag- gressiveness against anybody who is not trying to be witty, any kind of seriousness being taken almost as a threat that has to be di- minished, run down and ridiculed.

CREELEY: That's very much a New York scene, you can understand that situation when you are still very young, when you are feeling very questioning and threatened by the authorities surrounding you, then there is almost sadly a physiological paranoia before you have any sense of situation that gives you any place to be.

*Faas*: That's what I liked about Robert Bly, that he was almost apologetic about what he'd written about Olson, expressing an at- titude very much like the one you're describing right now, just as he's very relaxed about this whole controversy with James Dickey.

CREELEY: Bob Bly is such an easy man to get along with, I like him. He is just like the old time classic Minnesota farmer. It's so lovely that he should be the great defender of the Great Mother, being like the old time patriarch himself, a lovely paradox. [Both laughing]

*Faas*: Somewhere you have stated that the "pace of [your] writing is concerned with the speed with which [you] can type" and that with two fingers you "type actually as fast as [you] can talk."

the writing process

CREELEY: I just write it down, I mean, I could show you notebooks and stuff, it's just physically writing. I mean I think a lot, I think endlessly with a consciousness of trying this on and trying that on. That really is attractive to me in Wittgenstein, that constant preoccupation with thinking.

*Faas*: But are you aware of observing your mind process while writing?

CREELEY: Oh yes.

*Faas*: So it would not be altogether different from Ginsberg's graphing the movement of his mind?

CREELEY: No, because writing gives me that curious detachment.

*Faas*: I have always been puzzled by the fact that Ginsberg frequently adduces Gertrude Stein as an antecedent for his own way of writing whereas to me she seems to have been propelled by language . . .

CREELEY: Right.

*Faas*: . . . while Allen Ginsberg is really concerned with the dynamics of the mind. And in that dichotomy, I think, you would be much closer to Gertrude Stein.

CREELEY: Yes, I agree. I am fascinated with what words say and how that saying stimulates one to move in them. I feel like I'm moving in words.

*Faas*: Although you don't seem to go quite as far as Gertrude Stein in letting the language take its own course.

CREELEY: She was more syntactically oriented than I am.

*Faas*: When does a poem come to a close?

poetic closure

CREELEY: When the energy drops. It's like Pound's law of discourse: say what you have to say and then just shut up. Sometimes when I was younger I tended to overwrite, that is to write beyond the impulse. And then I would frequently find that I'd go back and cut off the last verse and the center of the poem was clear.

*Faas*: So there is a kind of center related to the impulse of creation.

CREELEY: Right.

*Faas*: William Stafford once said that his poems usually come to a close when his powers to homogenize an experience come to a close.

CREELEY: In what *I'm* doing I certainly don't know that I am homogenizing. My wife has a recollection of that movie in which you see the doctor arriving through the pouring rain, coming home, and he says: Tonight history was made, I've just delivered Louis Pasteur. [Both laughing] That kind of trip, yes.

*Faas*: What are your criteria for evaluating your own work? I mean what makes you decide whether or not you are going to publish a poem. You have often emphasized that you never revise.

evaluating his own poetry

CREELEY: The important thing is that they should *feel* right. If in reading them, what's getting done, seems to me moving, appropriate and revealing, then I tend to trust them.

*Faas*: Revealing in terms of content?

CREELEY: Things that I respect are high energy states and/or some situations where the words are so relating that that constitutes an interest. It could be like a pun or a sing-song or some very minimal event possibly in that way. I use myself as the only measure that way and I will, as I said, use friends, like Duncan specifically, I'd use his advice. But usually if it feels right, then I trust it. I mean at times I've thrown away poems which later were published. For instance, I'd written a poem called "The Name" and threw it away, and then my wife happily asked me what I was doing and I recovered it from the waste basket and she said: That's really a moving poem. I don't know what caused me to throw it away, because now I can't quite see why I was dismayed by it.

*Faas*: Does concentration play any role in all that?

CREELEY: Yes, just physically, I'll show you one of my notebooks. [Fetches notebook] Like this is the poem on my mother's death. [Shows a manuscript without corrections, with very clean spacing and in beautiful handwriting]

*Faas*: It looks like a transcript.

CREELEY: No. That's the initial composition. That's primarily how a text will look. I remember when I sold the manuscript of *The Island* to Washington University one of the people there wrote me: We would like to know whether this is a copy of the actual manuscript or the actual manuscript. But that's truly the way I write. I must practise in my head in ways that I'm not quite able to articulate and to apprehend. There must be a lot of this going on in my head . . .

*Faas*: . . . before you write it down.

CREELEY: Yes. Not so much even the text itself, but it must be like playing chess games in your head endlessly.

*Faas*: But you wouldn't go ruminating on the lines, like Lowell or Snyder.

CREELEY: No. It's really written right there. [Shows further poems]

Here's a drunken night in a bar. [Both laughing] I don't rush *these* into print! And this is a poem that's really funny. I have a photographer friend, Walter Chappell, who told me he would like a poem to preface a collection of his photographs and he wanted it so it would fit on two pages, so I had two columns of twice four verses each, so it adds up to sixteen. [Laughing] So this poem is not only written straight out, man, but I'm counting as I go. [Laughing] Perhaps I should sit on a sidewalk and write poems to order.

Robert Bly

Photo: Layle Silbert

# ROBERT BLY  (1926 -          )

> There we go again! The Olsonite poets are always approaching poetry through technique; Creeley is a perfect example . . . When I have fought against what was weak in my own poems, I have often found myself fighting the American longing to lie down in technique and rest. . . I think Gary Snyder is right when he says that wherever we are is not where we're heading: we're going somewhere else. Talk of technique "throws light" on poetry, but the last thing we need is light. St. John of the Cross said, "If a man wants to be sure of his road, he must close his eyes and walk in the dark."

Of Norwegian descent, Robert Bly was born in Madison, Minnesota, a state he has lived in nearly all his life. He graduated from Harvard in 1950 and received his M.A. from Iowa University in 1956. Married since 1955, he started his turbulent literary career with the founding, in 1958, of the magazine *The Fifties* (later *The Sixties* and *The Seventies*), attacking American poets for their "elegant isolationism" and for failing to absorb the impulse of Surrealism like poets in Europe and South America. His translations of Trakl, Vallejo, Ekelöf, Neruda, Tranströmer, Rilke, Lorca, Jiménez and others, many of them published by his own Sixties Press, began to remedy these deficiencies long before his own poems. The first collection, *Silence in the Snowy Fields* (1962), shows little kinship with French or Spanish Surrealism, an impulse which, reinforced by the poet's political involvement, only became fully apparent in *The Light Around the Body*. This collection was published one year after Bly, in 1966, had taken the occasion of a reading at Reed College to launch American Writers Against the Vietnam War. Awarded the National Book Award for his second volume, he handed over the prize money to help young Americans "defy the draft authorities." A belligerent individualist all his life, his more recent involvement with Eastern mysticism seems to have brought Bly and his work (*The Morning Glory*, 1969; *Sleepers Joining Hands*, 1973) into closer contact with what he formerly saw as his opponents amongst the Beat poets and "Olsonites."

# Robert Bly

An owl on the dark waters
And so many torches smoking
By mossy stone
And horses that are seen riderless on moonlit nights
A candle that flutters as a black hand
Reaches out
All of these mean
A man with coins on his eyes

The vast waters
The cry of seagulls.

("Riderless Horses," B,L,58)

Poetry such as this gives Robert Bly an almost unique position in Anglo-American literature. With the possible exception of Philip Lamantia, one has, I think, to go back to *The Waste Land* to find lines that capture the phantasmagoria of the subconscious with comparable convincingness and magic:

A woman drew her long black hair out tight
And fiddled whisper music on those strings
And bats with baby faces in the violet light
Whistled, and beat their wings
And crawled head downward down a blackened wall
And upside down in air were towers
Tolling reminiscent bells, that kept the hours
And voices singing out of empty cisterns and exhausted wells.

("What the Thunder Said")

Even in Eliot's work, however, *The Waste Land* stands out as a unique and mysterious creation. Not surprisingly, it grew more and more alien to the author, to the point where he felt called upon to deprecate the poem as a "structureless" "piece of rhythmical grumbling" (E,IR,54) and a mere "relief of a personal and wholly insignificant

203

grouse against life" (E,F,1). And there is little else in Anglo-American poetry which, like parts of *The Waste Land,* compares with the work of poets such as Éluard, Lorca, and Neruda.

Among the minor poets, David Gascoyne has (before Bly) made the most energetic attempt to launch a Surrealist movement in the English-speaking world. But his poetry at best offers examples of the consciously manipulated dream-imagery that Breton himself had condemned as a pseudo-form of automatic writing. And the theoretical position stated by the 19 year old poet in his *Short Survey of Surrealism* (1935) was abandoned two years later in favor of the programmatic intent to narrate in poetry "the contemporary Zeitgeist of Europe" (Ra,M,167f.).

Among the major poets, Wallace Stevens welcomed "The Irrational Element in Poetry" and predicted its absorption into the mainstream of Western literature. But he was both too rational and too traditional a poet to contribute much to that tendency himself (Ra,M,309). William Carlos Williams praised the Surrealists as well as Gertrude Stein for their linguistic experiments, but he could hardly sympathize with their psycho-ideological claims and programs while propagating a philosophy of "no ideas but in things." Ezra Pound, after 1922 increasingly absorbed by socio-economic issues, was blind to the poetic and epistemological achievement of Surrealism and incensed by its later Communist orientation. In an ill-tempered diatribe he accused "The Coward Surrealists" (1936) of ideological escapism and compared their revolutionary stance with the "dim ditherings of the æsthetes in 1888" (Ra,M,185). If such party prejudice could do little to stop the influence of Surrealism in England and America, Eliot's well-informed controversy with its claims and theories, conducted over a period of several years, was considerably more successful in doing so.

After all, Eliot himself, while under psychiatric treatment in Lausanne, had produced, in a spurt of semi-automatic writing, some of the greatest and deservedly most famous Surrealist poetry in world literature. But *The Waste Land,* written after a serious nervous breakdown, was largely an efflux of that unconscious which Eliot, when in better control of his psyche, tried to exclude from poetic creativity. Poetry, he stated as early as 1919, "is not a turning loose of emotion, but an escape from emotion; it is not the expression of personality, but an escape from personality" (E,E,21). After composing *The Waste Land,* he, of course, had to admit that there were periods in his life, mainly during "some forms of ill-health, debility or anæmia," when poetry had come to him like a mere "efflux . . . approaching the condition of automatic writing" (E,U,144). On principle, however, he had "no good word to say for the cultivation of automatic writing as the model of literary composition" (E,E,405). When asked whether he had ever felt the need for a new language to express the experience of his night mind, he answered with a definite "*no,*" and added: "I am not, as a matter of fact, particularly interested in my 'night-mind'" (Ra,M,185).

It is tantalizing to speculate what might have happened to the life and poetic career of Hart Crane if he had ever come into contact with the Surrealist poetry of France, Spain, or South America. Instead, it was *The Waste Land,* as seen through the distorting lens of its academic interpreters, which became the much admired model for *The Bridge* (1930), and it is tragically ironic how the critical dictates of its author, disseminated by the New Critics, came to cripple a creative impulse which came closer to Surrealism than that of any other of the major Anglo-American poets, with the possible exception of Dylan Thomas. Crane dreamt of a poetry that would "express its concepts in the . . . direct terms of physical-psychic experience," raising "the entire construction of the poem . . . on the organic principle of a 'logic of metaphor,' which antedates our so-called pure logic." But despite the precedent of Whitman's *Leaves of Grass,* which, as Crane himself put it, was issued in a "number of editions, each incorporating further additions,"[1]* he felt compelled to fit *The Bridge* into the Procrustean bed of an obsolete unity concept. Analogously, his imagery and syntax, which occasional exercises in automatic writing could have infused with greater ease and naturalness, were all too often bogged down in the over-elaborate convolutions of a self-conscious rhetoric and in a willful striving after symbolism, meaningfulness, and complexity.

It is with these examples in mind that Robert Bly had reason to claim in *The Fifties* that unlike Europe and South America, England and North America have practically "had no bold new poetry since the astounding daring of *The Waste Land,*" because the "other poetries have passed through surrealism; we have not." And in both Eliot and Pound, "the mind won over the unconscious without too much struggle—the old Puritan victory." The result was that after the "rather dry flurry of leftist poetry in the thirties . . . poetry has been getting older every year" (B,F,3,7-9). According to Bly, a genuine rejuvenation of Anglo-American poetry must gain its impulse from the model of foreign poetries, from a return to the "fertile internationalism" of early Pound and Eliot (B,IJ,38) which their very followers among the New Critics had sacrificed to an "elegant

*Notes to this section on p. 222.

isolationism" (B,S,6,22). To be sure, Pound as well as Eliot, when drawing on the French tradition, had neglected the poetry with Surrealist elements (e.g., Rimbaud's "Le Bateau ivre") in favor of a more Objectivist kind of poem (e.g., Rimbaud's "Au Cabaret-Vert"). But it was their undeniable achievement to have drawn attention to poets such as Nerval, Lautréamont, Baudelaire, Rimbaud, and Laforgue, who were the first to adopt underground passages of association, to dare enter the "dark valley" of the unconscious and thus prepare the advent of a new imagination which finally, around 1910, began to appear "all over the world" (B,F,1,36). To Bly, this is the "jerky," "jumping," or "leaping" imagination, swiftly passing from the conscious to the unconscious and producing a poetry in which images become the very content of the poem. "It seems to me," he wrote in *The Fifties*, "that the greatest tradition of all modern poetry, and the *avant-garde* for a century has been the heavy use of images" (B,F,2,14). Bly tends to avoid the term "deep image," which Robert Kelly and Jerome Rothenberg coined in 1961 and which has since become the most common label for the kind of poetry written by himself and other poets under his influence. On the other hand, there is little in his critical writings which yields a clearer and more accurate description of the term "image." We can only guess that Bly may mean something like the "expression of psychic force which suddenly becomes language" (G. Bachelard), which thinks *for* the poet (P. Éluard) (Ra,M,49) and which is close "to the psychological archetype of Jungian analysis" (R. Duncan,D,C,29). Bly himself has repeatedly referred to Freud and Jung as the fountainheads of the new imagination and has criticized Imagism for its lack of psychological depth: "The Imagists were misnamed," he wrote in *The Fifties*, because "they did not write in images from the unconscious" (B,F,3,8). An image such as Pound's "Petals on a wet, black bough" is a mere picture, whereas true images like Lorca's "death on the deep roads of the guitar" (B,F,1,37-8) bring "together different thoughts by inexplicable means" (B,S,5,81).

Even if Bly was right in claiming that American poetry had failed to traverse the "dark valley" of the unconscious, there was little in his first volume to suggest that he would make this journey himself. Granted, the poems in *Silence in the Snowy Fields* (1962) frequently mention the wind with its numinous afflatus, or death and darkness in which man has to immerse himself for his psychic rejuvenation; and there are the ubiquitous assertions that we "want to go back, to return to the sea," dive "into the sea of death," "go back among the dark roots," that we are "returning now to . . . the depth of the darkness," or are "falling into the open mouths of darkness."

But such language is at best reminiscent of D. H. Lawrence, whereas the imagery which poets like Lorca and Neruda have gathered from these archetypal depths hardly disturbs the almost idyllic *Silence in the Snowy Fields*. Instead, there are similes such as "The bare trees more dignified than ever, / Like a fierce man on his deathbed"; images which tell a little story or fairytale (e.g., the snowflakes "like jewels of a murdered Gothic prince / Which were lost centuries ago during a battle"); or, even more elaborate, the conceit-like expansion of an initial image that determines the structure and meaning of an entire poem, such as "Waking from Sleep":

> Inside the veins there are navies setting forth,
> Tiny explosions at the water lines,
> And seagulls weaving in the wind of the salty blood.
>
> It is the morning. The country has slept the whole winter.
> Window seats were covered with fur skins, the yard was full
> Of stiff dogs, and hands that clumsily held heavy books.
>
> Now we wake, and rise from bed, and eat breakfast!—
> Shouts rise from the harbor of the blood,
> Mist, and masts rising, the knock of wooden tackle in the
>       sunlight.
> Now we sing, and do tiny dances on the kitchen floor.
> Our whole body is like a·harbor at dawn;
> We know that our master has left us for the day.
>
> (B,Si,13)

This is not to deny the aptness, beauty, and vividness of some of these images, or the mythopœic power of a stanza like the following:

> The strong leaves of the box-elder tree,
> Plunging in the wind, call us to disappear
> Into the wilds of the universe,
> Where we shall sit at the foot of a plant,
> And live forever, like the dust.
>
> ("Poem in Three Parts," B,Si,21)

However, there is little that is genuinely Surrealistic here, and even where Bly comes close to it, he is reminiscent less of Dali's minutely detailed hallucinatory psychographs than of Arnold Böcklin's late nineteenth century Romanticism with its weird, apocalyptic animals and statuesque mythic creatures inhabiting a crepuscular landscape of death:

> I know these cold shadows are falling for hundreds of miles,
> Crossing lawns in tiny towns, and the doors of Catholic
>     churches;
> I know the horse of darkness is riding fast to the east,
> Carrying a thin man with no coat.
>
> ("The Clear Air of October," B,Si,52)

This seems like the world of a man in love with death, and indeed no other theme is more central to the poet's early work. However, there is none of Böcklin's sickly fascination with a death that is terrifying, but instead an almost Zen-like acquiescence to death as an inevitable part of life which the poet has learned to fear and love as much as life itself. "Through our dark lives," we read in one of his poems, "Like those before, we move to the death we love" (B,Si,32). What at first seems full of darkness and gloom is finally revealed as a world of serene happiness which Bly expresses in the most direct and simple terms. For at its basis lies the conviction that our human life is embedded in the larger life around us, and that despite death, it will continue there:

> Oh, on an early morning I think I shall live forever!
> I am wrapped in my joyful flesh,
> As the grass is wrapped in its clouds of green.
>
> ("Poem in Three Parts," B,Si,21)

The final aim of Surrealism was a heightened level of consciousness from which "life and death," as Breton put it in the *Second manifeste du surréalisme* (1930), "le réel et l'imaginaire, le passé et le futur . . . cessent d'être perçus contradictoirement" (Br,M,76-7). The French Surrealists never reached that goal themselves. But they hewed a path through the obscure psychic woods of the Western subconscious from which later artists such as Jackson Pollock, Charles Olson, and John Cage have been able to emerge towards a new understanding of reality similar to that which Buddhist artists, for instance, have for centuries embodied in their music, painting, and poetry.

Before he began to publish his poetry, Bly spent several years in solitary self-confinement and analysis, a time he frequently remembers in his interviews and more recent poetry: "When I was alone, for three years, alone . . . in New York, in that great room / reading Rilke in the womanless loneliness" (B,Sl,58,59). It was here that he first found "the inward path I still walk on," and where one day he lost himself in the "curved energy" of an all-pervasive Godhead which "makes grass grow," "gives food to the dark cattle of the sea," or, as a kind of double, frequently invoked in Bly's poetry, shares the poet's own personality:

> There is another being living inside me.
> He is looking out of my eyes.
> I hear him
> in the wind through the bare trees.
>      ("Water Drawn Up into the Head," B,Sl,65)

Bly's first volume, *Silence in the Snowy Fields,* seems to show the poet emerging, as if from a shamanistic journey, into the light of this new, joyful consciousness. However, one poem, entitled "Unrest," stands out from the rest like an open wound, foreshadowing the world of Bly's future poetry. Here we have his first vision of the "strange unrest [hovering] over the nation" that was to become the central theme of his second volume, and which led him in 1967 to found, with David Ray, American Writers Against the Vietnam War. And here, for the first time, in a poem about his nation's society and politics, we find the Surrealist imagery absent in the poems about himself. Viewing the psycho-political disorder around him, the poet retreats into the *selva oscura* of the unconscious he was personally about to leave behind.

> A strange unrest hovers over the nation:
> This is the last dance, the wild tossing of Morgan's seas,
> The division of spoils. A lassitude
> Enters into the diamonds of the body.
> In high school the explosion begins, the child is partly killed.
> When the fight is over, and the land and the sea ruined,
> Two shapes inside us rise, and move away.
>
> But the baboon whistles on the shores of death—
> Climbing and falling, tossing nuts and stones,
> He gambols by the tree
> Whose branches hold the expanses of cold,
> The planets whirling and the black sun,
> The cries of insects, and the tiny slaves
> In the prisons of bark:
> Charlemagne, we are approaching your islands!
>
> We are returning now to the snowy trees,
> And the depth of the darkness buried in snow, through
>     which you rode all night

With stiff hands; now the darkness is falling
In which we sleep and awake—a darkness in which
Thieves shudder, and the insane have a hunger for snow,
In which bankers dream of being buried by black stones,
And businessmen fall on their knees in the dungeons of
    sleep.

(B,Si,25)

In using such images while writing about the outer world rather than about himself, Bly seems to depart from the original Surrealist impulse. And indeed, he has little interest in automatic writing. Breton's or Aragon's poetry appears to him "drab and squeaky" beside that of Lorca or Neruda, whose collection *Residencia en la tierra* he considers the "greatest surrealist poems yet written in a Western language." For Aragon and Breton "are poets of reason, who occasionally throw themselves backward into the unconscious, but Neruda, like a deep-sea crab, all claws and shell, is able to breathe in the heavy substances that lie beneath the daylight consciousness" (B,N,3) and at the same time he never loses his hold on concrete reality.

Bly himself heavily revises his own poetry, claiming that the approximately 1,000 lines of a recently published book, for instance, are based on about 100,000 actually written (B,IJ,30). Such conscious sifting and correcting, he is convinced, can probe deeper into the subconscious than any direct outpourings of the ego, while the process of creativity remains as open and unpredictable as in automatic writing. As he said in an interview, he often starts with a somehow striking line, "and then the unconscious keeps putting things in one after another that you were not quite aware of and at the end of the poem you feel amazed" (B,IL,63).

This process is reflected in the halting staccato of Surrealist images which in Bly's second volume, *The Light Around the Body* (1967), provide us with a nightmare vision of the American psyche. The fairy-tale world of his earlier work with its Arthur Rackham-like lyricism, Romantic oddity, and occasional cuteness (e.g., "This new snow seems to speak of virgins / With frail clothes made of gold, / Just as the old snow shall whisper / Of concierges in France," B,Si,16) has been transmogrified into the schizophrenic phantasmagoria of a painter like Richard Dadd. The bankers and businessmen who made their first appearance in "Unrest" are now part of a proliferating host of famous political figures, of types and characters from all walks of modern life, inhabiting a world of grotesque disfiguration, horror, and death, side by side with "strange plants," "curious many-eyed creatures," and other monsters. And all this is portrayed with such graphic precision and vivid plasticity that it evokes the illusion of a Surrealist wax figure cabinet.

Bly obviously had to sacrifice his hard-won personal serenity to achieve this vision. As he claims in his essay "On Political Poetry" (*The Nation*, April 24, 1967), the "life of a country can be imagined as a psyche larger than the psyche of anyone living," yet only the poet who has "such a grasp of his own concerns that he can leave them for a while" is able to penetrate into this socio-political unconscious and come back with a truly political poetry which (like Yeats's or Neruda's) transcends the mere versification of political opinions found in, for example, the works of Kenneth Fearing or Edwin Rolfe. As in "The Great Society," this Surrealist vision of contemporary life and politics ironically inverts the accepted image of that society, thus offering a critique of its actualities as powerful as any poetry of a directly polemical and propagandist orientation:

> Dentists continue to water their lawns even in the rain;
> Hands developed with terrible labor by apes
> Hang from the sleeves of evangelists;
> There are murdered kings in the light-bulbs outside movie
>     theaters;
> The coffins of the poor are hibernating in piles of new tires.
>
> The janitor sits troubled by the boiler,
> And the hotel keeper shuffles the cards of insanity.
> The President dreams of invading Cuba.
> Bushes are growing over the outdoor grills,
> Vines over the yachts and the leather seats.
>
> The city broods over ash cans and darkening mortar.
> On the far shore, at Coney Island, dark children
> Play on the chilling beach: a sprig of black seaweed,
> Shells, a skyful of birds,
> While the mayor sits with his head in his hands.

(B,L,17)

Of course, a poem like "The Great Society," except for the irony of its title, is not political in any exclusive sense. That aim is part of the much larger attempt to change the general bourgeois consciousness which Bly, not unlike the French Surrealists, holds responsible for our destructive politics and general life style. Just as the establishment culture is dominated by hypocritical moralizing, pragmatic reasoning, and future-oriented ideology, the new consciousness and the poetry which is its medium should be characterized by a non-moralistic, pre-rational, and a-teleological outlook.

It was in this sense that Bly defended his friend James Wright against the attacks levelled at *The Branch Will Not Break* (1963) (B,S,8,59 ff.). Thom Gunn had criticized Wright for deliberately excluding "the operation of the discursive reason," and Larry Rubin had attacked his "willful refusal to enter into the business of inter-preting experience . . . and attempting to show relationships." In his retort, Bly simply questioned the validity of these criteria. What Gunn and Rubin posit as absolutes, he argued, boils down to the demand that Wright should "relate what he is describing to the great ideas of the Western World." "This is called 'giving meanings'" whereas the demand for "discursive reasoning" in poetry more often than not results in the handling of "accepted ideas" and "moral platitudes." Such "poetry of 'relationships'" may still dominate the English-speaking world, yet Wright and himself, Bly argued, are far from alone in their refusal to impose rational order and meaning on reality. After all, Chinese poets have written in this way for 3000 years, and amongst his contemporaries there is "the generation of '62 . . . Creeley, Wright, Snyder, etc., [which] represents a watershed in American poetry."

The fact that James Dickey, whom shortly before Bly had hailed as a fellow traveller and the "exact opposite of the fashionable 'my healthy limitations school'" (B,S,7,55), is not mentioned as a member of this group was a portent of what was to follow. For shortly after his article on Wright, Bly launched a blistering attack against *Buckdancer's Choice* (1965) (B,S,9,70-9), whose author he called "a huge, blubbery poet, pulling out Southern language in long strings, like taffy, a toady to the government, supporting all move-ments toward Empire, a sort of Georgia cracker Kipling." For a man pretending to advocate a poetry free from the platitudes of Western ideology and moralizing, the attack seems curiously self-defeating.

Echoing his article on Wright, Bly grants that "a true work of art . . . moves into deep and painful regions of the memory, to areas most people cannot visit without wincing." When Dickey, in "The Firebombing" and "Slave Quarters," portrays feelings of self-protective apathy and gloating joy over Western racial superiority and the destructive power provided by our technology, he not only, it seems to me, fulfills that function but extends it into the realm of his nation's psyche. And though his method is non-Surrealistic, it is no less truthful than Bly's in poems such as "Unrest" and "The Great Society." Bly criticizes Dickey's poetry for its "easy acceptance of brutality" and concomitant repulsiveness. Yet how could Dickey's poems be considered more repulsive than Bly's? And where in "Unrest" or "The Great Society" do we find "the real grief . . . [the] masculine and adult sorrow" which, according to Bly, can alone redeem that repulsiveness? It is the very absence of any such philanthropic attitudinizing which saves these poems from the "kitsch" Bly has attributed to "Slave Quarters," and which gives them the terrifying and cathartic power they possess.

The issues at stake here are as old as the genre in which Dickey's poems are composed. It is true that the speakers in "Slave Quarters" and "The Firebombing" are not as clearly individualized as the personæ of Robert Browning, and that it is often difficult to dissociate them from the author. Yet even Victorian dramatic monologues, as nineteenth-century critics were the first to realize, are characterized by a strange amalgam of "subjective objectivity." Just as the most confessional of poets has to resort to some "oblique, objective, or dramatic way of expression,"[2] so Browning, giving words to a murderer and sexual psychopath like Porphyria's Lover, could only do so by transmogrifying, through his empathetic imagination, what was part of himself into the character of his poem. Although he was far more concerned than Dickey to invest his personæ with all the trappings of an autonomous individuality, there were enough critics who identified these characters with the author and accused him of the cynicism of Bishop Blougram or the dissoluteness of Fra Lippo Lippi.

The confusion persists, and Bly, while making fun of the "jabber about 'personæ,'" hardly clarifies the issue by declaring that in "Slave Quarters" "the umbilical cord [between author and speaker] has not been cut. Mr. Dickey is not standing outside the poem." It is far more convincing when Dickey, in an indirect answer to these charges, points out that

> Every poem written—and particularly those which make use of a figure designated in the poem as "I"—is both an exploration and an invention of identity. . . . A true poet can write with utter convincingness about "his" career as a sex murderer, and then in the next poem with equal conviction about tenderness and children and self-sacrifice. As Keats says, it is simply that the poet "has no personality." I would say, rather, that he has a personality large enough to encompass and explore each of the separate, sometimes related, sometimes unrelated, personalities that inhabit him, as they inhabit us all. (Di,S,155,161)

To be sure, Bly's criticism, if taken *cum grano salis*, is not entirely irrelevant. For a poet using personæ without the techniques of multiperspective fragmentation developed by Pound, Eliot, and Williams, or without the self-transcendence achieved by D. H. Lawrence, somehow remains caught within a closed ego system. In other words, it seems doubtful whether anybody writing in the second half of this century can adopt a genre as obsolete as the dramatic monologue without falling into patterns, clichés, and sentiments typical of a previous age and alien to our literary sensibility as well as to our understanding of man in our time. And indeed, if poems such as "Slave Quarters" avoid these pitfalls by the compelling urgency of their subject and sheer technical brilliance, there are other poems by Dickey which sound like unintentional parodies of Browning. Keats' prophetic notion of the "chameleon poet" without a personality found an embodiment, appropriate for its time, in the Victorian poet and the proliferating multitude of "men and women" he projected in his dramatic lyrics. But modern man has learned to see his ego as immersed in Jung's collective unconscious, as only another object or event in Whitehead's open-ended universe of interrelated forces, or even as the final emptiness of Eastern philosophy. And it is possible that no great poetry can be written now which precludes an awareness of such insights.

In "The Teeth Mother Naked at Last" from a more recent volume of verse, *Sleepers Joining Hands* (1974), Bly attempts a solution for some of these problems. A combination of Neruda's Surrealism with Ginsberg's Whitmanesque rhetoric and Pound's techniques of fragmentation, the poem in its indictment of the Vietnam war reads like an indirect answer to "The Firebombing" and its "easy acceptance of brutality." "The Firebombing," Bly had written, "has no real anguish. If the anguish were real . . . we would stop what we were doing, we would break the television set with an axe, we would throw ourselves on the ground sobbing" (B,S,9,74). Yet it is exactly where it translates these gestures into verse that "The Teeth Mother" has the least effect on the reader:

> If a child came by burning, you would dance on a lawn,
> trying to leap into the air, digging into your cheeks,
> you would ram your head against the wall of your bedroom
> like a bull penned too long in his moody pen—

> If one of those children came toward me with both hands
> in the air, fire rising along both elbows
> I would suddenly go back to my animal brain,

> I would drop on all fours, screaming,
> my vocal chords would turn blue, so would yours,
> it would be two days before I could play with my own children
>     again.
>
>                                         (B,SI,25)

My anguish is far more real when I consider the diabolic destructiveness in the following lines from "The Firebombing," regardless of whether the speaker voices the poet's own feelings or not. For if he does, it is only to Dickey's credit that he portrayed himself with the unflinching objectivity even poets frequently reserve for the more attractive aspects of their personality:

> All leashes of dogs
> Break under the first bomb, around those
> In bed, or late in the public baths: around those
> Who inch forward on their hands
> Into medicinal waters.
> Their heads come up with a roar
> Of Chicago fire:
> Come up with the carp pond showing
> The bathhouse upside down,
> Standing stiller to show it more
> As I sail artistically over
> The resort town followed by farms,
> Singing and twisting
> All the handles in heaven kicking
> The small cattle off their feet
> In a red costly blast
> Flinging jelly over the walls
> As in a chemical war-
> fare field demonstration.
> With fire of mine like a cat
>
> Holding onto another man's walls,
> My hat should crawl on my head
> In streetcars, thinking of it,
> The fat on my body should pale.
>
>                                         (Di,P,184-5)

Bly must have come to recognize some of the contradictions pointed out when he declared, in 1972, that he "didn't criticize [Dickey] on moral grounds," and granted him the rank of an "extraordinary man, almost a genius" with "this quality of thinking about these negative things and trying to write about them." And it is easier to agree with Bly when he limits his criticism to the fact that Dickey's "imaginative form starts to collapse" and that "in terms of metaphor and action [he] has stopped going through the skin," which, according to Bly, separates Western man from his inner spiritual life (B,IL,59-60).

This change may partly be due to Bly's increasing immersion in Buddhist philosophy, which largely confirmed—but also deepened and modified—the beliefs he had held from the very beginnings of his poetic career. "In the last eight or nine, ten years," he confessed in 1972, "the thinking I've learned most from has been Buddhist" (B,IL,50). Buddhism also seems to have given him a maturity which is reflected not only in the softening of his attitude towards Dickey and others but in the greater complexity of his more recent poetry. Bly sounded convincing enough when in his earliest collection he wrote lines such as

> through our dark lives
> Like those before, we move to the death we love.
>
> (B,Si,32)

And his acceptance of death as well as the Zen Buddhist-like serenity derived from it may well have evolved from a long spiritual struggle. It is all the more admirable that Bly was ready to repeat, on the level of our socio-political consciousness, the journey through the "dark valley" of the subconscious, which he had personally already brought to a resolution. And the results speak for themselves. In lines like the following, which, in a fusion of his early and middle styles, seem to expose his hard-won serenity to the horror and suffering of the world around him, a new tone of harassing self-analysis and genuine sorrow emerges:

> I decide that death is friendly.
> Finally death seeps up through the tiniest capillaries of my
>     toes.
> I fall into my own hands,
>         fences break down under horses,
> cities starve, whole towns of singing women carrying to the
>     burial fields
>         the look I saw on my father's face,
> I sit down again, I hit my own body,
> I shout at myself, I see what I have betrayed.
> What I have written is not good enough.
> Who does it help?

> I am ashamed sitting on the edge of my bed.
>> ("The Night Journey in the Cooking Pot," B,SI,62-3)

Buddhism also must have brought Bly a clearer understanding of his own philosophical and poetical position and to some extent transformed his attitude towards those American poets who are engaged in a similar quest. In the past, for instance, he has often reprimanded Ginsberg for his obscenity, "unkindness," and "fear of the unconscious," or for giving up "all hope of imaginative precision and delicacy" (B,S,4,38;5,70;6,40). But more recently, he has hailed him as "the rebirth of a very powerful spiritual man" and as a fellow traveller in a common pursuit who, unlike Gary Snyder and himself, has gained his access to a new consciousness "not through the Tibetans and Japanese—but through the Hindus." With obvious approval Bly quotes Ginsberg's remarks about the psycho-physiological basis of poetic language, that "as soon as you have a new syntax," for instance, "you have a new way of breathing and as soon as you have that you have a new consciousness" (B,IL,54,59).

These, of course, are insights closely akin to, if not inspired by those of Olson. Yet, ironically, it is the latter's position, above all, which seems to have eluded Bly in his search for a new poetry and poetics. Bly's accusation that Olson embodies the "formalist obsession" of American poetry hardly needs refuting, while his contention that both form and content are "expressions of a certain rebellious energy rising in the psyche" (B-M,P,163-4) is not too far a cry from Olson's (or rather Creeley's) famous dictum that "form is never more than an extension of content" or that "if one taps, via psyche, plus a 'true' adherence of Muse, one does reveal 'Form'" (O,W,16,29). And in the light of Buddhist philosophy it should be easy to understand that Olson's Objectism does not imply a positivist approach to nature or an evasion of self, but a quest complementary rather than opposed to that of Bly or Surrealism generally.

To Bly, however, Objectivism is no more than the theoretical formula for a failing more widespread than any other in American poetry—for the absorption in things, which, as he wrote in *The Sixties*, "is shared by almost all the poets in America today. . . It is the quality that the poetry of Lowell and of Merwin has in common with that of the Beats, as well as with the poetry of the Black Mountain group, who after Charles Olson and William Carlos Williams emphasize 'objects' and 'objectivism'" (B,S,4,39). All this may be true, though even Williams, the most famous and uncompromising practitioner of such thingyness in verse, at least *strove* for the inwardness Bly finds lacking in his poetry. "A life that is here and now is timeless," he wrote in 1939. "That is the universal I am seeking: to embody that in a work of art, a new world that is always 'real'" (W,E,196). Such timelessness reached by an absorption in the *hic et nunc* has, of course, been the universal aim of mystics of all traditions and is a notion central to most Eastern philosophies. The Zen Buddhists, for instance, call it *ekakṣaṇa*, which in Suzuki's paraphrase is the "eternal Now" or "absolute present" (Su,W,268) reflected in the "momentariness of *sumi* paintings and *haiku*" (Wa,W,199) as well as of most Sino-Japanese art and poetry. In this way the famous Chinese poet Tu Fu, whom Bly quotes as a model for real inwardness (B,S,4,39), might well have preferred Williams' poetics to the Surrealist manifestoes or to Rimbaud's plea that the poet should "par un long, immense et raisonné *dérèglement* de *tous les sens*" try to immerse himself into the unknown of "l'âme universelle" (R,W,306-8). And where, one might ask, does a lyric like the following by Tu Fu differ markedly from any of Williams' shorter "Objectivist" poems?

> The catkins line the lanes,
>     making white carpets,
> And leaves on lotus streams
>     spread like green money:
>
> Pheasants root bamboo shoots,
>     nobody looking,
> While ducklings on the sands
>     sleep by their mothers.[3]

Yet, granting the ultimately mystical orientation of Williams' poetic aims, there remains the more serious question of whether he or any of his Western peers can, like some Eastern poets, reach this goal by a mere empathetic immersion in objective reality. It is the very model of Zen Buddhism which has led many of his followers to the erroneous belief that such a shortcut to a new consciousness is generally accessible.

Zen teaches its disciples to ignore and avoid hallucinations and dreams and instead to focus on the pre-conceptual suchness of reality. Yet such a seeming rejection of the unconscious is the outcome of a struggle that lasted more than two millennia, so that the "participation mystique" (Lévy-Bruhl) with the subconscious, which may be a matter of painful and strenuous therapeutic effort for a Westerner, has long been a readily available experience for the Buddhist. And even Suzuki, a more recent exponent of the doctrine, defines *ekakṣaṇa* as "the awakening of consciousness out of the darkest recesses of the unconscious" (Su,W,268); while the pre-Christian

*Lankavatara Scripture*, the most important of the Sutras for the evolution of Zen Buddhism, reads like a running commentary on what, in Jungian terms, we would now call the collective unconscious—that "memory of . . . discriminations, desires, attachments and deeds [which] is stored in Universal Mind since beginningless time, and is still being accumulated," that "habit-energy" which "like a magician . . . causes phantom things and people to appear and move about" (Go,B,300 ff.). The "intuitive mind" which is able to penetrate beyond the conscious and unconscious world helps us understand the dream-like emptiness of both: "The discriminating-mind is a dancer and a magician with the objective world as his stage. Intuitive-mind is the wise jester who travels with the magician and reflects upon his emptiness and transiency. Universal Mind keeps the record and knows what must be and what may be." Yet, again and again, it is emphasized that the final insight into the unruffled quietude of Universal Mind can only be reached by traversing the unconscious to the point of a sudden "'turning about' at the deepest seat of consciousness."

It is only beyond this stage that all dichotomies of good and evil, past and future, inward and outward, and, above all, the duality of subject and object cease to be seen as opposites—not, however, by an extinction of the mind but by its tranquilization. Just as the "old body" continues to operate, so the "mind-system, because of its accumulated habit-energy, goes on functioning." To talk of the egolessness of either the self or the non-self would therefore be as pointless as to assert their essentiality. Both are "neither real nor unreal," so that their relationship, as one Zen expert puts it, "becomes a real relationship, a mutuality in which the subject creates the object just as much as the object creates the subject. The knower no longer feels himself to be independent of the known; the experiencer no longer feels himself to stand apart from the experience" (Wa,W,120).

Modern quantum mechanics teaches a similar lesson, and it was from its combination with the Eastern philosophy he knew through reading Jung that Olson derived his theory of Objectism. According to Heisenberg's Indeterminacy Principle, which the poet repeatedly invokes in his writings, "it is impossible to measure the simultaneous place and speed of a nuclear particle with absolute exactitude" for (in Olson's paraphrase) "a thing can be measured in its mass only by arbitrarily assuming a stopping of its motion, or in its motion only by neglecting, for the moment of measuring, its mass" (O,W,61). As Heisenberg points out in more general terms, we can only gather knowledge about our relationship to nature, never about nature as

separate from the observer, so that rigid dichotomies such as internal versus external, soul versus body, and subject versus object lose
their validity.[4] Objectism—which in his "Projective Verse" essay of
1950 Olson defined as "the getting rid of the lyrical interference of
the individual as ego, of the 'subject' and his soul"—is a reinterpreta-
tion of Williams' and Zukofsky's Objectivism in the light of these
insights. In contrast to Objectivism, Objectism is not conceived of as
the opposite of subjectivism, nor is man seen in contrast to nature.
For man, as Olson says, "is himself an object" (O,W,24).

Analogously, Olson, in his lifelong concern with the poetic
image, held a position not at all unlike Bly's. Needless to say, Olson
opposed "the suck of symbol which has increased and increased
since the great Greeks first promoted the idea of a transcendent
world of forms" (O,W,61) and he tried to limit the use of that term to
what he believed to be its original meaning: "Greek *symbolon*, 'a sign
by which one knows or infers a thing'" (O,M,11). In this way, Olson
was fond of quoting a slightly altered sentence from the Taoist
treatise *The Secret of the Golden Flower* as the sum total of what he "had
to offer": "That which exists through itself, is what is called meaning" (originally: "the Way [Tao]") (O,T,61).[5] Meaning, in other
words, is identical with, not referential to, pre-conceptual reality or
suchness—identical with things viewed (as Shao Yung, another
Taoist put it) "not subjectively but from the viewpoint of things"
(Ba,C,451). A Western poet in search of such reality, however, must
first traverse the "dark valley" of the unconscious, and then, in the
attempt to express himself, contend with the final incommunicabil-
ity of such insight.

Olson, albeit vaguely, seems to have been aware of both these
problems. He knew that it was only by using images, and avoiding
allegory, symbolism, and discursive logic, that the poet could stay
close to the suchness of things, and that his images, in order to
express this "meaning," have to be imbued with both the world of the
conscious and of the unconscious. This, I think, is the meaning of a
cryptic note Olson jotted down in 1955: "An image is truth, not
image, except as without image it is impossible to present truth (An
image may be defined as any proximate object to which there is a
flow of feeling) The conversion of archetypes to working images."[6]
In insisting on the fluidity and dynamism of such imagery, Olson
again almost seems to anticipate Bly's plea for a poetry that evokes
"that swift movement all over the psyche, from conscious to unconscious, from a pine table to mad inward desires" (B-M,P,163). To
Olson an image should not be a static picture, but a "vector." "As the
Master said to me in the dream, of rhythm is image / of image is

knowing / of knowing there is / a construct" (O,U,121).

Of course, it is one thing to explicate Olson's poetics and another to evaluate its general influence. And no doubt it was the latter which inspired and, to a degree, justified Robert Bly's criticisms. In this way, his single-minded and sometimes over-aggressive attacks on Olson and the "elegant isolationism" (B,S,6,22) of American poets generally, have performed a salutary function. The image of Bly as the Surrealist opponent to Objectivism may therefore soon come to be replaced by that of the poet who helped relate American open form poetics back to some of its European origins.

[1]See Hart Crane, *The Letters*, ed. B. Weber (Berkeley: University of California Press, 1965), p. 239; *The Complete Poems and Selected Letters and Prose*, ed. B. Weber (London: Oxford University Press, 1968), p. 221; J. Unterecker, *Voyager: A Life of Hart Crane* (New York: Farrar, Straus and Giroux, 1969), p. 590.

[2]See E. Faas, *Poesie als Psychogramm* (Munich: W. Fink Verlag, 1974), pp. 11, 143 ff.

[3]"Wandering Breezes: 8," *Li Po and Tu Fu*, ed. A. Cooper (Harmondsworth: Penguin Books, 1973), p. 205.

[4]*Das Naturbild der heutigen Physik* (Hamburg: Rowohlt Verlag, 1972), pp. 18, 28.

[5]See also *The Secret of the Golden Flower*, ed. R. Wilhelm (London: Routledge and K. Paul, 1972), p. 21.

[6]Quoted by R. von Hallberg, "Olson, Whitehead and the Objectivists," *boundary 2*, 2:2 (Fall 1973 - Winter 1974), 85-111,107.

# Robert Bly

*Faas*: To what degree do you acknowledge Philip Lamantia and David Gascoyne as predecessors for your own attempts to introduce Surrealism into Anglo-American poetry?

BLY: My view of Surrealism came entirely from Spanish and South American Surrealism.

*Faas*: It seems to me that in your earlier poetry collected in *Silence in the Snowy Fields* you are influenced by D. H. Lawrence.

BLY: No. *Silence in the Snowy Fields* looks back to Synge; and a couple of translations that Frank O'Connor made of medieval Irish work which moved me greatly; and then there is Antonio Machado. He is the father of that book.

D. H. Lawrence

*Faas*: And you hadn't read D. H. Lawrence at all at the time?

BLY: I had read a few poems, but among the English, Wordsworth is a much deeper influence.

*Faas*: But then there is all that imagery of going into the depths, into the dark and into the sea of death, etc., which seems exactly like Lawrence.

BLY: No link. I never read much of D. H. Lawrence's poetry until someone gave me the three-volume edition four or five years later. The only one I knew well was "Bavarian Gentians," which I think is a great great great great poem.

*Faas*: That's the poem I was thinking of, actually.

BLY: I still learn much from Lawrence, not from his poetry, but from the motion that he made from the intellect and down into the body.

*Faas*: So you do respect him.

BLY: Oh tremendously. The essay in the middle of *Sleepers Joining Hands* is full of mad generalizations for which I first saw the possibility in *Fantasia of the Unconscious*. Why not? A book of unsupportable generalizations about things that interest us. I don't think my essay would exist without *Fantasia of the Unconscious*.

*Faas*: There is an interesting book about Surrealism by C. Kellerer,

223

who claims that Western art, after a transitional period of Surrealism, or after crossing the "dark psychic woods of the
unconscious," as you would call it, is moving closer and
closer to a Zen Buddhist approach to reality. Does that
kind of general overview make sense to you? Kellerer
describes Pollock as approaching Eastern calligraphic painting
techniques, for instance.

*Surrealism and Zen*

BLY: We could imagine a poetry in which a great "flowing" consciousness is present, and the outer world is also present. In ancient
Buddhist art the world is very very very very present. The artist is
aware of it all the time. Such an artist would never do as Pollock does
and scatter it around like this, because in doing so he has dissolved
the world, he has returned to the state of the infant in which the
world is not clear. I respect Pollock a great deal, but I would think he
is the *end* of a Western tradition and that he has nothing to do with
the calligraphers, because the calligraphers are dealing with content.
When they are doing a calligraphy, every one of their curves to them
has the shape of a mountain or a moon in mist.

*Faas*: And you don't think that the impulse of action painting could
finally incorporate that concreteness?

BLY: I don't know. The tendency now is for everything in art to
break the link with the adult energy of the unconscious, if you can
say such a thing, and instead to proceed back towards the crib. The
baby is also spontaneous. So you have two movements
here, which appear alike, but are not. There is a very
interesting book entitled *Man-Child: A Study of the Infantilization of Man* by David Jonas and Doris Klein. It is an
impressive book. If the infantilism continues, all the things Lawrence stood for will be destroyed. I've just translated a poem by H.
Martinson about D. H. Lawrence:

*infantilization*

> You waited for the hour when all things would take on soul
>     again,
> and taste, feeling, and soul would touch them,
> as the day of inwardness came.
>
> But the world was extroverted.
> Only misunderstanding really thrived.
>
> The new deep communion you sang of did not happen.
> The interior table was set,
> but only a few came
> and only a few of those were capable of eating.

The rest came out of a meaningless curiosity.

The church in the body had to be locked up.
Now it stands open to the storm of steel, given over
to the demons of extroversion.

It's a good poem, and it gives another way to understand pop art. Pop art makes sense to me in terms of infantilization. The sense of adulthood is weak with us; it is stronger in the European psyche, and even more so in the Chinese. They imagine adulthood as the ability to balance *yin* and *yang*.

Let's return to Surrealism and open form. Both are launch points into the unknown. We launch out, and go away from patriarchal form, and then what happens? There is a powerful magnet over there, not far away, near the wall. It is the magnet of the crib, or the cradle, or "the Primitive man." It is too strong in America; it's too strong! It pulls art down into the crib, it pulls it backward. The "New York School" of recent years in art and poetry has not gone forward into the union of *yang* and *yin* as the ancient Chinese art and poetry did. Chinese artists moved for a thousand years into adult minglings of *yin* and *yang*, of mist and discipline. We go a little way away from the patriarchal and start to curve down. The lethargy in the colleges is a form of infantilism.

*Faas:* You once said that "the road to the new brain goes through the forest." That, in a way, seems to summarize what you have been talking about right now.

BLY: Yes, following that imagery, what we do is we find a gingerbread house in the forest and stay there. We never bother to put the witch into her own oven. We just ask for more cookies.

The Sufis and the Buddhists leave the gingerbread house and aim for an adult consciousness. But in order to reach that, the soul has to go through the mammal brain, which means it has to go into human suffering and into the body, into a deep sexual life. Lawrence says a man, like a flower, is "fertilized" by a strong sexual experience.

As Americans, we have to go through the mammal brain, but we don't want to do that. We went into the Vietnam war and did all that reptile killing and we now refuse to go through the mammal grief. I ended the reading last night with poems of Kabir, and the students' faces lit up all over the room. It was beautiful. That ecstasy is what they want more than anything, but they don't want to or know how to go through the mammal brain in order to get there.

*Faas:* Of course, that's an impression that one frequently gets in America, that people think they can take a shortcut to the new consciousness.

BLY: And one has to say in favor of Ted Hughes that he goes through the mammal, though he may not arrive at the new brain . . . The new brain is not so prominent in him. As Marie Louise von Franz would say, he is a little "caught" by black magic, and black magic hates the new brain. He's a little "caught" there. That's expressed by the crow, which is black. He wants someone to take him and bring him out, someone to bring him out of that. But there is nobody that's that far in, so nobody can help him. I see him as a suffering mammal, a great suffering mammal.

*Faas:* Are there any contemporary artists whose work parallels what you are trying to achieve in poetry?

BLY: I feel a strong kinship with Morris Graves, Max Ernst, de Kooning, Jean Arp, and with some work of Rauschenberg. To me Max Ernst is great, inexhaustible. I don't know any recent Surrealist poetry that comes near his *Une semaine de bonté.*

Surrealist art

*Faas:* But isn't that still deep "in the forest"?

BLY: Certainly, oh yes.

*Faas:* But do you see any glimpses of light from the open country on the other side?

BLY: There is something luminous about his paintings, the open country is floating all through them. The open country lives in Jean Arp's sculpture also.

*Faas:* But I was thinking of more recent art.

BLY: Well, Rauschenberg, I think, is a genius—sometimes!

*Faas:* But how about your criticism of pop art?

BLY: Rauschenberg is not only a pop artist.

pop art

*Faas:* I remember your saying that pop art—in Lawrence's terms—is putting the umbrella up again where Surrealism had taken it down.

BLY: Did I? Lawrence said that when you look up, in most centuries, you do not see the black sky with stars, but instead an opened umbrella on which artists have painted some stars. Humanity prefers that, it is less scary. A strong artist will tear holes in the umbrella so you can see the stars again. Eliot did that, so did the Surrealists. The whole Andy Warhol school is just putting the umbrella up again. I like Lawrence's image—it explains a lot to me. None of Warhol's movies tear open anything, just as pornography never tears open anything, it closes instead. The point of commercial pornography is to prevent you from experiencing. This is only my opinion; most people don't agree with me.

*Faas:* No, I wouldn't either.

BLY: Most people think Andy Warhol is part of the avant-garde, I don't.

*Faas:* To me, your poetic development shows a curious reversal of the development we talked about in relation to Kellerer's book. In this way, *Silence in the Snowy Fields* seems to have been written, not by a man "deep in the forest" of the unconscious, but by one who has traversed that forest and has come out the other side. You have often referred to a period of depression, solitude, and self-analysis, in New York, I gather, before you began to write poetry, and I wondered how that period relates to your first collection of poetry and what kind of experiences you went through during that period.

poetic development

BLY: I'd rather not talk about that very much. But you're right in your sense of the order. I did write some Surrealism before *Silence in the Snowy Fields*. I didn't put it in because I didn't want to break the tone of *Silence*.

*Faas:* So biographically speaking your development doesn't really reverse the general historical one in which Surrealism seems to precede the kind of consciousness which must have inspired *Silence in the Snowy Fields*.

BLY: But then there is no reason that Surrealism cannot return later. At any point it may be necessary for you to return to the confusion of the unconscious again.

*Faas:* But you don't want to talk about that period in New York.

BLY: I describe it in the autobiographical poem in *Sleepers Joining Hands* as well as I can. I was simply living in a small room, very poor. [Pause] Anyway it wasn't a period in which I did much writing. I understood Sartre's *Nausea* very well in those days. I didn't care for Sartre at all until I had been there for about two years, until I picked it up. I read the first five pages and I felt weak, almost fainted.

*Faas:* Most American poets seem to bypass the crisis described in *Nausea*, I mean the whole consciousness and language crisis which had such a devastating effect on many European poets—actually destroyed them as poets. Like Hugo von Hofmannsthal, for instance, who was probably the first to undergo that experience. He wrote all his greatest poetry before he turned 24, then suffered the crisis he describes in his famous "Lord Chandos Letter" (1902), and after that just stopped writing poetry. Of course, what Gary Snyder says concerning this

the language crisis

whole problem makes sense to me: that a poet like Hofmannsthal really wanted to be some kind of philosopher-magus.

BLY:  That language crisis involves the emotion of disgust. "You are defiled by what comes out of your mouth."

*Faas:*  That's like the phrase Hofmannsthal uses in the "Lord Chandos Letter": that words seemed to disintegrate in his mouth like mouldering mushrooms . . . What I'd like to discuss is your concept of the image.

the "deep image"    BLY:  I'm not fond of the term "deep image."

*Faas:*  Yes, I noticed that you avoid it in your criticism. But you have never given a detailed description or definition of what you mean by image.

BLY:  Let's try to make a distinction between "projection" and "image." Pound and Eliot both believed that a feeling is best kept fresh in art by being "projected" onto the outer world. "Smells of steaks in passageways" becomes an objective correlative of a certain feeling of mingled fatigue and despair Eliot experienced when he entered rooming houses. The substances "smells," "steaks," and "passageways" can all be taken out of the work of art and re-inserted back into the world. So they are "objective." Eliot doesn't use projection exclusively, he uses it mostly. Then, if "smells of steaks in passageways" is a projection of an inner fatigue out onto objects, what is an "image"? I'll quote some lines of Lorca, and then of Trakl:

> I want to sleep for half a second,
> a second, a minute, a century,
> but I want everyone to know that I'm still alive,
> that I am the little friend of the west wind,
> that I am the elephantine shadow of my own tears.

Somehow the psychic energy has remained inside the psyche, and there it created a new substance, "the elephantine shadow of my own tears." Trakl says:

> On silver soles I climbed down the thorny stairs, and I walked into the white-washed room. A light burned there silently, and without speaking I wrapped my head in purple linen; and the earth threw out a child's body, a creature of the moon, that slowly stepped out of the darkness of my shadow, and with broken arms dropped over a stony waterfall, fluffy snow.

You notice that the psyche is in a state of great energy. Moving with its own immense energy, it becomes equal to the world. Instead of depending on the outer world for support, it begins somehow to create a third world, neither "physical" nor "inner."

It's as if a human being and a badger together would give birth to an angel. Or as if an angel and a tree give birth to a bridge. It's as if a bull woke up one day with so much energy, he ignored the fence-posts and barn-door of his pasture and created Assyria instead.  creating a third world

We're so used to "fence-post and barn-door poetry" we don't recognize what Lorca is doing. We all write barn-door poetry. Most political poetry is barn-door poetry, and most love poetry now.

The phrase "deep image" suggests a geographical location in the psyche. It misses what the bull does. So I didn't feel that Robert Kelly caught the physicalness of the image in his "deep image" essay. Kelly has a wonderfully strong mind, but it's not especially physical. Rothenberg's mind is more physical.

*Faas:* I spent a day with Rothenberg several months ago, and liked him a lot.

BLY: He and I were friends, and still are, and we had conversations and planned magazines in which we tried to bring forward ideas of this sort. He did "Poems of the Floating World" . . .

*Faas:* Let me quote a few phrases by Duncan, who says that the image should be "close to the psychological archetype of Jungian analysis" or that it should be an "evocation of depth . . . not unrelated to the neo-Platonic images." Also he says that the image should be a "received sign of the great language in which the universe itself is written."  Duncan on image

BLY: I like the last one best. I get sick of hearing Plato's name spoken of in every discussion of the image. I agree an image can be "close" to an archetype, but the way to ruin a poem is to put in a lot of archetypes. I insist the image is a physical thing, and Plato doesn't know a thing about that.

We don't have to work on this. [Pointing to his brain] We become "successful" through *this,* but the mysterious thing is that art is created with this. [Pointing to his heart] What was the last one again?

*Faas:* The image is a "received sign of the great language in which the universe itself is written," which is really an Orphic concept.

BLY: And Orpheus, as you know, decided to go down here. [Pointing to his body]

*Faas:* The first one makes most sense to me.

BLY: They all make "sense," but it's a question of tone.

*Faas:* So you would hesitate to formulate a phrase or definition like that.

BLY: I would try to avoid it.

*Faas:* Like associating the image with Jungian archetypes and so forth.

BLY: I hate the word archetype.

*Faas:* Can you make any statement as to how images originate in your consciousness?

BLY: No.

*Faas:* Why not?

BLY: I don't *want* to make any statements on that. If I do, in this rapid tone, I'd make it with my thinking function. It wouldn't be just to the experience to describe it with one-fourth of the brain!

*Faas:* Did you know that Duncan has criticized Imagism in almost the exact same terms you use?

BLY: I'm not surprised.

*Faas:* How does your admiration for Chinese poetry relate to all this? After all, there don't seem to be many images like "death in the deep roads of the guitar" in Chinese poetry.

BLY: On the contrary, there are lots, and we can't get them through the English language, because the translators are used to "projection" poetry and they translate the poems into the barn-door poetry they know. Until Trakl's and Lorca's true image poetry penetrates to the minds of the scholars who translate Chinese, until that happens, we will be blind to Chinese poetry. In the meantime we have A. C. Graham's translations of *Poems of the Late T'ang.* In Li Ho you'll see images almost too wild to be disguised.

Chinese Surrealist poetry

*Faas:* So you would say that there is a very strong element in Far Eastern poetry of what in Western terminology we'd call Surrealist imagery?

BLY: Oh yes, very strong. Another way of talking about their sophistication would be to talk of the union of the senses. Here is a little poem of Basho's. He is listening to the temple bells in his garden.

> The temple bell stops,
> but the sound keeps coming
> out of the flowers.

Basho has taken a sound and changed it into an odor. That's someting that an Imagist couldn't do, or at least has not, to my knowledge, done. This art belongs to the whole area of changing of substances and transforming them. The ancient Chinese and Japanese poetry is far ahead of ours. American students in the poetry workshops have a hard time bringing an odor in its natural form into a poem, so we smell it as an odor. It's rare to hear a sound that's not a language sound in an American poem! It's rare to see green in a poem! Imagine being so at home in them that you could transform them!

*Faas:* How do you relate to Breton's concept of automatic writing? Do you think it's a useful exercise?

BLY: No.

*Faas:* My feeling is that exercises in automatic writing, even if they wouldn't have produced the actual poetry, could have had a very liberating effect on Hart Crane, for instance.

automatic writing

BLY: Automatic writing to me has more to do with Freud than with poetry.

*Faas:* That's more or less how T. S. Eliot felt about it, although he had to admit that parts of *The Waste Land* were composed in an efflux of poetry approaching the condition of automatic writing.

BLY: That's probably why it doesn't hold together as a work of art. Automatic writing evidently comes from fragmented parts of the psyche; and they are not connected to the whole and they are just like men at the edges of the raft crying, trying to make one realize that they're out there; and he brought too many of them into *The Waste Land;* the result is that it falls apart as a work of art. Its victory was a human victory, of compassion and listening.

*The Waste Land*

*Faas:* Of course, later he became almost ashamed of his poem, calling it a mere piece of rhythmical grumbling.

BLY: That's so typical. What he's gone through he feels obliged to deny to others. But there are real images in *The Waste Land:* "bats with baby faces in the violet light / Whistled, and beat their wings / And crawled head downward down a blackened wall . . ."Bats with baby faces in the violet light cannot be inserted into the universe or taken away. The are something insane, from another world.

*Faas:* At the beginning of my essay I compare these lines with some of yours.

BLY: I'd like to see it. I love that passage, love it, love it.

*Faas:* I'd like to come back to your concept of creativity for a moment. In my studies of Chinese æsthetics I found that the ancient literati talk a lot more about painting techniques than about poetic creativity.

Chinese æsthetics

BLY: It's not really worth investigating maybe; it would be different for every poet.

*Faas:* Whereas the painter calligraphists seem to be talking about the same thing most of the time: a kind of gestural automatism, a complete fusion with the subject matter, etc.

BLY:  Lovely, but I don't think we are advanced enough to do that.

*Faas:*  I wondered if there might be any analogue to that in poetic creativity.

BLY:  Probably.

*Faas:*  And I thought it was Olson's great contribution to have redis-covered this physiological basis of poetic creativity, this genuine spontaneity in contrast to the fictitious spontaneity of Romantic nature poetry.

Olson

BLY:  On the other hand, there are no real objects in Olson's poetry, perceived without the intrusion of the intellect or the ego.

*Faas:*  That's exactly what he criticized in Pound.

BLY:  It's a problem with intuitive types. There are no cows, a cow is a symbol for some part of his psyche. There are no horses, every horse is a symbol of part of his psyche. In a way, Jung is like that.

*Faas:*  And Surrealism would avoid that, in your opinion.

BLY:  Although in *most* Surrealism the author is again using only the intuitive part of his intelligence. It's possible that a great work of art cannot come out through using only one of our "functions" or "intelligences." It's as mistaken as Yvor Winters' trying to use only his thinking function. In good Spanish or South American Surrealism the world is often present, as well as the inner impulses from the unconscious. I'm not sure where Breton is in this. I don't feel "the world" so much in his poems. His younger

impure
Surrealism

followers evidently feel that the Surrealism is more in-tense and daring and more genuine if the world itself is left out. That is one reason they hate Neruda. Several American Surrealists have written me letters attacking me for translating Neruda. Some Surrealists feel also that if the Vietnam war appears in a poem otherwise Surrealist, it is a violation of the ideals of Sur-realism. The Puritan wishes to control the interior of his world, the American Surrealist wishes to control the interior of *his* world. Neruda is wise to call for "impure poetry." I think a Surrealist who tries to shut off in his own poems political comment is involved in Puritanism. Of course, he sees his point of view as wildly anti-Puritanical. But we all have many surprises for each other.

*Faas:*  But is there any principle as to how *you* make images intercon-nect?

BLY:  There, you are doing it again. I don't *make* images intercon-nect. If they don't and I notice it, I throw the poem away.

*Faas:*  And how do you notice it?

BLY: Reading the poem.

*Faas:* So again you wouldn't like to make an analytical statement about that?

BLY: No.

*Faas:* In an interview from the year 1972 you stated that the thinking which in the last eight or nine years you have learned most from has been Buddhist, and I wondered if Buddhism has also influenced your writing and creativity.

BLY: You are asking questions in a pre-Lawrence way, you are trying to fragment the psyche too much, and you are forcing me to think of myself as a third person. It's wrong to try and pin down religious influence. Perhaps an intelligent theory of meter could be discussed. But Buddhism, if it has influence, influences the entire psyche, it has to do with the integration of previously disconnected parts of the psyche, therefore you can't point to any one thing.

*Faas:* I was mainly thinking of my own comparison between action painting and Chinese calligraphy, that in both cases the artist abandons himself to the autonomous movements of his body.

BLY: Buddhism doesn't do that, Buddhism is very disciplined, they hate that kind of stuff.

*Faas:* I would speak of disciplined spontaneity.

BLY: Mu Ch'i made an ink wash of five pears. They are done with ink, I take it, and so could not be corrected. I suppose it took maybe 35 seconds.

*Faas:* Quite.

BLY: But this is preceded by fifteen years of this discipline. In the West we want to have "autonomous movement of the limbs" before the fifteen years are over.

*Faas:* I couldn't agree more. One can see some of that disciplined spontaneity in the work of Peter Brook and Jerzy Grotowski when compared with most Happenings.

BLY: Happenings belong to the history of infantilism, in my opinion. I repeat that I feel a danger in your questions, namely that you are drawn to the work of Lawrence and after, but approach it in a pre-Lawrence way.

*Faas:* But how does one avoid that?

BLY: How would Lawrence ask a question?

*Faas:* But you know, I'm not Lawrence. I'm just a University-trained European intellectual. [Both laughing]

BLY: Oh, now don't give me that modesty stuff!

*Faas:* I'm not really trying to be evasive. I know the shortcomings of what I'm doing, or rather of the way I'm doing it, only too well.

*[margin notes]* influence of Buddhism

disciplined spontaneity

BLY:   I don't mean shortcomings. I mean that you have a responsibility to Lawrence if he is one of your heroes. He says it is important to approach a problem from the point of view of the whole psyche. He opposes his new approach to the old fragmented or intellectualist approach. You're asking me for intellectualist formulations of various experiences which are bound to fragment the experience. I like your intellectual energy. But you might try to ask the questions in a Lawrence or post-Lawrence way. You might have to interpret the answer. I don't know what it would be like. But I sense it's harmful to your own psyche to ask intellectualist questions.

*the new critical approach*

*Faas:*   As a motto for one of your books you use those beautiful lines by Bashō:

> The morning glory —
> another thing
> that will never be my friend.

I think that's an example of what one can learn from Zen Buddhism or Eastern philosophy generally.

BLY:   I agree.

*Faas:*   In one of his interviews Ginsberg explains how the gaps between his images make the concrete world of the poem transparent for the final emptiness of the Absolute, the "blissful empty void" or *śūnyatā*, as the Buddhists call it. Does that notion make sense to you?

BLY:   What makes me vomit is that last thing, the "blissful empty void" or *śūnyatā*. We are all tourists of the East, all Westerners are, and we take their concepts and we misuse them constantly because of our crude psychological development. I've done it many times myself, I'm sure, I misuse them crudely, but somewhere there's a line which one shouldn't pass, and *śūnyatā* is an extremely serious concept or state. I think no Westerner has ever experienced it except perhaps San Juan de la Cruz or Santa Teresa de Avila. Now to have this dragged over and stuck into a little passage about poetry is revolting. I feel the same way about the phrase "Dharma Bums," can't stand it. It's exploitation not different from what the American soldier did in Vietnam, and Ginsberg doesn't realize, in my opinion, that when he uses a phrase like this he is violating the Buddhist religion in the same way that American marines violated a village.

*tourists of the East*

*Faas:*   Would the same apply to Gary Snyder as well, in your opinion?

BLY:   No, no. Once in a while, maybe. It applies to me too once in a while. But Gary has worked on the problem, he has worked hard, very hard. And these concepts need to be brought in, they are very valuable, but somehow the concepts are being destroyed. The poet's job is to keep language fresh, and Ginsberg is aware of that. And yet he takes a word like *śūnyatā* and throws it in any old place; he's cheapening language. Why does he do that?

Snyder

*Faas:* You've often attacked Ginsberg.

BLY: I don't attack him.

*Faas:* At least there are various critical remarks throughout your prose writings. You spoke of his "lack of gentleness."

attacking Ginsberg

BLY: Where did I say that?

*Faas:* Somewhere in *The Sixties,* I think, I could find it for you.

BLY: Ginsberg's lack of gentleness?

*Faas:* Yes. Then you criticize him for his use of four-letter words and shocking subjects.

BLY: That must have been in 1958, in *Fifties* No. 1.

*Faas:* And then you accused him for giving up "all hope of imaginative precision and delicacy."

BLY: When was that?

*Faas:* I don't have the exact reference here, but somewhere in *The Sixties,* I think. I could quote a lot more. [Both laughing]

BLY: That's interesting.

*Faas:* But recently you have called him the "clear rebirth . . . of a very powerful spiritual man" and have approvingly quoted his remark that "as soon as you have a new syntax, you have a new way of breathing and as soon as you have that you have a new consciousness." Has there been any change in your attitude towards Ginsberg?

change of attitude towards Ginsberg

BLY: There has. I wrote an article for *The American Poetry Review* recently giving examples in poetry of the "four intelligences" Jung talks about. They are thinking, feeling, grasp of the senses, and intuition. I gave Louis Simpson as an example of a thinking man basically. I mentioned that the hostility early on that thinking types felt towards Ginsberg was connected with the perception that he was urging them to develop their weak feeling function. I think that's true of my early hostility to Ginsberg.

*Faas:* So you're really saying your *peccavi* here.

BLY: Yes, of course . . . But at the same time we all notice that Ginsberg's spiritual gift is mingled with some sort of sloppy language. I mentioned that earlier. You see the problem. I feel two people in him. One is spiritual, one not. Recently I have been able to separate those two more. One part of Allen urges you on to develop your feeling areas, and since feeling is open on one side to the spirit, he is actually urging you to develop spirit. Then there's another being in him urging you to remain content with clutter. I'm thinking of the poem in his new book from a meditation retreat in Colorado describing his breath going out over the country to Lowell, Mass., then to Kyoto, Vietnam, etc. It is a sort of tourist poem, with a couple of anecdotes of each place. The poem loads us down with memory clutter so the poem somehow misrepresents meditation. One half of him is the grandmother, and the other half is the wolf! But the grandmother is so amazingly generous. It comes out in his singing, too.

*Faas:* So you have become friends.

BLY: Oh yes. Yes. We read together whenever we can. Once in my house, he saw a group of anthologies in a bookcase, and said, "Well, Robert, when we're both in all those anthologies, then what?" That's how wise the grandmother is.

*[I next read Bly the passage from my essay dealing with his attack on James Dickey. This led to a long and fascinating discussion of "The Firebombing" and "Slave Quarters" which Bly, however, preferred to delete from the typescript of the interview, saying there is too much criticism of others here. (E.Faas)]*

*Faas:* In your criticism you have mainly drawn attention to the poetries outside the Anglo-American tradition. Occasionally, but not very often, you mention Wordsworth, whom you compare with the Chinese poet Tao Yuan Ming, or Yeats as having the sense of "Gott-Natur," or Blake, who took a first step into the psychic forest. Are there any other English or American poets with whom you feel a deep affinity?

BLY: Besides Yeats and Blake—Chaucer, certainly. Even more the Grail poets, the Tristan poet, and the author of *Gawain and the Green Knight.* To me they are contemporary.

*Faas:* Duncan and, before him, Pound have argued that it was during the period of the "romances" that the Western mind, for a short phase at least, began to recuperate some of the energy and imagery repressed by Christianity.

medieval poetry

BLY: I'm just beginning to think of the possibility of the Grail poems being reworkings of Sufi literature. I have instead seen them as vigorous attempts to bring forward the feminine in man, in the male. Shortly after the Grail work, the movement was entirely crushed. The church moves in after the fourteenth century A.D. Respect for the feminine doesn't rise again until the Romantic age, but it appears once more in our time. Pound touched on Troubadour poetry, but

Pound doesn't seem involved in the spirit—or the link between the spirit and the feminine. What the Grail poems discuss even more is some strange creature who is wounded. He has a bit of steel or iron in his testicles, and he can't be healed; this wound remains unhealed century after century. So there is such a thing as    wound literature "wound literature." It is ignored through the whole eighteenth century. The European psyche knows it is wounded. It's a profound wound which will not heal, and in the eighteenth century people did not discuss it. They put a plaster or a bandage over it. In the nineteenth century, writers live out the agony of the wound. But they still will not investigate it, and it's only in our time that the wound is beginning to live and be lived again—also in words—

*Faas:* *The Waste Land* brings it up.

BLY: I think so.

*Faas:* Ted Hughes once described the poem to me as a love poem for this degraded and desecrated female spirit.

BLY: He's right surely. [Pause] Aristotle caused a wound and the Grail legends talk about that wound, now no work is of any value that does not face the wound . . .

*Faas:* You take Aristotle as being representative of Greek rationalism, I guess.

BLY: That kind of thing, yes. The Middle Ages centered around Aristotle, the whole mentality that led to the Ph.D. as well as to secularism. And I personally think that the Aristotle mentality is related to the mass-man also. Ortega y Gasset's *Revolt of the Masses*— what a powerful book! Underneath, Aquinas and Aristotle are much alike. One is the religious version, the other the secular version. The Grail legends describe the wound made by the Catholic Church that foolishly adopted Aristotle.

*Faas:* Ernst Topitsch has described how this fusion of Greek and Christian thought leads right up to Hegel and Marx . . .

BLY: . . . and leaves out an entire world, which is the world hinted at in the "romances." They are still secret literature, secret literature for a small group.

*Faas:* Duncan links that to Gnosticism, neo-Platonism, Hermeticism, and all the other heretical movements.

BLY: Yes. Bosch also. Centuries later Dürer appears with his great femininity, his combination of femininity and precision. In the twentieth century Antonio Machado. In between the two there is Blake. Blake talks about the wound in "Oh rose, thou art sick."

*Faas:* So you feel that Romanticism initiated Modernism.

BLY: I do surely.

*Faas:* Do you find that American poets of the last two decades have responded to your plea, made in the late fifties, that they must traverse the dark psychic woods of the unconscious before they will be able to write a truly great modern poetry?

BLY: I don't believe that it's possible to write post-Lawrentian poetry or "wound-poetry" or however you want to describe it without solitude; and when people in the universities try to write such poetry they often find the style without the way of life; it sends them off on just another sidetrack. I think that's what's happening. The style has been picked up but I don't see much deep change. I underestimated how much a style is a part of a way of life. Rilke is right at the end of his Apollo poem where he says that in order to write differently you have to change your *life*.

*Faas:* You have often criticized Olson for embodying the "formalist obsession" of American poetry. On the other hand, I find that your own position is not at all antagonistic to Olson's. I see it as complementary . . .

BLY: Sure, why not.

*Faas:* . . . rather than antagonistic to him. But why then did you have to attack him for something which is not even at the center of his poetics? I mean there is so much more to Olson than his concern with breath rhythm, prosody, and so forth. For instance, his concern with the physiological autonomy of the creative process.

controversy
with Olson

BLY: Several times—maybe those remarks are in interviews or essays you haven't seen—I've said about Olson that I respect his intellectual speculations tremendously.

I started my magazine to clear ground for myself and for other poets. By 1964 the ground was absolutely and entirely covered with Charles Olson bushes. There was not a spot of ground that was not shaded by a Charles Olson bush. Creeley, after a long correspondence with Charles Olson, formulated the dogma "form is never more than an extension of content." Olson praised it, and most writers since find it self-evident. But I don't think the statement is true at all.

form not an
extension
of content

I have the feeling that I sense Bach's mathematical form with one part of myself, and his ecstatic freedom with another part. That implies there are two separate forces meeting in a third body.

*Field* published a weird essay recently by Donald Hall, in which he suggested that some of the oral or breast sensuality of infancy goes into sound in poetry, and so into form. He suspects that poetic form is linked with archaic layers of the pleasure instinct, experienced first with depth in infancy. I add that some of the adult grasp of "the world" goes into content. We can see that such a visualization is incompatible with the accepted idea Olson has praised. Far from form and content being extensions, one of the other, it is more likely they are distinct and opposite forces, opposite in charge.

I wrote a letter to *Field* commenting on this issue, and I'll read you a couple of paragraphs:

> Charles Olson wonderfully understood that American poetic form could not be an imitation of English form, and that the roots of form go back to the body and its breath, not to English metrical habits. It seems though that he wanted the form to be adult—he was interested in the time after the invention of the typewriter, rather than the primitive time before the baby or the aborigine has ever seen a typewriter.
>
> His essay on projective verse makes the whole problem of form technical, post-industrial, needing ingenuity and a typewriter with a good spacer. I'm unjust to his intellectual liveliness, but there is some Puritanism, that is, dislike of childhood, in his essay. Russian poets don't seem to have that.

*Faas:* Even Duncan would partly agree with that, I think.

BLY: Suppose a work of art is a container of energy, a sort of battery, then bland formulations of the unity of form and content merely mislead young poets as to what a work of art is. There is something bland in much Black Mountain poetry.

*Faas:* You know, that at the Berkeley reading, being obviously quite drunk and stoned, he said that he was really in love with our lady of Christ.

BLY: I think he must have been a lively man. As a person, as a teacher, he was evidently extremely warm, with a fantastically big mammal brain. He taught Creeley an amazing number of things. But to go back, suppose we use open form. The sound sensuality question is how do you bring infantile pleasure or sound sensuality into an open form poem?

*Faas:* Snyder is very concerned with that.

BLY: Is he?

*Faas:* Oh yes. How do you get that rhythmic sensuality back into open form poetry?

BLY: Sensuality seems the right word to use.

*Faas:* You once said that Objectivism—and I don't think that's fair to Olson's Objectism—is an evasion of self. I feel that both you and Olson are rather more interested in a kind of self-transcendence.

BLY: Yes, yes.

*Faas:* You achieve it by delving into the unconscious, whereas Olson achieves it by trying to abandon himself to some kind of autonomous, automatic process of creativity akin to what Werner Haftmann calls the gestural expressionism of action painting—a physiological process which is larger than himself and in which he fuses with the flux of nature.

BLY: Absolutely right.

*Faas:* So I don't understand why you object . . .

BLY: When he says that we must try to avoid "the soul getting between us and the objects," I agree, and yet, what does it mean? It's a secular statement, an Aristotelian statement. So therefore I find him coming from two sides; he makes Aristotelian statements and yet he struggles against the Aristotelian box. By an Aristotelian I mean someone who encourages a naked confrontation between "mind" and "object," with the "soul" left out. That's vague, I know. But it's possible we *share* soul with objects. How could we then leave out soul as we try to get near objects? It's possible we're not the only beings who *have* soul!

Objectism

I do like the way he thinks from scratch. "I go down and look at the Mayan tombs and no one has ever looked at them with a fresh eye as I have." Pound looked at economics that way. The American apparently longs to be the amateur discoverer. It's a great weakness and a great strength. I do it too. I try to throw off the European mind background, and then I have to become an amateur psychologist if not an amateur archaeologist. You understand that impulse? It's very American, very American. It's all through Hemingway. Hemingway says: "The Europeans don't know anything about style. I found a style. I found it in the woods." That impulse is in all of us.

the American
amateur discoverer

*Faas:* Talking about the form of a poem, you once spoke of its "mysterious arbitrariness." You also said that it is obsolete to consider form as the most inportant thing about a poem. And finally, in a statement reminiscent of Pound and Lawrence, you said that a great work of art often has at its center "a long floating leap around which the work gathers like steel shavings around a magnet."

BLY: Magnetic energy gives so many possibilities for understanding art. In the leaping sentence I'm thinking of content. The substance of a poem arranges itself round the center leap. In the *Odyssey* the poem first leaps into the Great Mother, and

poetic form

then all the scenes such as visiting Circe, visiting the Cyclops, going down to the dead, center themselves naturally around the initial leap. The poem takes its form that way without mind-intervention.

*Faas:* Creeley claims that he usually writes a poem in one stretch, so that the order in which the words appear on the page reflects exactly the chronological sequence of creativity. Or Snyder told me that he often completes a poem in his mind and then just transcribes it onto the page. By contrast you once said that you wrote about 10,000 lines for the poem catled "Sleepers Joining Hands" and only published about four hundred. Do you    revising revise just by throwing things away, like Creeley, while leaving the rest untouched?

BLY: I revise by magnetics, see what holds on. In that poem, I didn't √ know what the poem was about so I worked in confusion for four years.

*Faas:* In a totally open process of creative discovery.

BLY: Evidently, that's why I wrote so many lines.

*Faas:* Of course, Snyder, likewise, uses a totally different way of writing in composing the various sections of *Mountains and Rivers without End.*

BLY: Yes. There must be other ways, too.

*Faas:* Last night you spoke of three levels of consciousness. In the lowest level there is a great deal of repression, violence, and isolation. On the second level the man or woman—you gave D. H. Lawrence as an example—moves out past his ego into creatures and trees. Then you read Kabir's ecstatic poems as    open form an example of work on the third level. How does "open form" relate to these three levels?

BLY: I haven't thought this over myself.

Let's say first that writing a good rhymed and metered poem means that the man or woman has learned how to repress successfully. Repressing well is a valuable art in civilization, as important as knowing how to build with wood. We repress constantly. When Breton, for example, allows angry lobsters with hair to come up, at the same second he is repressing tenderness. The problem is that when we're young, we don't choose what to repress. We repress firmly, but not wisely. In other words the material stays down. Poets who write a great deal of rhymed verse in their twenties have trouble growing, because their literary self-respect becomes associated with successful repression. We all know examples of that. Frost is one, on a wide scale.

Let's try to relate that idea to states of consciousness.    repression

and            The man or woman in the lowest stage—where we are
projection   most of the day—experiences constant projection. The
American man is not angry, other people are. He is not feminine,
Marilyn Monroe is. The American woman says: "I am not dark
inside, the blacks are dark." She is not obsessed with force, the
Russians are obsessed with force. But the marvellous discovery
Freud and Jung made is that only energies already pushed out of
sight are projected out onto others' faces. We can't get hold of our
energies, only see them on the faces of others. As a man, I can't get
hold of my female side, I can only see it on the faces of women. This
inability to get hold of our energies is an experience in the lowest
stage of consciousness. We have all had those experiences thousands
of times.

    To return then to rhymed and metered poems . . . The poet
says, "I am not orderly inside, the poem is." This projection, like all
projection, is dangerous when it becomes a habit. Frost's life got
more and more disorderly as that *habit* took hold.

    "Free verse" or "open form" then is not a literary technique—
that's why I dislike Olson's essay "Projective Verse"—that's odd—
Projective Verse!—but it is a step in growth. It is a way to encourage
us to let up a little in repression, ease up the projection, and move out
a bit from the lowest stage of consciousness. It doesn't always suc-
ceed, and those who write rhymed and metered poetry today don't
always stay in the lowest stage of consciousness, by any means. We're
dealing in tendencies, possibilities, only. Richard Wilbur did not stay
there.

    As a person moves from the first to the second level of con-
sciousness, he or she allows some repressed material to rise—just as
you are allowing it to rise in your hallucinations.
*Faas:* That's right.
BLY: Here's a possible visualization of it, that I see. Each time we
enter the second level there may be three sudden movements taking
place at the same instant. Energy pushed down rises up towards you
from below; then the brother of that energy sent off to live on the
faces of others descends down to you . . . at the same moment your
feminine soul appears as a speck on the horizon rushing toward you.
If a woman is writing the poem, or experiencing the second stage,
the movements are identical except that her masculine soul is what
the need for      appears far away hurrying towards her. There is a lot of
a new cycle   swift and vigorous motion, as of dancing, involved . . .
of repression      What "open form" and Lawrence's "we have come
and release   through" and Marianne Moore's intuitive joinings of dis-
parate material without "classical form" and Neruda's jumble in the

*Residencia* poems mean is not that repression is bad, but that we need a different cycle of repression and release than we have had.

From what I've said about release, we can guess what the third stage would be like. I suspect the idea of "open form" falls away in the third stage—the man's feminine side would be close to him, I think, and he would feel light for the first time. The woman's male side would be close to her—as the male side of Marie Louise von Franz has come very close to her. You feel in her prose that she's projecting very little. But some. We cannot enter paradise, we cannot in this life, we cannot have all the exiled material returned. Marie Louise has said that over and over—

*Faas:*  You think that some of Gary Snyder's poems reach that stage?

BLY:  Certainly.

*Faas:*  Would you identify the new brain with this third level?

BLY:  No, not really when I come to think of it . . . I don't think so. I would guess we need all our brains at that stage.

*Faas:*  I was a bit puzzled that you called Creeley a poet of "the steady light," who tended to remain in one brain when he writes. To me it seems that he is a poet fascinated by the void, like Mallarmé: "The poem supreme, addressed to/ emptiness."

BLY:  I don't know how to answer that. He has a weird     Creeley
path of his own. I don't really understand it, but I respect it. I feel very close to him—I kiss him when I see him—

*Faas:*  I am going to see him up in Buffalo in a couple of weeks.

BLY:  Then please tell him from me that I think his new poem about his mother in the hospital is marvellous.

# Allen Ginsberg

Photo: Gerard Malanga

# ALLEN GINSBERG (1926 -        )

> The problems confronted in attempting to graph the opera-
> tions of the mind in language and the problems confronted
> historically at this apocalyptic-end-of history time are so com-
> plex and so new and previously unexperienced by any culture
> . . . that no previous models of speech forms . . . just as no
> previous models of life style within memory are sufficient, and
> we're going to have to out of our own native genius invent our
> own, out of our own imagination, as Blake and Whitman
> proposed.

Ginsberg's deliberate efforts to destroy his charisma are, paradoxically, part of his personal magnetism. While forever paying homage
to his masters (Williams, Pound, Burroughs, Kerouac, Trungpa), he
has turned into the figurehead of a whole generation as America's
most internationally acclaimed poet since Whitman. The major data
of his life, many of them already shrouded in legend—his Blake
vision in Harlem, the reading of *Howl* at the San Francisco Six
Gallery, his reign and public arrest as King of the May in Prague, and
his involvement in numerous trials—seem to focus the literary as
much as culturo-political history of an entire era. A "Buddhist Jew
with attachments to Krishna, Siva, Allah, Coyote, and the Sacred
Heart," Ginsberg was born in New Jersey, the son of poet high-
school teacher Louis Ginsberg and his wife Naomi, a Communist
radical, whose death he lamented in *Kaddish* (1961). Educated in the
public schools of Paterson, New Jersey, he there made the acquain-
tance of Williams who taught him to listen to the rhythm of his own
voice. After temporarily suspending Ginsberg in 1945, Columbia
University finally granted him a B.A. in 1948. But his real education
was provided by older poet mentors like Burroughs and Kerouac. A
prolific poet since his teens (see *Empty Mirror*, 1961; *The Gates of
Wrath*, 1972), he found his own voice of "Hebraic-Melvillean bardic

breath" in *Howl*, a lament for his "generation destroyed by madness," dedicated to Carl Solomon, whom Ginsberg, in 1949, had met as a patient in the Columbia Psychiatric Institute. Widely known after an obscenity trial in which Judge Clayton Horn granted *Howl* "redeeming social importance," he began a life of global pilgrimages through South America, Europe, Israel, India, Japan and his own country. Much of his work published since *Kaddish (The Yage Letters,* 1963; *Planet News,* 1961-1967, 1968; *Indian Journals,* 1970; *The Fall of America,* 1972; *Mind Breaths,* 1977) gives an account of this ceaseless quest. For several years now, Ginsberg has been associated with Chögyam Trungpa's Naropa Institute where he is co-ordinator of "The Jack Kerouac School of Disembodied Poetics," teaching "poetics and meditation in the whispered transmission school of Milarepa (12th century Tibetan Buddhist yogi-poet)."

# Allen Ginsberg

> But at the far end of the universe the million eyed Spyder that
>     hath no name
> spinneth of itself endlessly
> the monster that is no monster approaches with apples, per-
>     fume, railroads, television, skulls
> a universe that eats and drinks itself
> blood from my skull.
>
> (G,K,86)

This evocation of the horrific aspect of Nature or the "Great Being" from Ginsberg's poem "Lysergic Acid" has many parallels, not only in the poet's own work, but in contemporary literature and art as a whole. Here, for instance, is a passage from Burroughs' *Naked Lunch* describing a scene from the blue movie shown at "A.J.'s Annual Party." What begins as a straightforward pornographic film à la *Deep Throat* suddenly turns into a Surrealist orgy of sadism and murder, in which Mary, the female participant, assumes the role of a bloodthirsty Ogress:

> She bites away Johnny's lips and nose and sucks out his eyes with a pop . . . She tears off great hunks of cheek . . . Now she lunches on his prick . . . Mark walks over to her and she looks up from Johnny's half-eaten genitals, her face covered with blood, eyes phosphorescent. . . .

Among the passages charged as "brutal, obscene and disgusting" in the Boston trial of 1962, this one is probably the most "offensive" in the entire novel.[1]* Yet it is hardly more so than much that for millennia has been an accepted part of the artistic canon of many non-Western cultures. Tantric, Hindu or Taoist art provides examples of the almost total absence of sexual tabus in specific cultures of ancient Tibet, India or China, while a few quotes from Heinrich Zimmer's *Myths and Symbols in Indian Art and Civilization* could have easily convinced Burroughs' judges that a gruesomeness

*Notes to this section on p. 268.

249

comparable to *Naked Lunch* is a common attribute of many Eastern divinities and, in the case of Black Kālī, of "the most cherished and widespread of the personalizations of Indian cult." "Innumerable representations of the devouring Black Kālī," Zimmer writes, "depict [the] wholly negative aspect of the Universal Mother." In a sculpture reproduced in the book, for instance,

> she appears as an emaciated, gruesome hag of bony fingers, protruding teeth, unquenchable hunger . . . [feeding] upon the entrails of her victim. And who among beings born is not her victim? She cleaves the belly and draws out and gobbles the intestines—that is what she is fond of—steaming with the last breath of expiring life.

Other representations show her "adorned with the blood-dripping hands and heads of her victims, treading on the prostrate, corpse-like body" of Shiva, her spouse and lover.[2]

Moreover, such monstrosities are by no means a specific obsession of one particular religion. The Great Mother in her "negative elementary character"[3] is common to many of the world's mythologies and her archetypal attributes are clearly evident when we compare Black Kālī with, for instance, the Aztec Coatlicue whose monumental sculpture, now in the Anthropological Museum of Mexico City, miraculously survived the destruction of Montezuma's Holy City at the hands of the Christian conquerors. Like the Indian Goddess, Coatlicue is adorned with the blood-dripping hands and torn-out hearts of her victims. In this she also resembles Vishnu, supreme deity of the Hindu pantheon, as depicted in the celebrated 11th chapter of the *Bhagavad Gita*. Like the latter's "Universal Form" as "Time," "the Destroyer of the worlds" equipped with many faces, eyes, arms, bellies, legs, terrible teeth and devouring mouths (B,G,229), the Mexican Earth Mother and mother of all the Aztec divinities has myriad eyes, multiple serpent faces and devouring jaws, several bodies and claws as well as fearsome arrays of tusks.

Western culture proves to be different from most others in excluding such notions from the accepted part of its religious consciousness. Here, Heraclitus was both the first and last of the great philosopher prophets (before Blake or Nietzsche) who, in his famous proposition that "war is the father and king of all," affirmed the horrific as an intrinsic part of the divine. But such wisdom was obscured by the advent of Greek idealistic philosophy and Judæo-Christian eschatological thinking which reinforced each other in "the illusion that good may exist without evil,"—either in a Platonic realm of ideas or in a heavenly hereafter in which "there shall be no more death, neither sorrow, nor crying" (Wa,G,48). Evil was explained as an incomplete self-realization of the ideal or was relegated to the infernal region of the fallen angels, while on the level of secular religion the Great Mother was gradually replaced by "Frau Welt" whom Chaucer's contemporary, the preacher John Bromyard, describes as a beautiful lady with her back full of worms and festering sores.[4] By the late Middle Ages this image, which also adorns the outside of many cathedrels, had acquired the ubiquity of a literary *locus communis*.

What to most religions is an unalterable part of the divine is explained by Christianity as the result of man's sinfulness. Thus God assumes the role of a judge to whom the horrific, by a further twist of the same cosmological notion, becomes the justification for punishing man for the evil which is an inherent part of all creation. As if modelled on this scheme, the segregating, torturing and exterminating of large groups of people for their sinfulness, unorthodox beliefs, impure race or ideology has been one of the most obvious hallmarks of Western spiritual history. Ironically, the most frightening excesses of this kind have tended to occur in periods of enlightened ideologizing such as our own which, coincident with the breakdown of traditional values, has witnessed the total unleashing of the demonic forces ignored or suppressed by idealistic philosophy and Judæo-Christian religion. The concentration camps of this century may thus be seen as a secularized extension or psychological enactment of the horror world which Dante and others have portrayed with such zestful detail and ingenious precision.

The actual holocausts of recent decades were paralleled and often heralded by an unprecedented emergence of the horrific in art. It is the final irony of our tragic misconception of evil that such art was denounced as decadent and corrupt by the very ideologists who began to stage its imagined horrors in the barbed wire infernos of the German and Russian concentration camps. Of course, there were others who clearly recognized the function of this artistic phenomenon in the spiritual development of our time. Not long before the Nazi exhibition of decadent art in Munich opened its gates to innumerable visitors from Germany and abroad, a large Picasso retrospective in Zurich and the stir it had created caused C. G. Jung to write an essay about the artist (1932). To the psychiatrist it is a symptom of the general emergence of the "antichristian and Luciferian forces . . . in modern man" that Picasso follows "the demoniacal attraction of ugliness and evil," thereby dissolving the "accepted ideals of goodness and beauty" into "fragments, fractures . . . [and] disorganized units." Despite its obvious schizophrenic tinge, the painter's work (just like Joyce's *Ulysses*) complies to the fullest extent with the "social significance of art" in its time. For the latter, as Jung had written as early as 1922,

> is constantly at work educating the spirit of the age, conjuring up the forms in which the age is most lacking. The unsatisfied yearning of the artist reaches back to the primordial image in the unconscious which is best fitted to compensate the inadequacy and one-sidedness of the present.[5]

Eastern literature showed Jung that the images emerging in this process often resemble the symbols of various non-Western mythologies. As he found in 1938, the sequence of events described in *The Tibetan Book of the Dead*, for instance, "offers a close parallel to the phenomenology of the European unconscious when it is undergoing an 'initiation process,' that is to say, when it is being analysed" (BT,xlix). Even Jung, however, might have been surprised to see how closely a description such as the following of the "blood-drinking wrathful deities" which the soul encounters on her journey after death comes to paralleling the horrific in the art and literature that began to emerge towards the end of his life (1875-1961):

> from the south-east, the Red Pukkase, holding intestines in the right [hand] and [with] the left putting them to her mouth . . . from the north-west, the Yellowish-White Tsandhalî, tearing asunder a head from a corpse, the right [hand] holding a heart, the left putting the corpse to the mouth and [she then] eating [thereof]; . . . from the north-west, the Black Crow-Headed One, the left [hand] holding a skull-bowl, the right holding a sword, and [she] eating heart and lungs. (BT,142-3)

For although Jung's insights were preceded by artistic developments originating with "the Romantic Agony,"[6] it was only after World War II that the horrific began to dominate modern art. The full extent of this phenomenon and of its origins is as yet uncharted, but it is sufficient to mention names such as Francis Bacon or Edward Kienholz, Ted Hughes or William Burroughs to remind us that the horrific, far from being the subject matter of outsider visionaries such as Bosch, Goya or Blake, now holds center stage in the imaginative world of present-day art and literature. Among North American poets, Allen Ginsberg no doubt has had the strongest impact in this realm, and it may contribute to our understanding of modern art in general to follow the poet through his arduous struggle with the demons which loom so frighteningly in our contemporary consciousness.

The fourth book of *Paterson* reprints a letter which Ginsberg sent Williams, along with some poems, shortly after his release from a New York mental hospital. One of the poems, later published in *Empty Mirror* (1961), has the mysterious title "The Shrouded Stranger." As Ginsberg explained to Williams, it was based on a real dream about "a classic hooded figure" and "the void," a dream which had "become identified with [his] own abyss" (W,P,205). Thus inspired, the poem not only seems to prefigure a more than fifteen year long search for the hidden divinity, but to anticipate some of its ultimate fulfillment:

> I dreamed I was dreaming again
> and decided to go down the years
> looking for the Shrouded Stranger.
> I knew the old bastard
> was hanging around somewhere.
>
> I couldn't find him for a while;
> went looking under beds,
> pulling mattresses off,
> and finally discovered him
> hiding under the springs
> crouched in the corner:
>
> met him face to face at last.
> I didn't even recognise him.
>
> "I'll bet you didn't think
> it was me after all," he said.
>
> (G,M,46-7)

Before Ginsberg, fulfilling his own dream prophecy, could face up to the "Shrouded Stranger" in real life, he had to subject himself to shamanistic rituals of self-destruction and learn to accept his bodily self in a "universe that eats and drinks itself" (G,K,86). What launched him on this fearsome journey was his 1948 Blake vision which Ginsberg, like a latter-day Ancient Mariner, has told and retold ever since. Even in this first of many hallucinatory experiences, the attainment of "cosmic consciousness," the exhilarating awareness that "existence itself was God," is overshadowed by dread and doom. As the poet recalled in 1965,

> I experienced "The Sick Rose," with the voice of Blake reading
> it, as something that applied to the whole universe, like hear-
> ing the doom of the whole universe, and at the same time the

inevitable beauty of doom. I can't remember now, except it
was very beautiful and very awesome. But a little of it slightly
scary, having to do with the knowledge of death—my death
and also the death of being itself, and that was the great pain.

The experience left Ginsberg with no doubt that he "was born to
realize . . . the spirit of the universe." But in his repeated attempts to
fulfill this mission he more and more came to resemble Dr. Faustus
who yearns to see God, yet only succeeds in conjuring up the devil.
Shortly after the Blake vision, when once again he tried to invoke the
"Great Spirit," it did indeed appear to him, but in the shape of "some
really scary presence, it was almost as if I saw God again except God
was the devil." And although Blake seemed to urge him on "To find a
Western Path / Right through the Gates of Wrath," Ginsberg "got
scared, and thought, I've gone too far" (Pl,W,304,305,308,311).

None of these early visions found direct expression in the poet's
published verse, and to judge from their actual descriptions there
was, in fact, little visual detail to record. Subsequent drug experiments, however, not only brought back the hallucinations, but filled
them with an eerie phantasmagoria of archetypal images embodied
in the concrete realities of modern life. Such a fusion is documented
in Ginsberg's report of an experience which inspired the second part
of *Howl*:

> I had an apt on Nob Hill [San Francisco], got high on Peyote, &
> saw an image of the robot skullface of Moloch in the upper
> stories of a big hotel glaring into my window; got high weeks
> later again, the Visage was still there in red smokey downtown
> Metropolis. (A,P,416)

But how could such visions be turned into poetry, without
"thought of transcription," as Ginsberg put it later, "haz[ing his]
mental open eye" (G,H,25)? From about 1945, when the 19 year old
poet wrote "big long poems about a last voyage looking for Supreme
Reality" (Pl,W,301), up to the composition of *Howl*, it took Ginsberg
an entire decade to find a satisfactory answer to this question. The
early poems, collected in *Empty Mirror* (1961), *Reality Sandwiches*
(1963) and *The Gates of Wrath* (1972), many of which discuss the
writing of poetry itself, bear witness to the formal ingenuity
Ginsberg unfolded in this search as well as to the many impasses he
encountered along the way. One such poem records how he abandoned the concentrated precision of his early manner under the
influence of poets like Wyatt or Williams:

I attempted to concentrate

the total sun's rays in
each poem as through a glass,
but such magnification
did not set the page afire.

(G,M,18)

As if to ensure himself of a possible alternative, Ginsberg gave the
poem a motto culled from Thomas Hardy's introduction to *Poems of
the Past and the Present* (1901). "The road to a true philosophy of life,"
it reads, "seems to lie in humbly recording diverse readings of its
phenomena."

Yet neither Hardy nor any contemporary poet seemed to
suggest a satisfactory medium for such recording. Instead, Cézanne
(to whom he was introduced by his Columbia University teacher
Meyer Schapiro) gave him the exact effect of "a catalyst to visionary
states of being" he tried to achieve in poetry. Looking at the paintings Ginsberg "got a strange shuddering impression," a "cosmic
sensation" resembling his Blake vision, as if he "could see *through*
[the] canvas to God" (Pl,W,291ff.). He immediately set about to
investigate the painter's techniques and found several which, he felt,
were directly transferable to poetry. Instead of using perspective,
Cézanne simply juxtaposed one color against another, for instance,
or instead of *imitating* reality, he *recreated* it by processes of reduction
and reconstitution:

> So, I was trying to do similar things with juxtaposition like
> "hydrogen jukebox" . . . Cézanne is reconstituting by means of
> triangles, cubes, and colors—I have to reconstitute by means
> of words, rhythms . . . phrasings . . . The problem is then to
> reach the different parts of the mind, which are existing simul-
> taneously, the different associations which are going on simul-
> taneously, choosing elements from both, like: jazz, jukebox,
> and all that, and we have the jukebox from that: politics,
> hydrogen bomb, and we have the hydrogen of that. (Pl,W,206)

Somewhat later, Ginsberg found that this method of compressing "basically imagistic notations into surrealist or cubist phrasing"
(Kr,G,166) is related to the poetics of Fenollosa's *The Chinese Written
Character as a Medium for Poetry*, and that his use of dashes, the most
obvious hallmark of this method, can be seen in the light of *haiku*
technique which, in Pound's terms, is characterized by "a form of
super-position . . . one idea set on top of another" (P,G,89). In
Ginsberg's own words, a dash or ellipse—"the hair-raising awareness
in between two mental visual images"—can give us a glimpse of
*śūnyatā*, of the "blissful empty void" of Buddhism "to which the Zen
finger classically points" (Pa,C,57).

With these issues solved, there remained the more difficult problem of embodying his prophecies in an adequate new prosody and texture. Unaware of Olson's "Projective Verse" essay (1950) at the time, Ginsberg again found little that was of help in this search. Not even Williams' prosodic experiments, let alone the "ridiculous limited little accent or piddling syllable count" of traditional verse seemed to offer a satisfactory model. There was nothing Ginsberg felt sure about except that he was "sick of preconceived literature and only interested in *writing* the actual process" (Kr,G,170). But by 1951 Kerouac had settled down in front of a typewriter fed by a stolen role of U. P. teletype paper, to venture on an almost non-stop marathon of automatic prose composition, later published as the novel *On The Road* (1957). This gigantic effort of "the new Buddha of American prose" (G,H,3), who also trained Ginsberg's sensibility to the "eccentric modulations of long-line composition displayed by Smart, Blake, Whitman, Jeffers, Rimbaud, Artaud & other precursors" (B-M,P,221), taught the poet how to graph the movement of his mind in disregard of literary, grammatical and syntactical inhibitions. This was achieved by a physiological automatism close to Olson's breath rhythm poetics. As Kerouac protested in a 1968 interview, he "formulated the theory of breath as measure, in prose and verse, never mind what Olson, Charles Olson says, I formulated that theory in 1953 at the request of Burroughs and Ginsberg" (Ke,IR,83).

By 1955, all these methods, which Ginsberg had been testing and evolving over the years, finally fused in the poet's imagination to produce his first major poem and one of the most influential works of twentieth century literature. *Howl* itself, in an indirect homage to Cézanne, speaks of "the use of ellipse," or of the poet

> who dreamt and made incarnate gaps in Time & Space
> through images juxtaposed, and trapped the archangel of
> the soul between 2 visual images and joined the elemental
> verbs and set the noun and dash of consciousness to-
> gether jumping with sensation of Pater Omnipotens
> Æterna Deus.

$$(G,H,16)$$

In the second part of the poem, this "Pater Omnipotens Æterna Deus" is also portrayed in his negative aspect, the "robot skullface of Moloch," as Ginsberg had visualized it from his apartment window in downtown San Francisco:

Moloch whose mind is pure machinery! Moloch whose blood is

running money! Moloch whose fingers are ten armies!
Moloch whose breast is a cannibal dynamo! Moloch whose
ear is a smoking tomb!
Moloch whose eyes are a thousand blind windows!

(G,H,17)

One of Ginsberg's most detailed and revealing self-interpretations explains how here, for the first time, he succeeded in capturing one of the visions which ever since 1948 had been haunting his imagination with a sense of doom and destruction. To sum it up in terms of the poet's general concept of creativity, the vision is turned into poetry by a rhythmical articulation of the feelings it engenders in the body. By arranging themselves around this "definite rhythmic impulse" the words may, to the poet's own amazement, take their own illogical and unexpected course.

> The poetry generally is like a rhythmic articulation of feeling
> . . . At best what happens, is there's a definite body rhythm that
> has no definite words, or may have one or two words attached
> to it . . . And then, in writing it down, it's simply by a process of
> association that I find what the rest of the statement is . . .
> [B]efore I wrote "Moloch whose eyes are a thousand blind
> windows," I had the word, "Moloch, Moloch, Moloch," and I
> also had the feeling DA de de DA de de DA de de DA DA. So it
> was just a question of looking up and seeing a lot of windows
> . . . So Moloch whose eyes—then probably the next thing I
> thought was "thousands." O.K., and then thousands *what*?
> "Thousands blind." And I had to finish it somehow. So I
> hadda say "windows." It looked good *afterward*. (Pl,W,289-90)

In his introduction to *Howl*, Williams expresses surprise at Ginsberg's "ability to survive," for literally, as he remarks, Ginsberg, "from all the evidence, [has] been through hell." Yet the worst was still to come. To assure his survival, the poet, only 29 at the time he screamed out his "howl of defeat" (Williams), could either flee or accept the demons he had summoned from his subconscious. In this archetypal situation he resembled the soul in the *Bardo Thödol* who is advised not to fear or flee the Wrathful Deities it is about to encounter. Because met in the right spirit of self-abandonment, they are recognized to be no other than the Peaceful Deities in disguise, and like those, mere emanations of one's mind:

> the fifty-eight flame-enhaloed, wrathful, blood-drinking
> deities come to dawn, who are only the former Peaceful Deities
> in changed aspect . . . the least of the least of the devotees of
> the mystic *mantrayāna* doctrines, as soon as he sees these

> blood-drinking deities, will recognize them to be his tutelary
> deities, and the meeting will be like that of human acquain-
> tances. He will trust them; and becoming merged into them, in
> at-onement, will obtain Buddhahood. (BT,131-2)

As if following such advice, Ginsberg decided to face the demons.

The crucial event in what followed was the death of the poet's
mother. In and out of mental hospitals for most of Allen's childhood, she had turned into a living incarnation of the awesome
divinity he later was to encounter in his vision—into the "fatal Mama,"
the "old woman of skulls" (G,K,27,31), whose traumatic impact on
the young boy finds expression in a ruthlessly realistic anecdote
from *Kaddish*, the elegy on Naomi's death:

> One time I thought she was trying to make me come lay
> her—flirting to herself at sink—lay back on huge bed that
> filled most of the room, dress up round her hips, big slash of
> hair, scars of operations, pancreas, belly wounds, abortions,
> appendix, stitching of incisions pulling down in the fat like
> hideous thick zippers—ragged long lips between her legs—
> What, even, smell of asshole? I was cold—later revolted a little,
> not much—seemed perhaps a good idea to try—know the
> Monster of the Beginning Womb— (G,K,24)

The hold which this and similar experiences had on Ginsberg was all
the stronger since he knew himself to be closer to his mother than
any other member of his family. Her "mad idealism," her visions of
God, her very insanity prefigure or even parallel ("I was in bughouse
that year 8 months," G,K,24,25) the poet's own experiences. Yet
given his willingness to face evil and destruction, this "madness" now
becomes the very means to redeem the media-perverted consciousness and Moloch-inspired violence which caused it and which, like
many others who "suffered death and madness," had

> murdered my mother
> who died of the communist anticommunist psychosis . . .
> complaining about wires of masscommunication in her head
> and phantom political voices in the air
> besmirching her girlish character.
> ("Wichita Vortex Sutra," G,N,132)

In this way *Kaddish* can celebrate "the Monster of the Beginning
Womb" in her positive aspect of the "holy mother" whose "world is
born anew" and thus becomes the source of the poet's inspiration:

> O glorious muse that bore me from the womb, gave suck

first mystic life & taught me talk and music, from whose
pained head I first took Vision—

Yet such acceptance of suffering is still far from the abiding
equanimity of the "devotee of the mystic doctrines," and in the very
passage that follows, the redemptive power of the poet's visions is
again called in doubt:

> Tortured and beaten in the skull—What mad hallucina-
> tions of the damned that drive me out of my own skull to seek
> Eternity till I find Peace for Thee, O Poetry.

> (G,K,29)

So the search for the hidden divinity becomes ever more frantic
and self-destructive. In the footsteps of William Burroughs,
Ginsberg visits Peru to try the hallucinogenic Ayahuasca in the
company of the natives. His visions, recorded in the descriptions and
drawings of the *Yage Letters* to his older friend, were the strongest
and most frightening since his "Merry Visions of Blake" in Harlem.
Still ruminating about his mother who died "in God knows what state
of suffering," the poet experiences "the Great Being, or some sense
of It, approaching [his] mind like a big wet vagina," and during a
subsequent session

> got nauseous, rushed out and began vomiting, all covered with
> snakes, like a Snake Seraph, colored serpents in aureole all
> around my body . . . like a snake vomiting out the universe—
> or a Jivaro in head-dress with fangs vomiting up in realization
> of the Murder of the Universe—my death to come—
> everyone's death to come—all unready—I unready. (G,L,52)

Ginsberg tried to preserve his sanity by somewhat artificially treating
these hallucinations as a "temporary illusion," but the "fearful" and
"almost schizophrenic alteration of consciousness," caused by the
drug, proved to defy such psychological self-persuasion. "I don't
know if I'm going mad," he reports to his friend. "I hardly have the
nerve to go back, afraid of some real madness; a Changed Universe
permanently changed." Burroughs' reply to Ginsberg's plea for help
ultimately turned out to be the right advice: "There is no thing to
fear. Vaya adelante." Yet for Ginsberg such acceptance of the Wrathful Divinities was not to be achieved before several more years had
gone by (G,L,53-64, see also Ginsberg's drawings of "The Great
Being" and "The Vomiter" reproduced below).

The poems inspired by the Peruvian adventure read like one
agonized howl of yearning, fright and despair. "[R]eady for [the]

disintegration of [his] mind," the poet throws himself at the mercy of the "Creator and Eater of Mankind," imploring him to "devour [his] brain," to "attack [his] hairy heart with terror" and to "transfigure [him] to slimy worms" ("Magic Psalm," G,K,92,93). Yet though the "Ever-Unknowable" fulfills the poet's longing for self-sacrifice, doom is his ultimate answer, and the shamanistic journey never penetrates beyond the valley of death and destruction:

> No refuge in Myself, which is on fire
>> or in the World which is His also to bomb & Devour!
> Recognise His might! Loose hold
> of my hands—my frightened skull
>> —for I had chose self-love—
> my eyes, my nose, my face, my cock, my soul—and now
>> the faceless Destroyer!
> A billion doors to the same new Being!
> The universe turns inside out to devour me!
> and the mighty burst of music comes from out the inhuman
>> door—
>> ("The Reply,"G,K,97-8)

Ginsberg's journey through India (1962-3), which he had hoped would prove to be his "promised land," only led him into the lowest region of this inferno. Though it was reassuring for him to note that the *Bhagavad Gita* representation of Vishnu in his negative aspect of "world-destroying Time" resembled what he had "seen often on LSD, etc.," he was only too well aware that "fearful Allen" had never lost his fear "in the face of that monster."

Because I am still clinging to my human known me, Allen
Ginsberg—and to enter this thing means final, complete
abandonment of all I know of my *I am* except for this outer-
seeming otherness which requires my disappearance.
(G,J,28-9)

Tantrism, a religion devoted to the worship of the Great Mother
in her negative elementary character, teaches that this self-
abandonment can only be achieved through a detached, though
fully sensual, acceptance of one's physical passions and desires. "A
whole series of India holy men" Ginsberg consulted on his journey
gave similar advice, directing him "back to the body—getting *in* the
body rather than getting out of the human form." Such words
turned the tip of the scale. Years of shamanistic self-destruction led
Ginsberg into an ever deepening despair in which, bereft of love,
hope, even "sacred poetry," the meaningless suffering of himself
and those around him seemed to provide the only sense of existence:

> Skin is sufficient to be skin, that's all
> it ever could be, tho screams of pain in the kidney
> make it sick of itself, a hollow dream
> dying to finish its all too famous misery
> —leave immortality for another to suffer like a fool,
> not get stuck in a corner of the Universe
> sticking morphine in the arm and eating meat.
>
> *Bankok - May 28, '63*
> Chinese meats hanging in shops— . . .

This is the state reached at the end of the Indian journey—a state of
despondency so complete that it could transcend its proper bounds
and reach out into a new realm beyond despair. This aloneness, as
Ginsberg himself observed, "is like a returning home" (G,J,208-10).

It also marked the turning point in his quest of the "faceless
Destroyer" who, elusive and threatening in his cosmic aloofness till
then, is now forced to reveal himself in his own creation. This
epiphany was recorded in "The Change: Kyoto - Tokyo Express,"
dated 7/18/63, on a subsequent journey through Japan.[7] "Seeking
the Great Spirit of the / Universe in Terrible Godly / form," the poet
still sees himself and the rest of mankind as the Destroyer's victim:

> O suffering Jews
> burned in the hopeless fire
> O thin Bengali sadhus adoring

> Kali mother hung with
> nightmare skulls O Myself
> under her pounding
> feet!

Yet accepting his own body and suffering, the poet, like the enlightened soul of the *Bardo Thödol*, recognizes such phantoms as mere projections of his agonized self:

> Who is, who cringes, perishes,
> is reborn a red Screaming
> baby? Who cringes before
> that meaty shape in
> Fear?

> In this dream I am the Dreamer
> and the Dreamed I am
> that I am.
> (G,N,59-60)

And the "Destroyer of the World" who several years before had answered his "Magic Psalm" with a "Reply" of doom now appears as the "sweet lonely Spirit" who, eager to follow the poet's conjurations, seems ready to reveal himself in his own creation, forceful yet benign, with a gesture of "fear not" and ultimate peace:

> Come, sweet lonely Spirit, back
> to your bodies, come great God
> back to your only image, come
> to your many eyes & breasts,
> come thru thought and
> motion up all your
> arms the great gesture of
> Peace & acceptance Abhya
> Mudra Mudra of fearlessness
> Mudra of Elephant Calmed &
> war-fear ended forever.
> (G,N,61)

The epiphany on the Kyoto - Tokyo express left Ginsberg a man "in mid-age, finished with half desire / Tranquil in [his] hairy body" ("A Vision in Hollywood," G,N,106):

> Joy, I am I
> the lone One singing to myself
> God come true—
> ("Wichita Vortex Sutra," G,N,113-4)

As if by miracle, all monster visions vanished from the poetry written after "The Change" and even failed to reappear when Ginsberg decided to resume his drug experiments. While in his 1965 *Paris Review* interview he claimed to have renounced all use of hallucinogenics, a footnote to this statement, added in 1966, reports that subsequent LSD experiments had produced no "monster vibration, no snake universe hallucinations" (Pl,W,312). Another such experiment inspired the "Wales Visitation" which Ginsberg describes as his "first great big Wordsworthian nature poem" (Kr,G,22). Here, the multiple million eyed "Monster of the Beginning Womb" has been replaced by the Great Mother of creativity and harmonious balance:

> O great Wetness, O Mother, No harm on thy body!
> Stare close, no imperfection in the grass,
>> each flower Buddha-eye, repeating the story,
>> the myriad-formed soul
>
> . . . . . . . . . . . . . . . . . . . . . . .
>
>> & look in the eyes of the branded lambs that stare
>> breathing stockstill under dripping hawthorn—
> I lay down mixing my beard with the wet hair of the mountain-
> side,
>> smelling the brown vagina-moist ground, harmless,
>> tasting the violet thistle-hair, sweetness—
> One being so balanced, so vast, that its softest breath
>> moves every floweret in the stillness on the valley floor,
>> trembles lamb-hair hung gossamer rain-beaded in the
>> grass,
> lifts trees on their roots, birds in the great draught
>> hiding their strength in the rain, bearing same
> weight.
>
> (G,N,141)

The lines, of course, bespeak an eagerness to proclaim the newly found happiness which belies the serenity they profess. But such exuberance is easily understood considering what preceded it, and nobody more than Ginsberg himself was aware of this self-defeating over-assertiveness. So "Autumn Gold: New England Fall" from *The Fall of America* (1972) completely reverses our expectations of another "Wordsworthian nature poem" and, instead, gives a humorous self-portrait of the poet as the self-complacent saint and quester after "the spirit of the universe":

> I thought I was my body the last 4 years,
> and everytime I had a headache, God dealt me
>> Ace of Spades—

I thought I was mind-consciousness 10 yrs before that,
    and everytime I went to the Dentist the Kosmos disap-
    peared,
Now I don't know who I am—
    I wake up in the morning surrounded
        by meat and wires,
    pile drivers crashing thru the bedroom floor,
War images rayed thru Television apartments,
Machine chaos on Earth,
    Too many bodies, mouths bleeding on every Continent,
    my own wall plaster cracked,
      What kind of prophecy
        for this Nation.

                    (G,F,50-1)

Ginsberg's recent development resembles Robert Bly's to the point where they could join hands in a common cause. Having come to terms with their psycho-religious problems, both began to devote more and more time to public issues, such as fighting the Vietnam war or the socio-political consciousness which caused it. The latter is the central theme of *The Fall of America*, in which the poet seems to refocus his concern with the horrific by directly analysing the destructive forces in our time. "Earth pollution," as Ginsberg put it in one of the poems of this "epic containing history,"

      identical with Mind pollution, conscious-
      ness Pollution identical with filthy sky,
    dirty-thoughted Usury simultaneous with metal dust in wa-
    ter courses
    murder of great & little fish same as self besmirchment
    short hair thought control.

                    (G,F,142)

Such new concerns also demanded a new language—a language which could oppose the corrupt rhetoric of politicians and public media. A reader of Wittgenstein, Fenollosa and Eastern philosophy, Ginsberg had always been keenly aware of the insufficiencies of human language generally and of the fallacies of Platonic essentialism and Aristotelian rhetoric in particular. Language to him is "a vehicle of feeling . . . itself [it] doesn't mean anything—Wittgenstein and the Diamond Sutra agree on that" (G,R,7). And such a purely emotive medium was the "language-inner-thought-monologue-abstraction" or "mental-image-mathematical-abstraction" in which he had expressed his cosmic visions. But even that had degenerated into a sterile and "fixed habit" and as such into "a block to further awareness." Thus by 1961, the poet finds himself unable to compose

anything but dream notations and diaries and, again inspired by
Wittgenstein, wonders if perhaps "we've reached point in human or
unhuman evolution where art of words is oldhat dinosaur futile, &
must be left behind" (G,R,10).

In this quandary Ginsberg consulted his friend William Burroughs who in the meantime had devised his "cutup" method based
on the model of ideograms and hieroglyphs. In contrast to Aristotelian logic—"one of the great shackles of Western civilization"—this
technique, as Burroughs explained in an interview, tries to juxtapose "what's happening outside and what you're thinking of,"
thereby recording a "psycho-sensory process that is going on all the
time anyway" (Pl,W,154-7). Of course, Ginsberg was unlikely to
adopt the actual scissors-pasteboard dissections and remodellings of
human consciousness involved in this pursuit, and as if to confirm this
fact, Burroughs rejected his former disciple, disclaiming the bond of
their previous friendship. As Ginsberg wrote after his visit to Burroughs in Tangiers following the Peruvian adventure, the novelist

> was cutting up [his art] with a razor as if it weren't no sacred
> texts at all, just as he was cutting up all known human feelings
> between us, and cutting up the newspapers, and cutting up
> Cuba & Russia & America & making collages; he was cutting
> up his own consciousness & escaping as far as I can tell outside
> of anything I could recognize as his previous identity.
> (G,R,8-9)

The only result Ginsberg gained from his visit was the additional
fear of perhaps being a mere "degenerate robot under the mind-
control of the mad spectre of Burroughs" (G,R,10), an image which
continued to haunt him during his journey through India.

Yet while the spiritual change which finally culminated in the
Kyoto-Tokyo express epiphany was still germinating, Ginsberg already began pondering "radical means" towards a new poetic breakthrough such as "Composition in Void: Gertrude Stein," "Association: Kerouac & Surrealism," "Random juxtaposition: W. S. Burroughs" and "Arrangement of Sounds: Artaud, Lettrism, Tantric
Hantras" (To P.O.—July 8, 1962, G,J,39). To explore the relations
"between poetry and mantra chanting by means of the yoga of
breath" (G,IS,12) has proved to be the most fruitful of these propositions for Ginsberg's subsequent development. As he announced in
"Wichita Vortex Sutra," his first major poem after "The Change,"

> I search for the language
> that is also yours—
> almost all our language has been taxed by war.
> . . . .
> I lift my voice aloud,

> make Mantra of American language now,
> pronounce the words beginning my own millennium,
> I here declare the end of the War!
>                                        (G,N,125-7)

Not being a musician himself, Ginsberg found models in the rock music of Dylan and others, music which to him marks the full re-entry of a physiologically determined poetry into Western art. It can thus be related to Pound's principle of the "tone leading of vowels" or to Artaud's discovery that "certain rhythmic frequencies of music or voice might alter molecular patterns in the nervous system" (G,B) as well as to a system as ancient as Sanskrit prosody which to Ginsberg is based on "patterns of physiological reactions built into the language" (G,P,20). As the poet formulated it on September 10, 1966,

> Mantra repetition—a form of prayer in which a short magic formula containing various God names is chanted hypnotically—has entered Western consciousness & a new Mantra-rock is formulated in the Byrds & Beatles.
> (B-M,P,221)

Where previously Ginsberg had exorcised his private demons by accepting his bodily self, his new body-mantra-poetics was devised to dispel the public demons controlling our present-day consciousness. And Blake who had launched him on his long quest

> To find a Western Path,
> Right through the Gates of Wrath,

was also there to welcome the quester upon his return. It was "The Sick Rose" which 21 years earlier—"with the voice of Blake reading it" to him in his Harlem flat—had brought about Ginsberg's first cosmic vision.

> O Rose, thou art sick!
> The invisible worm
> That flies in the night,
> In the howling storm,
>
> Has found out thy bed
> Of crimson joy:
>
> And his dark secret love
> Does thy life destroy.

Ginsberg immediately recognized that the poem "applied to the whole universe." Yet it took him one and a half decades to make Blake's vision—which, in a way unique for the West, portrays the horrific as an unalterable part of all life—an accepted part of his own experience. Similarly, he had always felt that his "physiologic ecstatic experience had been catalysed in [his] body by the physical arrangement of [the] words." Yet only much later did he recognize that "The Sick Rose" represents an example of "pure Mantra" within English poetry—"as penetrant & capable of causing Transcendental Knowledge as any Hindu Hare Krishna or Hari Om Namo Shivaye." To make this impact complete, Ginsberg, by way of an exercise for his future creativity, finally set about to reinvent the unrecorded melodies to which Blake himself used to sing his *Songs of Innocence & Experience* "unaccompanied at friends' houses." As the poet-composer explains on the blurb of his album:

> The purpose in putting them to music was to articulate the significance of each holy and magic syllable of his poems . . . I hope that musical articulation of Blake's poetry will be heard by the Pop Rock Music Mass Media Electronic Illumination Democratic Ear and provide an Eternal Poesy standard by which to measure sublimity & sincerity in contemporary masters such as Bob Dylan, encouraging all souls to trust their own genius Inspiration.
>
> For the soul of the Planet is Wakening, the time of Dissolution of Material Forms is here, our generation's trapped in Imperial Satanic Cities & Nations, & only the prophetic priestly consciousness of the Bard—Blake, Whitman or our own new selves—can Steady our gaze into the Fiery eyes of the Tygers of the Wrath to Come. (G,B)

Have his past shamanistic experiences provided Ginsberg with the Bodhisattva consciousness necessary for this task? His poetic testimony leaves little doubt as to how to answer this question, although the poet seems to be well aware of the fact that human achievements, and especially those of the spirit, are rarely final or absolute. Asked to sing "The Tyger" at a Blake Poetry Class in 1971, Ginsberg replied:

> I've worked on "The Tyger"—the rhythm is the same as heartbeat—but that's like revolution, or the total wrath to come, so I'm not quite capable of looking it in the eye yet. (G,A,23)

[1](New York: Grove Press, 1966), pp. viii, 97; punctuation as in the novel.

[2]Ed J. Campbell. Bollingen Series VI (Princeton, N.J.: Princeton University Press, 1972), pp. 212-3, 215.

[3]See E. Neumann, *The Great Mother. An Analysis of the Archetype*, Bollingen Series XLVII (Princeton, N.J.: Princeton University Press, 1974), pp. 147-208.

[4]*Summa Predicantium*, 2 vols. (Venice, 1586), II,90v-91.

[5]*The Spirit in Man, Art, and Literature*. Bollingen Series XX (Princeton, N.J.: Princeton University Press, 1972), pp. 82-3, 138-9.

[6]The title of the well-known study by Mario Praz.

[7]See G,IR,6-7: "My poem *The Change* is a renunciation of this first vision, as I'd got hung up on it abstractly, and it had become an obsession. So I'd had to remove it into my own body again. The realization that the whole visionary game was lost came to me on a train leaving Kyoto—at which point I started weeping and sobbing that I was still alive in a body that was going to die. Then I began looking around on the train and seeing all the other mortal faces, 'with their noses of weakness and woe,' and I saw how exquisitely dear they all were—we all were—so I pulled out my notebook, while the illumination was still glowing in my body, and, while my breath was still fitted to weeping, scribbled everything that came into my thought-stream—all the immediate perceptions of the moment in the order in which I could record them fastest. Later on, that becomes known as a poem. The mind supplies the language, if you don't interfere. That's something I learnt from Jack Kerouac,—how to let the mind supply the language."

# Allen Ginsberg

*Faas:* Did you write "The Shrouded Stranger" before or after your Blake vision?

GINSBERG: I think that's after. The concept came before though.

"The Shrouded Stranger"

*Faas:* It was based on an actual dream, wasn't it?

GINSBERG: Well, I had a series of related dreams since I was three.

*Faas:* About the Shrouded Stranger?

GINSBERG: Yes. Kerouac had a very similar thing in *Dr. Sax;* that in fact was *his* Shrouded Stranger.

*Faas:* I haven't read that novel.

GINSBERG: Well he talks about the Shrouded Stranger there too. And we'd discussed that book quite a bit, discussed how to end it and everything like that. That was one of my favorite books, because he enlarges on the Shrouded Stranger.

*Faas:* A similar figure occurs in the *Waste Land.*

GINSBERG: Yes, it's an archetype, the boogie man, the Hooded Stranger.

*Faas:* In *Empty Mirror* you have one stanza beginning "I attempted to concentrate the total sun's rays" and so forth, with the motto from Thomas Hardy . . .

GINSBERG: . . . which suggests doing the opposite.

*Faas:* Yes, quite. I assume that these lines are referring to a particular style you practised before you started publishing your poetry.

early development

GINSBERG: They refer to the poems in *The Gates of Wrath,* and particularly to the poem that begins "I cannot sleep, I cannot sleep." I was just trying to arrange and rearrange sort of symbols of mystical experience, like the words "light," "skull," which were really very vague. They referred to something Gnostic, but they didn't really describe anything seen. So it was "reference" rather than "presentation." I thought at the time that I would be able to write a poem that was so dense and would have so much symbolic significance that it would be able to penetrate anybody else's consciousness.

*Faas:* In the way the New Critics taught people to write.

GINSBERG: Yeah, well, I didn't have that in mind, but it was influenced by that kind of practise.

*Faas:* Were there any poets and artists besides Cézanne, Kerouac and Burroughs who helped you develop the mode of expression used in *Howl?*

GINSBERG: William Carlos Williams.

*Faas:* But didn't you have to go beyond Williams in order to write that poem.

GINSBERG: No, I only expanded on his style and then got to work from there. The poem I read tonight [March 28, 1974] "Transcriptions of Organ Music," was really basically Williams's practise. What Williams presents is facts, which I put together in a Surrealist way, but they are still facts, like "hydrogen jukebox."

Williams' influence

*Faas:* The image you discuss in the *Paris Review* interview.

GINSBERG: It's the most obvious as "Surrealism." But at the same time it is jukebox, hydrogen bomb and so forth.

*Faas:* What inspired your notion of ellipse, of the gap between two images which gives you a flash of awareness of *śūnyatā* or the final emptiness of the absolute?

GINSBERG: That comes from the *haiku.* You know the books by Blyth on the *haiku,* that's the best sample, the work in four volumes. That's the book Kerouac and Gary and I used, the basic text to study to get an idea of what was possible.

*Faas:* And Cézanne?

GINSBERG: Well, the Cézanne stuff was actually [pause] '48. The model for *Empty Mirror,* the first book of my earlier poems I published, was Williams. And the models for *The Gates of Wrath,* those are rhymed poems, was Andrew Marvell.

*Faas:* Thomas Wyatt—

GINSBERG: Yes, and Raleigh, Christopher Smart. And my father.

*Faas:* How about the influence of Walt Whitman?

GINSBERG: I knew Whitman before I wrote *Howl,* but I didn't really sit down and read his entire poetic output, all through *Leaves of Grass,* until *after* I had written *Howl,* and then I saw that it was important.

Whitman's influence

*Faas:* And yet everybody seems to take it for granted that *Howl* was directly inspired by Whitman.

GINSBERG: No, it's more a combination of Williams and Hart Crane—and Shelley. The Moloch section—"Moloch whose eyes are a thousand blind windows"—the Moloch section which is the strongest thing in *Howl,* I think, is more like that dizzying dance foot that you would get in Shelley's [pause]—

*Faas: Epipsychidion?*

GINSBERG: Yes, "One life, one death, one heaven, one hell, one immortality and one annihilation," which I knew from my father as a kid, or from Poe or from Hart Crane's "Atlantis" or from Shelley's "Ode to the West Wind" or from the end of "Adonais" or from some Wordsworth like "A sense sublime of something far more deeply interfused"—that long breath which continues. A lot of that I got from Kerouac, that sense of a long breath in a builded rhyme, in a builded rhythm.

*Faas:* Lawrence, too, you began to study *after* the completion of *Howl?*

GINSBERG: I didn't study him, I just read him. You see , after picking up on what Williams was doing, I read his contemporaries and poets generally that were writing in a kind of open form. So I went and looked up works by Louis Zukofsky and Pound and later by Charles Reznikoff and the Objectivists and the Activists and the Imagists and Marsden Hartley and Lawrence, and then Christopher Smart and anybody that wasn't writing just rhymed stanzas, I just started reading anything that would apply—the Bible—

Faas: Did you have any personal contact with Olson in those years?

GINSBERG: No, not until 1958. Met him in '57, knew of him in '55 through Black Mountain people. I didn't meet Creeley or Duncan until '55. contacts with Olson

*Faas:* That was in San Francisco, wasn't it? But the real coming together happened at the Vancouver poetry conference in 1963, I guess.

GINSBERG: Well we'd met and we knew each others' work but till then we didn't actually have a convention, so to speak.

*Faas:* You have described how everything seemed to join at Vancouver, how Olson said to you: "I feel I am one with my skin" and Creeley: "I am in my place" and how you yourself had, as it were, returned to your own body.

GINSBERG: And now, I think, for the same concept I would use the word "space," which I get from Chögyam Trungpa. I'm taking the language from Trungpa because it means the same thing as all the others and, yet, it doesn't have the hang-ups of body or body-mind, and at the same time it's the classical yogic and Buddhist term for appreciation of the actual space, and the emptiness of space, the infiniteness and the emptiness. That's what the mantra "Ah" is. "Ah" before the place or space, that we breath into, "Ah." So it's almost literal appreciation and use of space. And traditionally it is the seed syllable mantra for purification of speech, as well as the appreciation of space like the color blue of the sky.

*Faas:* I don't quite understand that yet.

GINSBERG: Okay, let's see. You can understand Creeley's use of "place," as "we'll all get to heaven and everybody will have a smile on their faces."

*Faas:* That's right, and we also will have "beautiful chairs to sit in"—

GINSBERG: "And we'll likewise all have places." To come back to the place meaning as Williams, to come back to *this* place to see what is here rather than wandering off with the imagination. So you could also say, interchange the word, come back to *this* space here in the apartment and the space in which the apartment sits and the space through which the planet moves, and the space into which we breathe, as being the one common element that holds all of us together, and also the one element that is open and free which does not stop us; to which we can speak, into which we can breathe. It's sort of the womb of being. They say *dharma-kāya* is space and at the same time the host which holds us all together and the place where we exist. So an appreciation of that space place means an awakenedness to the fact that we are here and that there is no paranoia closing down and imprisoning all of us.

*Faas:* It seems to me that Creeley has only found that kind of space more recently.

GINSBERG: He always used the word "place" in that way, I thought.

*Faas:* But then in his early poetry you find this almost obsessive pursuit of emptiness, this reduction of self and of all concrete things to a zero. And more recently he has suddenly started to grope around for objects, counting them . . . But let's go back to Lawrence for a moment. Has he had any major influence on your work?

Lawrence's influence

GINSBERG: I think I am indebted to Lawrence more indirectly through Kerouac and Burroughs. At one point I read a lot of his poetry, and some of his prose.

*Faas:* His critical writings as well?

GINSBERG: Well, his thing on Whitman in *Studies in Classic American Literature* is interesting.

*Faas:* I find him to be one of the greatest pioneers of open form poetics and philosophy.

GINSBERG: Except, you see, one problem with what we call open form and that's one problem with Lawrence's poetry, is that it is completely open and completely loose, but because he's got a literary mind in his head and he thinks he's writing poetry, he has a tendency to be slightly pompous or artificial, a little bit deliberative in his statements rather than accidental or inadvertent or caught or embarrassed or funny or Surrealist on account of that's the way the mind is, you know, putting things together fast without realizing why or how. And then there is also not too much interest in the musical part, not too much interest in balancing lines like in Pound or Williams, not much interest in the measure of the line. And in open form poetry there still is an interest in measuring the line, open form or free poetry, spontaneous poetry.

*Faas:* In 1961 while discussing Wittgenstein and Burroughs' cutup method you wondered whether perhaps we have "reached a point in human or unhuman development where art of word is oldhat dinosaur futile and must be left behind." How do you feel about that now?

Borroughs' cutups

GINSBERG: It seemed like an apt perception for that time because it did seem to me that Burroughs' cutup things are very similar by hindsight now to regular mindfulness meditation procedure. That is, in *vipassana* meditation where what you do is switch attention to the breath going out of your nostrils thus interrupting and cutting up thought forms and so taking a distance from thought forms rather than getting entangled in them; and thus observing thought forms comma anger comma sleepiness comma discursive fantasy and finding, paying attention to the gaps between two thoughts and mixing mind with space. Actually the traditional explanation by Gampopa, so I'm told, is mixing breath with space, mixing mind with breath, mixing mind with space, which is very similar to Burroughs' proposition of "all out of time and into space." So the exercises that Burroughs was using to cut himself out of language, which is to say out of the conceptual prison or projection, or projective fantasies, fantasy projections—out into space, is very similar to the description of meditation by both Zen and Tibetan teachers, in particular, Chögyam Trungpa. I was taking it at that time perhaps a little too literalistically, in a little upside down way.

*Faas:* Yes, you said that Burroughs was cutting up his art with a razor just as he was cutting up all human feelings between you, and then a little later that you feared you might be a mere robot under the mind control of the mad spectre of Burroughs.

GINSBERG: There was a certain amount of humor in that, I mean. [Laughing] It was one of the possible fantasies of the situation which I was able to deal with objectively by putting it on paper and saying: "I'm a robot under the mind control of the mad spectre of Burroughs." It's in that kind of voice, I mean, that's comedy also.

*Faas:* Did you really have a break with Burroughs at that point?

GINSBERG: Yes, I did, I mean somewhat of a break, nothing permanent. I had known him already for fifteen years, and I was to know him for another fifteen years, so it was just like in any relationship, a temporary disequilibrium. Because for one thing he was really going into something very radical in terms of introspection of his consciousness and something

break with Burroughs

which I didn't get myself into until many years later, though at the time I saw the relation between what he was doing and what I understood ideologically of Tibetan practise. I even had a dream about this which is somewhere in my journals [Grove Press (New York, 1977), pp. 154-7]. Burroughs is almost a Tibetan Lama *sangha* type, but working independently.

*Faas:* I got the impression that you were repelled by his coldly analytic approach to language and experience, dissecting everything.

GINSBERG: That was one aspect of my thought about it. The other was, like, a great deal of interest in it and preoccupation which I carried around for several years.

*Faas:* You mentioned that your "monster vibrations" completely disappeared after a certain point—1966, was it?

GINSBERG: Yeah.

*Faas:* How do you explain that?

monster visions    GINSBERG: Well there was always a shadow over me of the recollection of the mystical experience I had in 1948 connected with hearing Blake's voice. There was a series of visionary moments of intermittent sort of cosmic perceptions relating to Blake's *Songs of Innocence and of Experience,* and the last one was scary, as traditionally it's described sometimes: there are, you know, hellish visions as well as heavenly visions. And then I had the idea that what I was seeing was my egoless death state and it scared me. The monster vibration is described in the *Yage Letters.* There is even a symbolic picture I drew, the equivalent of the "Vomiter" or the "Blind Eye" or something, that little *mandala* in the book. And it's similar to the horrific deities of the Tibetan pantheon. So I was getting vibes like that. But rather than seeing their function I was seeing them as a threat; or actually I was seeing them as representative of a divine order, but feeling that I was too afraid to go into it, and afraid to accept that, afraid to accept that as part of myself or something. But I was in the wrong relation with them. And I simply came into a better relation with that aspect of nature later on, probably because I had been sort of insistently imposing on myself an ideal of a state of consciousness that was ecstatic and celestial, and I was looking for that. And because I was pushing that so hard (and it was only a figment of memory really, an imagination), I was coming up with the opposite side of that, which was non-celestial and murderous.

*Faas:* But don't you feel one has to live with these monsters permanently?

GINSBERG: They are just little *māyā* day-dreams. Even Buchenwald is a little *māyā* day-dream.

*Faas:* Why then are they worshipped in India and Tibet, for instance?

all *māyā* day-dreams

GINSBERG: Because people think they are real. Well, it's very complicated, the practise of relating to these deities goes through various stages, some is worship, but then the other is annihilation of them and mastery of them. Some of the Tibetan practises include becoming them. And then after becoming them, realizing that they are just creations of your own mind and that they are like little fantasy doggies, too, say, but that they are illusory in the sense that both heaven and hell are illusory, aren't they? I think it was at a certain point around '67, when I stopped seeking a divine vision in acid, that I ceased getting demonic visions. And it's the same thing, I think, in Zen or in Tibetan practise, if you stop seeking *satori,* stop seeking illumination, you've sort of arrived at the end of the search.

*Faas:* In other words you can't find *satori* as long as you are consciously looking for it.

GINSBERG: In other words there is no *satori.* Just to put an end to it, there is no *satori.* And there is no hell. Or if you want, you could turn it around and say that *satori* consists in the realization that there is no *satori.* So you don't have to seek any further. So everything is complete and everything is perfect then.

*Faas:* You have often described your Blake vision but never really given a detailed account of what happened to you on the Kyoto-Tokyo express.

"The Change"

GINSBERG: Well, it was just about as much as I could remember, it wasn't anything quite as full, it was simply a realization that I had been pushing it too hard to regain my "vision," pushing myself too hard to go into the demonic, thinking that it was real, in order to get to some kind of *satori.* And pushing myself too hard with guilt, thinking that I should be taking acid to really cleanse out my soul, and making too much strain and effort in order to seek for some kind of illumination. I began realizing that the very effort I was making was a burden, and was preventing me from being present in my own mind.

*Faas:* When you look back on the years of depression and creative sterility which preceded that experience . . .

GINSBERG: That would be from about '61—

*Faas:* —to '63?

GINSBERG: Yeah. What I actually finally did was cut up my own illumination as Burroughs recommended. I finally abandoned or cut up or cut out of my obsession of becoming the divine center of the universe.

*Faas:* You don't feel that you repressed anything instead of absorbing and accepting these former visions.

GINSBERG: Well, I don't think we're really understanding each others' language yet. There is still a hang-up. I had some sort of a mystical experience, the nature of which I don't understand, which was both heavenly and hellish, okay. Then I kept trying to recapture those experiences while still being afraid of experiencing the hellish ones. But I was hung up on getting a heavenly experience, and then I used the acid for that purpose. And the more I strained to have a heavenly experience the more I'd get a hellish experience, because the hellish experience was the fear of being left out of heaven.

the demons
non-existent

*Faas:* Like Dr. Faustus trying to conjure up God and instead conjuring up the devil.

GINSBERG: No. [Laughing] It's too Romantic you're making it. It's something much simpler. The hellish experience existed in the fear of not making it into heaven. But, there is really no heaven. So that I was trying to get to somewhere that didn't exist. And because I failed, I kept feeling I was in hell. So I had imagined a heaven, so to speak, or was in the process of imagining a heaven, or trying to remember a heaven which is the same thing: to synthesize a heaven by my thought or my effort or my activity. And because I could not successfully do that I kept thinking then that I was in hell and doomed. Once I realized that there was no heaven to strain for then there was no hell to fall into, to be worried about. I realized I wasn't missing anything. So it's not a question of absorbing the demons, but it's a question of realizing that the demons don't really exist, in a sense, that they are self-created, out of a fear of missing the big event.

*Faas:* In the sense of the *Bardo Thödol* . . .

GINSBERG: Anyway, I have never been there, it's just a book. [Laughing]   Oh, I am sorry, go on,   "in the sense of the *Bardo Thödol* . . ."

*Faas:* I meant, in the sense of the *Bardo Thödol* which teaches the soul to just accept these wrathful divinities as projections of the mind . . .

GINSBERG: Right.

*Faas:* . . . and as unreal.

GINSBERG: Yes. I found a tremendous number of people who freaked out on acid; they freak out because they think that what they see on acid is real, and then try to incorporate that into their everyday life.

*Faas:* What was Gary Snyder's reaction to that? You mentioned that he went through a similarly horrific experience.

GINSBERG: I think once in a while or so when younger before he went to Japan, he visioned a little bit, though he had a long period of meditation and so, according to his traditional Zen understanding, he was probably a lot freer than I was of that kind of preoccupation. Actually it's only, I think, last fall [i.e., of 1973] that I finally got over the whole, really got completely through with the whole process by simply renouncing any idea of obtaining *satori* or illumination. I gave up on trying to get into heaven entirely. In the course of attending this Buddhist seminary and sitting ten hours a day and having a chance to examine every single minute thought that I was having about the idea of getting illuminated, I realized that I wasn't getting any more illuminated than the fact that I was sitting. And once I gave up substituting an imaginary heaven for the present reality, then heaven and hell were off my shoulders like a weight fallen off.

*Snyder*

*Faas:* And that occurred a few months ago?

GINSBERG: Half a year ago. It occurred in stages, it was progressive. I'd had some sort of a brain seizure, "frantic light does seize my brain"—writ by Blake when he was fourteen. I had some sort of a hallucination perhaps when I was young, 22, and clung to that as a reality, because it seemed so complete and heavenly, it was only after renouncing heaven that you can be where you are. I wouldn't even want to say that you only have to renounce heaven and you get to heaven, because again that would be deceptive.

*Faas:* That's a new way you put it now. Previously you used to speak about getting back to the body.

GINSBERG: Yes.

*Faas:* But then, I suppose that would be a kind of simultaneous process.

GINSBERG: Yes, although I was too involved in a false dichotomy between mind and body. In my experience, let's see. My awareness and understanding of the process of self or non-self changes over the years. I'm sorry I have led people up blind alleys. [Laughing] I finally led people up as many blind alleys as I've been up. So that what Burroughs recommended at the end of *Yage Letters,* his telegram or his letter to cut out completely, cut up the Word, cut up my own Word, was very good advice. But it took me about fifteen years to finally realize how or what or why. Because I didn't want to cut out because I was senti- mentally attached to the idea of being a saint in heaven, or some- thing. It was just "a projection of my own ego."

*Burroughs' advice*

*Faas:* But even now your own mode of expressing all that is quite different from Burroughs's, isn't it?

GINSBERG: Well yes, because it's a different situation, a different person, a different set of experiences that we're dealing with.

*Faas:* Can we switch to your attempt "to make *mantra* of American language." In *Improvised Poetics* you say that one shouldn't take that statement too literally.

GINSBERG: I forgot why I said that. Oh yes, because somebody else was taking it too literally. I don't know, there was an essay on it by Paul Carroll.

*mantra* poetics    *Faas:* In *The Poem in its Skin?*

GINSBERG: Yes. I have a lot of correspondence with him in that book about that. So *Improvised Poetics* is probably referring back to that. Yes, look at that, because we had a real correspondence about what I meant by that.

*Faas:* But you're still pursuing that path, I gather.

GINSBERG: Yes.

*Faas:* Robert Bly writes that a poet who wants to write a true political poem has to have such a grasp of his own psyche that he can leap up from it into the higher sphere of the national or political psyche. Does that notion make sense to you?

GINSBERG: Well, not entirely. If the grass and narcotics police try to set me up for a bust, my personal private life and my house is connected quite directly with the police bureaucracy, and so there is no disjunction between the political and the personal, there, in that case. Ah, so, as I am, so to speak, a cocksucker, there are laws about sex which are political and therefore personal to the extent that they impinge on my private life.

*Faas:* Yet would it make sense to you to speak of a national psyche? I recall several passages in your poetry where you treat a nation as if it had a psyche.

the national    GINSBERG: Yes, I think it's possible to do that, especially in
psyche          an electronic age where everybody is subjected to con-
                tinuous bombardment with the same images and thought
forms. Like, I'll give you an instance, right this minute [March 27, 1974]—the idea current in U.S.A. that "the war is over in Vietnam" seems to me just like an individual suppressing realization of a conflict going on around the house. It's like, you know, his mother and his father having a deadly battle around the house and they might shoot each other, and the son didn't want to recognize it. So right now there is this vast war going on in Vietnam which we are funding and which we are completely responsible for and which everybody is acting as if unconscious of, and which is not referred to

in polite political discourse or private life as it *was* three, four, five years ago. Everybody is pretending it's over, so to speak, but they know it's not over. So in that sense there is a national psyche, in the sense that the electronic network of communications is not bringing that war up into front page, front-brain, picture consciousness right now, but is relegating it to third and fourth page, and only with stories that are neutral and not charged emotionally. Or, for instance, see the Cambodian bombing was much more violent and illegal than any of the Watergate stuff. And yet everybody, the whole national consciousness—I should say, national media consciousness—is concerned with Watergate wire tapping on that slight level and has not yet been willing to confront this real heavier violence of the Cambodian bombing and the illegality of that which was just as illegal as the plumbers' activities—much more illegal!—mass murder, violation of the Constitution, violation of the tradition and everything, violation of what's supposed to be the tradition. So by nation-psyche I really mean, I suppose, the accumulated composite consciousness formed by all the interlocking mass media and their effect on people's everyday conversation and thought forms.

*Faas:* Including their own private thoughts.

GINSBERG: Well, thought forms inside the brain couldn't be more private.

*Faas:* I have tried to figure out some of the changes in style and content your poetry has undergone since "The Change."

GINSBERG: Yes, I've gone through quite a few since.

*Faas:* I wondered if you could make any comments as to how your style has changed.

development since "The Change"

GINSBERG: Well, I would say "The Change" is prophetic of a more literal change later on, say in the last year. A final abandonment of the pursuit of heaven, of—I should be more literal—final abandonment of the attempt to reconstruct the Blake vision I once had, and live by that. Because, finally, the memory of the Blake vision left such a strong impression of universal consciousness that it didn't seem right to abandon it. In fact, my first thought when it happened to me was "I must never forget this." But it sort of now appears by hindsight to be somewhat, say, like the Temptation of St. Anthony. You know, if you get a vision of heaven you might get hung up on that, and meanwhile, you know, you don't feed the beggar next door or don't feed your cat, or whatever. You see, theoretically a complete universe of consciousness would be total attention to "minute particular" detail around you, complete present attention. Wouldn't that be so?

*Faas:* In a Zen Buddhist sense.

GINSBERG: Well, when you look at all the descriptions of religious experience there is really always an absorption in seeing the universal in the particular. I mean it's always "No ideas but in things" finally. Not only in Zen but even in Christian mysticism I think you find it.

Faas: One finds that mystical attitude in William Carlos Williams.

GINSBERG: Well, but a Zen type mystical attitude.

Faas: Quite.

Williams' mysticism

GINSBERG: In which the mysticism is "No ideas but in things." So, what I'm trying to say is that clinging to a memory of a mode of consciousness that I wanted to obtain or attain prevented me from obtaining that very mode of consciousness, because I was substituting memory for present attention, and constantly referring every perception I have now or had back to 1948, and what would that look like *sub specie æternitatis*, so that finally the vision, the memory of the vision became a hang-up. And now I'm even beginning to wonder, but maybe I should just say that I just had a freak out hallucination, to get rid of it, you know.

Faas: Your poetry since "Wichita Vortex Sutra" seems to be characterized by a more rhythmic *mantra*-like language which at the same time is more fact-oriented.

GINSBERG: Yeah. I suppose, I haven't really figured that one out. Yes, ideally it would be interesting to be able to compose rhythmic articulation, a sequence that would be exciting rhythmically, yet contain nothing but the facts, and at the same time have a kind of subtle interconnectedness and harmony that would appear from the outside to be divine, so to speak.

Faas: Do you feel that *The Fall of America* is a completed poem?

the end of *The Fall of America*

GINSBERG: No, well, I have a lot of fragments and long poems since then, that connect with that. I don't think it will ever have a completed form unless it arrives by accident. But a sort of completed form did arrive to the *Cantos*, simply by Pound pursuing to the end his preoccupations and registering his changes of sensibility. Maybe the end of *The Fall of America* will be: What the fuck am I getting so hung up on symbols of war and politics, I want to go back and sit on a mountain. [Laughing] I mean that might be the end for all I know. I mean I might finally realize that that's the point where—what it's all about. Or maybe I can go into exile or something like that. I think the police state is going to get worse and worse, I can't see how it's ever going to improve, because it's so built-in now.

Faas: I really can't see you doing that.

GINSBERG: Well I can't see it either. But what if the police came round knocking on my door? Well I can't see myself hanging around and going to jail forever. But I'm saying that the police state in America is really getting badder and badder, you know there's a hundred million dollar budget, the most right wing military people are now in control of the army and intelligence agencies, and they are not at all affected by the whole Watergate scandal. In fact, it's almost like the scandal itself will make people feel that they have done something to purify the government, while in fact the entire police bureaucracy and intelligence-military-industry are stronger than ever and more vicious than ever, and they are getting interconnected up by computers, so everybody's got dossiers, so the end of *The Fall of America* might be the abandoning of America finally.

*Faas*: You have recently propagated a poetry whose "root lies in neolithic tribal earth knowledge."

GINSBERG: A lot of that I get from Gary Snyder, it's like adaptations of his language, because I'm very imitative in that way.

*Faas*: One also finds these notions in D. H. Lawrence who in part derived them from the North American Indians.

GINSBERG: I don't think necessarily one will have to go back to . . .

*Faas*: Lawrence?

GINSBERG: No, to the Indians, something may emerge out of this situation here. I mean it might wind up with people of East Tenth Street where I live with no more heat, no more light, living in the ruins, and gathering in the streets every night for community block consultations and people meditating, singing, dancing and prophesizing on the brick and stone ruins of New York.

*Faas*: What criteria do you have for evaluating your own work? Somewhere, you say, for instance, that in a poem each syllable should have a place and a purpose; or you claim that each poem should have an emotional feeling center. [evaluating his own poetry]

GINSBERG: Well, I write a great deal, and my habit of writing is to write in journals and notebooks, generally, not all the time, but that's the general habit. And then I cull from the notebooks things that seem to be complete poems.

*Faas*: And what's a complete poem?

GINSBERG: Well, something that seems to have a beginning, a middle and end. [Laughing] Or something that embarrasses me because of the truthfulness, or something that seems quite clear and hard, the images seem hard in the sense of precise and not abstract, not generalized, but composed of "minute particulars"; or if the sound is coherent, the vowel structure is clear. Since each poem has a different form more or less, there is no way of knowing it in advance. But by hindsight I can look at a piece of writing and say: That's interesting. But for criteria very specifically, almost the highest criterion I know is, if I weep while writing it's generally good writing—weep for the truthfulness of what I'm writing. And if I'm embarrassed by it, it very often turns out to be a really good poem, in which I'm reclaiming areas of my awareness which I hadn't admitted to myself or others.

*Faas*: That, I suppose, is what you call "present temporary form," which, you say, is all that form can ever be.

GINSBERG: I'd rather qualify this by saying: for this kind of writing. For instance, I've been doing a lot of blues lately and that has a very regular form of three lines, there are twelve bars and an aaa rhyme.

*Faas*: It seems that just like Duncan or Snyder, you seem reluctant to use the term open form.

open form    GINSBERG: Well, no, it's a usable phrase. It's just that I don't think I heard it until when? I don't know. When did it come into circulation?

*Faas*: Maybe with books like Umberto Eco's *L'opera aperta*, that is to say in the early sixties.

GINSBERG: Well, I had done most of my work in what you might call "open form" from 1950 to 1960 so I went into the habit of using that phrase, but I didn't think of it in those terms.

*Faas*: What were the terms in which you thought of "open form" in the '50's?

GINSBERG: "Spontaneous poems . . . scribbles . . . writings . . . ditties . . . Williams modern . . . Kerouac free style . . . free verse . . . etc."

*Faas*: You spoke of your poems as having a beginning, a middle and an end.

GINSBERG: Yes, where the thought process begins, where there's a middle, and where [laughing] I don't know, well, beginning, middle and end. I'm thinking of a poem I wrote recently, a description of breathing, and I have the breath go over the Grand Teton Mountains to Northern San Francisco into Hawaii and Australia and Saigon through the Indian Ocean and Africa and Marseille and on top of the Eiffel tower and then through the Atlantic to New York to Paterson, N.J. onto the Midwest finally arriving back in Teton village where it first began breathing. So [laughing] it had a beginning, a middle and an end. And that's a pretty good poem because it had that much clarity. But it's just the beginning of a series of thoughts and an end of a series of thoughts, a definite emotional end I guess and conclusive.

*Faas*: So it's really the beginning and end of a thought process.

GINSBERG: Right.

*Faas*: William Stafford says that his poems usually come to an end when his powers to homogenize an experience come to an end.   beginning, middle and end

GINSBERG: I don't quite know what that means. I don't mind it actually, if I knew what it meant.

*Faas*: I think it means to impose some kind of order upon an experience or reality, to make an experience shapely.

GINSBERG: But then I don't know what that means either. In other words the experience one has while writing is the experience of one's own mind and to *put* order into it wouldn't that mean to rearrange one's normal sequence of thought-reflection?

*Faas*: Anyway, I didn't mean to defend that statement.

GINSBERG: No, but I don't even know what it means because, well, I'm saying quite literally, I don't know what it means. I would also put order into my thoughts if I knew a way of doing that without violating the nature, the natural structure of the thought. I do feel that thought has a natural order of its own, so it's a question of transcribing the thought in its own order, and in that sense a beginning, a middle and an end.

*Faas*: But of course it would be very difficult to describe that kind of . . .

GINSBERG: Not too hard. For instance, you know my book called *Empty Mirror*. There is this little poem that begins "How sick I am!" called "Marijuana Notations." So I got high and thought ahah at the beginning of a thought feeling sensation, and then made several ruminations about it, "does everybody feel this way?," and then suddenly switched the mind from that kind of introspective self-persecution to: "It is Christmas almost and people are singing Christmas carols down the block on Fourteenth Street." So that was the end, shifting the mind   the thought process completely to something more real. It was a lot of subjective thought about my being sick or not being sick, very vague really, representative of a twenty year old or a twenty-four year old talking to himself. But then suddenly the mind comes down, suddenly I realize, you know, it's hopeless, and switched the thought like a cutup almost, or like you switch back to the breath attention in mindfulness meditation. Suddenly I switched back to observing something real at the outside of myself, outside of my subjective babbling. So in that sense it has a beginning, a middle and an end. In almost like ah . . .

*Faas*: But always in terms of actual experience.

GINSBERG: Well in terms of the experience of the mind.

*Faas*: Of actual thought process.

GINSBERG: Yeah, I would think that would be the criterion. Like one poem that does not have a beginning and an end is at the beginning of *Planet News*, a long poem called "Journal Night Thoughts" which is just sort of discursive free association. It's almost not a poem, but I included it because it's a specimen of that poetical mode, I mean it's very intense language, but at the same time it doesn't have any subject at all except the thoughts of the moment of that day, the thoughts at the moment of writing, recollecting all the thoughts of that day.

*Faas*: It seems that you avoid the term automatic writing, preferring to speak of spontaneous writing.

automatic versus transcriptive writing

GINSBERG: Well, automatic writing has to me the association that you are not completely conscious of what you are writing.

*Faas*: Not completely conscious of what you are writing?

GINSBERG: Yes, just the hand moving and just the unconscious coming out as if dictated by voices or from the unconscious but, you know, the hand moving and creating words that the mind is not aware of.

*Faas*: So graphing the movement of the mind, as you understand it, would imply a high degree of consciousness.

GINSBERG: Yes, depending . . . the process would be observing what is going on in the mind and writing it down, as simple as that, rather than to attempt to separate yourself from awareness of what your thought forms were. I would speak of spontaneous writing as writing down your thought forms as they occur. Automatic writing, I think, is a technical term which implies that you don't know what you're writing at the time. You really don't know, it might be ghost voices, and I think certain Surrealist practices were attempting to approach that.

*Faas*: With the assumption that if you have a poetic genius whatever comes out might be a great poem, I suppose.

GINSBERG: I would have the same assumption about recording the thought forms of spontaneous mind and really if you are a poetic genius, if your mind is shapely, then what comes out will be shapely. In other words if you see clearly into your mind, if you remember and recollect clearly what you were thinking, it would be thoughts in minute detail, thoughts of minute detail, it will have objects and it will have real describable things in it. It won't be sort of vague moods, it will be actual buses passing by, yellow street signs, those of Tenth Street.

*Faas*: I am puzzled by the fact that you frequently mention Gertrude Stein

Gertrude Stein

trude Stein as a model for your technique of graphing the mind-movement. At one point when a well-known psychiatrist wrote that she was doing automatic writing, she replied that the man was wrong.

GINSBERG: We are still having this confusion about automatic writing. I didn't say she was doing automatic writing, I said that she was writing down the sequence of verbal sounds.

*Faas*: Exactly, like an unfolding of language . . .

GINSBERG: . . . that occurred to her during the time of composition.

*Faas*: But I don't think she graphed the movement of her thoughts the way you do.

GINSBERG: No, she wasn't interested in memory, she wasn't interested in the future, she had a specific subject which was a few sentences like "Napoleon ate ice cream on Elba" and then she would recombine the words over and over again in the normal order that they came to her. Actually "the graph of the mind-movement," that poetry is a "graph of a mind moving" is not my phrase, it's Philip Whalen's from his poetics statement at the end of Don Allen's anthology. Philip Whalen once read Stein's "Composition as Explanation" to me aloud about ten years ago and it seemed exactly on the line of what I was interested in. Gertrude Stein made a lot of different kinds of art experiments, but her experiments were all with the present consciousness during the time of composition.

*Faas*: I would distinguish between two kinds of automatic writing.

GINSBERG: You keep calling it automatic writing, I don't see anything automatic about it. If I am recalling what I am thinking, that's not automatic, it's very deliberate. I would say transcriptive more than automatic—stenographic transcription of mind thought, of how the mind thinks.

*Faas*: All I was really trying to say was that Gertrude Stein wasn't interested in "graphing the mind-movement."

GINSBERG: I think in certain compositions she was. That's what I was saying, she made a great many different kinds of experiments in present consciousness, experiments in present consciousness during composition. She was interested in the present consciousness during composition, would we agree on that?

*Faas*: Well, I don't know Gertrude Stein's work *that* well.

GINSBERG: You have to read her aloud.

*Faas*: When does a line break? It wasn't clear to me what you say about that in your *Improvised Poetics*. Sometimes you say it's determined by the page . . .

GINSBERG: That's Creeley's method . . . Basically breath-stop.    the line break

*Faas*: . . . or that the thought breaks.

GINSBERG: Well, when you talk and then after a while like you run out of thought and words, and then you're gonna stop and take a breath and continue. So that's when you have your breath-stop. Breath-stop and the thought-division could be the same.

*Faas*: Which would imply a new kind of thinking, wouldn't it?

GINSBERG: No, only an *observation* of your thinking. Same thing as usual, except you're observing it, and see where it stops, and there's a gap, and where a new thought begins. Because if you observe thought, it actually does stop and there are gaps in between. It's like a movie, it looks continuous, but actually it's a lot of different frames. And thought is the same way.

*Faas*: Graphing the movement of the mind, while, I suppose, standing back from your own stream of consciousness.

GINSBERG: Observing it or recollecting it.

*Faas*: I just don't have any personal experience of graphing the movement of my mind, so it's difficult to understand.

GINSBERG: Well, I'll show you. Really, it's very simple. Sit up with your back straight. Now, the primary attention could be on the breath coming out of the nostrils, so that—keep your mouth closed so there's no air pocket, and instead of thinking about the conversation or about me, or looking at me or anything like that—look toward *there* maybe [pointing to the kitchen wall]—so we don't get tangled in some kind of subjective thing, pay attention to the flow of breath out through the nostrils for maybe five breaths. Can you do it for five breaths just on the out-breaths? Forget about what's going on inside you on the in-breaths or any other time. And really sit up straight—Yeah, now—Okay. [Pause] Now are you able to put your complete attention on your breath going out . . . or do thoughts interrupt?

*Faas*: I have an image of the hair in my nose.

GINSBERG: Okay, so pay attention to breath after it leaves your nose and the space in front of your face, into which the breath flows, for five breaths.

*Faas*: Pay attention to the air coming out? and flowing into space?

GINSBERG: Yeah, into space and dissolving in space, or identify with the breath going out and dissolving. [Pause] Okay now, you're paying some attention to that.

*Faas*: Yes.

GINSBERG: What else were you thinking about?

*Faas*: Sort of an image of a balloon coming out of my nose as in comic books, and then I was also thinking about telling you about it.

GINSBERG: Okay, so there's three separate things going on. Now can you pay attention to the invisible space not in the form of a balloon. [Pause] I don't mean invisible but transparent. [Pause] Now during

graphing the
mind movement

the last few breaths, what other thoughts came into mind? Anything about Frankfurt or anything like that?

*Faas*: No, you see, when I meditate I usually try to concentrate on one image: a clock outside the town gate of Eibelstadt, a German medieval town I used to live in, and that sort of came into my mind.

GINSBERG: Okay, fine. Well, try one more time, and when the clock rises, switch your attention to your breath again. [Pause] So your thought is separated between the clock and the breath, and it's really discontinuous. There is a gap in between.

*Faas*: I see. [Both laughing]

GINSBERG: Just literally speaking, there is a moment of shift, that's almost a fraction of a second. So if you do meditate and continue to practise attention to breath, you never can stop your mind from thinking and wandering and travelling in space, but you keep interrupting it, bring it back to the breath and the space in front of you.

*Faas*: I suppose that's what I'm trying to do with the clock.

GINSBERG: Yeah.

*Faas*: I mean I can never stay with that image for any longer than say thirty seconds.

GINSBERG: Okay, so that in that sense thought is discontinuous, I mean there are jumps and gaps in between the thoughts, and there are actually complete gaps in between for only a micro-second, but . . .

*Faas*: And that's where you talk about *śūnyatā*.

GINSBERG: Well, a gap is—that is Chögyam Trungpa's terminology—that gap in which we are just sitting in space or in just empty space. Now, if you practise that kind of thing either for meditation or just trying to recollect what you were just thinking about when you are writing you notice you get a lot of different thoughts with gaps in between, and in that sense thought is discontinuous, like movies, in the sense writing a line of Ginsberg poetry of the cinema, you know with twenty-four or fifteen frames a second. So you might have like three or four thoughts a second, or maybe one thought a second, but in between—and the thoughts jump around, so obviously you were thinking of a clock, but then you might think from a clock to the . . . Beats, your paper or your nostril. So that's all I mean when I say remembering or recollecting. So the process of writing for me is remembering and recollecting the thoughts I was just having while writing.

*Faas*: And the writing is a kind of stepping back from that.

GINSBERG: Well, the mind steps back, and the writing registers it fast, you just scribble it fast. The first words that come to your mind, the first flashes of what it was, your clock, a hand, a gingerbread hand, iron letters, roman numerals, roof, grey tiles, those were the first things . . . So that's "clock roman numerals iron letters roof grey tiles," and you've got a line of Ginsberg poetry. That's exactly it, you see. It's the first thoughts, whatever you can get. I have a whole scene of clocks and roofs and whatever I remember from Munich or wherever I saw a clock, just picking up, you know, like when you sketch very fast.

*Faas*: Yet these are still only fragments. How do you put them together? The way they come out?

GINSBERG: Like a *haiku*: "clocks iron letters."

*Faas*: No, I mean once you have written a line.

GINSBERG: You move on to the next.

*Faas*: Add them up, just in the order in which they came out?

GINSBERG: Move on to . . . yes.

*Faas*: And never shift them around.

GINSBERG: No no no no no. No you couldn't—then you'd be stopping the whole process.

# Bibliography & Abbreviated References

A,P  Allen, D. M. *The New American Poetry.* Edited by D. M. Allen. New York: Grove Press, 1960.

Ab,M  Abrams, M. H. *The Mirror and the Lamp. Romantic Theory and the Critical Tradition.* New York: Norton, 1958.

Ab,S  ——. *Natural Supernaturalism. Tradition and Revolution in Romantic Literature.* New York: Norton, 1971.

B,F  Bly, Robert, ed. *The Fifties.* (Journal)

B,IJ  ——. "An Interview with Robert Bly." *Tennessee Poetry Journal,* 2, No. 2 (Winter 1969), pp. 29-38.

B,IL  ——. "Interview." *The Lamp in the Spine,* 3 (Winter 1972), pp. 50-65.

B,L  ——. *The Light Around the Body: Poems.* New York: Harper & Row, 1967.

B,N  ——. *Neruda and Vallejo: Selected Poems.* Edited by Robert Bly. Boston: Beacon Press, 1971.

B,R  ——. "Reflections on the Origins of Poetic Form." *Field,* 10 (Spring 1974), pp. 31-36.

B,S  ——, ed. *The Sixties.* (Journal)

B,Si  ——. *Silence in the Snowy Fields.* Middletown, Conn.: Wesleyan University Press, 1962.

B,Sl  ——. *Sleepers Joining Hands.* New York: Harper & Row, 1974.

Ba,C  Baskin, W., ed. *Classics in Chinese Philosophy.* Totowa, N.J.: Littlefield, Adams & Co., 1974.

Bi,A  Birch, C., ed. *Anthology of Chinese Literature.* New York: Grove Press, 1967.

Br,M  Breton, André. *Manifestes du surréalisme.* Paris: Gallimard, 1972.

Bs,D  Barthes, R. *Le degré zéro de l'écriture.* Paris: Éditions Gonthier, 1970.

289

Bs,E \_\_\_\_\_. *Essais critiques.* Paris: Éditions du Seuil, 1964.

Bu,L Bush, S. *The Chinese Literati on Painting. Su Shih (1037-1101) to Tung Ch'i-Ch'ang (1555-1636):* Harvard-Yenching Institute Studies XXVII. Cambridge, Mass.: Harvard University Press, 1971.

BG Anonymous. *The Bhagavad Gita As It Is.* With Introduction, Translation and Authorized Purport by A. C. Bhaktivedanta Swami. London: Collier-Macmillan Ltd., 1969.

BT Anonymous. *The Tibetan Book of the Dead.* Edited by W. Y. Evans-Wentz, with a Psychological Commentary by C. G. Jung. London: Oxford University Press, 1960.

B-M,P Berg, S. & R. Mezey, eds. *Naked Poetry: Recent American Poetry in Open Forms.* Indianapolis: Bobbs-Merrill, 1969.

C,B Creeley, Robert, *A Day Book.* New York: Scribner, 1972.

C,C \_\_\_\_\_. *Contexts of Poetry: Interviews 1961-1971.* Edited by D. Allen. Bolinas, Cal.: Four Seasons Foundation, 1973.

C,Cr \_\_\_\_\_. *The Creative.* Los Angeles: Black Sparrow Press, 1973.

C,D \_\_\_\_\_. *The Gold Diggers and Other Stories.* New York: Scribner, 1965.

C,F \_\_\_\_\_. *The Finger: Poems 1966-1969.* London: Calder and Boyars, 1970.

C,G \_\_\_\_\_. *A Quick Graph: Collected Notes and Essays.* Edited by D. Allen. San Francisco: Four Seasons Foundation, 1970.

C,IR \_\_\_\_\_. "Interview." By L. Wagner and L. MacAdams, Jr. *Paris Review,* 44 (Fall 1968), pp. 154-187.

C,P \_\_\_\_\_. *Poems 1950-1965.* London: Calder and Boyars, 1966.

C,W \_\_\_\_\_. *Words.* New York: Scribner, 1967.

Ce,B Coleridge, Samuel Taylor. *Biographia Literaria.* Edited by G. Watson. London: Dent, 1965.

Ch,C Chang Chung-yuan. *Creativity and Taoism: A Study of Chinese Philosophy, Art, and Poetry.* New York: Harper & Row, 1970.

D,A Duncan, Robert. *Audit/Poetry,* IV, No. 3 (1967). Featuring Robert Duncan.

D,C \_\_\_\_\_. "The H.D. Book," II, 2. *Caterpillar,* 6 (January 1969), pp. 16-38.

D,F     ———. "Ideas of the Meaning of Form." *Kulchur*, 1, No. 4 (1961), pp. 60-74.

D,I     ———. *An Interview.* By George Bowering and Robert Hogg. Toronto: Beaver Kosmos Folio, 1971.

D,S     ———. "The H.D. Book," 1, 5. *Stony Brook*, 1/2 (1968), pp. 4-19.

D,T     ———. *The Truth and Life of Myth: An Essay in Essential Autobiography.* Fremont, Mich.: The Sumac Press, 1968.

D,W     ———. "Changing Perspectives in Reading Whitman," *The Artistic Legacy of Walt Whitman.* Edited by E. H. Miller. New York: New York University Press, 1970, pp. 73-101.

Di,B     Dickey, James. *Babel to Byzantium: Poets and Poetry Now.* New York: Farrar, Straus, and Giroux, 1968.

Di,P     ———. *Poems 1957-1967.* New York: Collier Books, 1967.

Di,S     ———. *Sorties.* Garden City, N.Y.: Doubleday and Co., 1971.

E,E     Eliot, T. S. *Selected Essays.* London: Faber and Faber, 1966.

E,F     ———. *The Waste Land: A Facsimile and Transcript of the Original Drafts etc.* Edited by V. Eliot. London: Faber and Faber, 1971.

E,IR     ———. "Interview." *The Paris Review*, 6, No. 21 (Spring-Summer, 1959), pp. 47-70.

E,P     ———. *On Poetry and Poets.* London: Faber and Faber, 1969.

E,U     ———. *The Use of Poetry and the Use of Criticism.* London: Faber and Faber, 1967.

E,W     ———. *The Sacred Wood: Essays on Poetry and Criticism.* London: Faber and Faber, 1969.

F,C     Fenollosa, Ernest. *The Chinese Written Character as a Medium for Poetry.* Edited by E. Pound. San Francisco: City Lights Books, 1968.

G,A     Ginsberg, Allen. *Allen Verbatim: Lectures on Poetry, Politics, Consciousness.* Edited by G. Ball. New York: McGraw-Hill, 1974.

G,B     ———. *Songs of Innocence and Experience.* By William Blake; tuned by Allen Ginsberg. MGM Records: FTS-3083.

G,F     ———. *The Fall of America: Poems of These States, 1965-1971.* San Francisco: City Lights Books, 1972.

| | |
|---|---|
| G,H | ———. *Howl and Other Poems*. Introduction by William Carlos Williams. San Francisco: City Lights Books, 1971. |
| G,IO | ———. "Interview." *Unmuzzled Ox,* iii, No. 2 (1975), pp. 14-25. |
| G,IR | ———. "Mystery in the Universe" (1965). *Rogue,* 10, No. 3 (June 1965), pp. 1-9. |
| G,IS | ———. "Interview." *Spectrum,* 21, No. 34 (20 November 1970), pp. 5, 12. |
| G,J | ———. *Indian Journals: March 1962-May 1963*. San Francisco: City Lights Books, 1968. |
| G,K | ———. *Kaddish and Other Poems, 1958-1960*. San Francisco: City Lights Books, 1961. |
| G,L | ———. *The Yage Letters: William Burroughs and Allen Ginsberg*. San Francisco: City Lights Books, 1971. |
| G,M | ———. *Empty Mirror: Early Poems*. Introduction by William Carlos Williams. New York: Totem Press-Corinth Books, 1961. |
| G,N | ———. *Planet News, 1961-1967*. San Francisco: City Lights Books, 1968. |
| G,P | ———. *Improvised Poetics*. Buffalo, N.Y.: Anonym Press, 1971. |
| G,R | ———. *Prose Contribution to the Cuban Revolution*. Detroit: Artists' Workshop Press, 1966. |
| Go,B | Goddard, D., ed. *A Buddhist Bible*. Boston: Beacon Press, 1970. |
| G-R,W | Goedl-Roth, M., ed. *Weltkulturen und moderne Kunst*. München: Verlag Bruckmann, 1972. |
| K,L | Keats, John. *The Letters*. Edited by M. B. Forman. London: Oxford University Press, 1952. |
| Ke,B | Kerouac, Jack. *The Dharma Bums*. New York: Viking Press, 1958. |
| Ke,IR | ———. "Interview." *Paris Review,* 11, No. 43 (Summer 1968), pp. 61-105. |
| Kh,S | ———. Kherdian, D. *Gary Snyder: A Biographical Sketch and Descriptive Checklist*. Berkeley: Oyez, 1965. |
| Ko,N | Kornbluth, J., ed. *Notes from the New Underground*. New York: Viking Press 1968. |
| Kr,G | Kramer, J. *Allen Ginsberg in America*. New York: Random House, 1970. |

| L,B | Lowell, Robert. Review of R. P. Warren's *Brother to Dragons*. *Kenyon Review*, 15 (1953), pp. 619-625. |
| L,IR | ——. "A Conversation." *The Review*, 26 (Summer 1971), pp. 10-29. |
| L,W | ——. "William Carlos Williams." *Hudson Review*, 14 (1961/62), pp. 530-536. |
| La,A | Lawrence, D. H. *Apocalypse*. With an introduction by R. Aldington. London: Heinemann, 1972. |
| La,C | ——. *Selected Literary Criticism*. Edited by A. Beal. New York: Viking Press, 1956. |
| La,E | ——. *Selected Essays*. Harmondsworth: Penguin Books, 1968. |
| La,F | ——. *Fantasia of the Unconscious and Psychoanalysis and the Unconscious*. Harmondsworth: Penguin Books, 1971. |
| La,M | ——. *Mornings in Mexico and Etruscan Places*. Harmondsworth: Penguin Books, 1971. |
| Li,T | Liu, J. J. Y. *Chinese Theories of Literature*. Chicago: University of Chicago Press, 1975. |
| Lv,P | *Levertov, Denise. The Poet in the World*. New York: New Directions, 1973. |
| M,Œ | Mallarmé, Stéphane. *Œuvres complètes*. Paris: Gallimard, 1951. |
| M,E | ——. *Selected Prose Poems, Essays, & Letters*. Edited by B. Cook. Baltimore: Johns Hopkins Press, 1956. |
| N,C | Novik, M. *A Writing Biography and Inventory*. Unpublished Doctoral Dissertation on Robert Creeley. University of British Columbia at Vancouver, 1973. |
| O,I | Olson, Charles. *Call Me Ishmael: A Study of Melville*. London: J. Cape, 1967. |
| O,L | ——. *Letters for Origin: 1950-1955*. Edited by A. Glover. London: Cape Goliard Press, 1970. |
| O,M | ——. *Maps*, 4 (1971). Featuring Charles Olson. |
| O,P | ——. *Proprioception*. San Francisco: Four Seasons Foundation, 1965. |
| O,R | ——. Review of E. A. Havelock's *Preface to Plato*. *Niagara Frontier Review* (Summer 1964), pp. 40-44. |
| O,T | ——. *Poetry and Truth: The Beloit Lectures and Poems*. Edited by G. F. Butterick. San Francisco: Four Seasons Foundation, 1971. |

O,U — . *Human Universe and Other Essays.* Edited by D. Allen. New York: Grove Press, 1967.

O,V — . *The Special View of History.* Edited by Ann Charters. Berkeley: Oyez, 1970.

O,W — . *Selected Writings.* Edited by R. Creeley. New York: New Directions, 1966.

Os,A — Ossman, D. *The Sullen Art. Interviews with Modern American Poets.* New York: Corinth Books, 1963.

O'C,P — O'Connor, F. V. *Jackson Pollock.* New York: Museum of Modern Art, 1967.

P,B — Pound, Ezra. "Epstein, Belgion and Meaning." *The Criterion,* 9 (Oct. 1929-July 1930), pp. 470-475.

P,G — . *Gaudier-Brzeska: A Memoir.* Hessle, East Yorkshire: Marvell Press, 1960.

P,L — . *The Letters: 1907-1941.* Edited by D. D. Paige. New York: Harcourt, Brace & World, Inc., 1950.

P,P — . *Selected Poems.* Edited by T. S. Eliot. London: Faber and Faber, 1964.

Pa,C — Packard, W., ed. *The Craft of Poetry.* Garden City, N.Y.: Doubleday and Co., 1974.

Pl,W — Plimpton, G., ed. *Writers at Work: Third Series.* New York: Viking Press, 1967.

R,W — Rimbaud, Arthur. *Complete Works: Selected Letters (English and French).* Edited by W. Fowlie. Chicago: University of Chicago Press, 1966.

Ra,M — Ray, P. C. *The Surrealist Movement in England.* London: Cornell University Press, 1971.

Rg,A — Rothenberg, J. & G. Quasha, eds. *America a Prophecy. A New Reading of American Poetry from Pre-Columbian Times to the Present.* New York: Random House, 1974.

Rg,T — Rothenberg, Jerome., ed. *Technicians of the Sacred. A Range of Poetries from Africa, America, Asia, & Oceania.* Garden City, N.Y.: Doubleday and Co., 1968.

Rn,P — Robertson, B. *Jackson Pollock.* New York: H. N. Abrams, 1960.

R-G,R — Robbe-Grillet, Alain. *Pour un nouveau roman.* Paris: Gallimard, 1963.

S,C      Snyder, Gary. *The Back Country.* New York: New Directions, 1967.

S,E      ———. *Earth House Hold.* New York: New Directions, 1969.

S,IA      ———. "Interview." By N. Tarn. *Alcheringa,* 4 (Autumn 1972), pp. 104-113.

S,IG      ———. "Interview." By D. Kozlovsky. *Modine Grunch,* 3 (January 1970), pp. 21-25.

S,IQ      ———. "Interview." By L. Bartlett. *California Quarterly,* 9 (Spring 1975), pp. 43-50.

S,IR      ———. "Interview."*Road Apple Review,* i, No. 4 and ii, No. 1 (Winter 1969-Spring 1970), pp. 59-68.

S,IT      ———. "Interview." By G. Fowler. *Literary Times,* iv, No. 2 (December 1964), p. 22.

S,M      ———. *Myths and Texts.* New York: Totem Press in association with Corinth Books, 1960.

S,R      ———. *Riprap, & Cold Mountain Poems.* Writing 7. San Francisco: Four Seasons Foundation, 1969.

S,T      ———. *Turtle Island.* New York: New Directions, 1974.

S,W      ———. *Regarding Wave.* New York: New Directions, 1970.

Sc,P      Scully, J., ed. *Modern Poets on Modern Poetry.* New York: McGraw-Hill, 1969.

Si,A      Sirén, O. *The Chinese on the Art of Painting.* New York: Schocken Books, 1971.

Su,M      Suzuki, D. T. *Mysticism: Christian and Buddhist.* World Perspectives. Volume Twelve. Planned and edited by R. N. Anshen. Westport, Conn.: Greenwood Press, 1975.

Su,W      ———. *Selected Writings.* Edited by W. Barrett. Garden City, N.Y.: Doubleday, 1956.

Su,Z      ———. *Essays in Zen Zuddhism. First Series.* New York: Grove Press, 1961.

W,E      Williams, William Carlos. *Selected Essays.* New York: New Directions, 1969.

W,P      ———. *Paterson.* New York: New Directions, 1963.

Wa,G      Watts, Alan W. *The Two Hands of God. The Myths of Polarity.* New York: Collier-Macmillan, Ltd., 1969.

Wa,W      ———.*The Way of Zen.* New York: Random House.

Wh,I     Whitehead, A. N. *The Interpretation of Science: Selected Essays.* Edited by A. H. Johnson. Indianapolis: Bobbs-Merrill, 1961.

Wh,S    ____. *Symbolism, Its Meaning and Effect.* New York: G. P. Putnam's Sons, 1959.

Wn,L    Whitman, Walt. *Leaves of Grass and Selected Prose.* Edited by J. Kouwenhoven. New York: Random House, 1950.

Y,B     Yates, F. A. *Giordano Bruno and the Hermetic Tradition.* New York: Random House, 1960.

Y,S     ____. "Magic in Shakespeare's Last Plays." *Encounter,* 44, No. 4 (April 1975), pp. 14-22.

Ekbert Faas was born in 1938 in Berlin. He studied in Munich, Paris, Madrid and London and holds a Ph.D. (1965) and a Dr.habil. (1971) in English literature. Besides articles, interviews and translations, he has published books on Renaissance literature, post-Romantic poetry and, more recently, on Modernist and non-Western æsthetics. At present he is writing critical studies of Ted Hughes and Robert Duncan. A writer as well as a teacher by profession, he has held appointments at European and North American universities and presently teaches at York University in Toronto.